4/13

CL

THE DISCOVERY OF THE
TITANIC

*Exploring the greatest
of all lost ships*

THE DISCOVERY OF THE
TITANIC

Dr. Robert D. Ballard
with Rick Archbold

Introduction by Walter Lord

**Illustrations of the Titanic
by Ken Marschall**

ORION

An Orion/Madison Press Book

Published in Great Britain in 1995 by Orion Books
The Orion Publishing Group Ltd.
Orion House
5 Upper St Martin's Lane
London WC2H 9EA

A CIP catalogue record for this book
is available from the British Library.

(Frontispiece) The Titanic *dressed with flags at the White Star Dock
in Southampton on Good Friday, April 5, 1912, five days before her
maiden voyage.*

Produced by
Madison Press Books
40 Madison Avenue
Toronto, Ontario
Canada M5R 2S1

Printed in Canada

CONTENTS

INTRODUCTION

BY WALTER LORD

WHAT IS THE MYSTIQUE OF THE *TITANIC*? IS IT THE SHEER immensity of the disaster — the largest ship in the world, proclaimed unsinkable, going down on her maiden voyage with appalling loss of life? Is it the element of Greek tragedy that runs through the story — if only she had heeded the warnings; if only there had been enough lifeboats; if only… if only. Is it the built-in sermon, the irresistible reminder that "pride goeth before a fall"? Or is it because she so eloquently symbolizes the end of the Edwardian era, a final nostalgic glimpse of a whole way of life?

Certainly all these elements are present, but somehow they are not enough. Recently, I received word that *A Night to Remember*, a small book I wrote about the *Titanic* more than 30 years ago, is about to have a Bulgarian edition. Surely there can't be that many Bulgars interested in the end of the Edwardian era.

No, the appeal must be more universal, and the thought occurs that the *Titanic* is the perfect example of something we can all relate to: the progression of almost any tragedy in our lives from initial disbelief to growing uneasiness to final, total awareness. We are all familiar with this sequence, and we watch it unfold again and again on the *Titanic* — always in slow motion.

There is the initial refusal to believe that anything serious is wrong — card games continuing in the smoking room; playful soccer matches on deck with chunks of ice broken from the berg. Then the gradual dawning that there is real danger — the growing tilt of the deck, the rockets going off. And finally, the realization that the end is at hand, with no apparent escape. Entranced, we watch how various people react: the Strauses embracing, the band playing, the engineers keeping the lights going. We wonder what *we* would do.

Whatever the explanation, the fascination continues; hence the universal excitement when word came in 1985 that an expedition led by Dr. Robert D. Ballard of the Woods Hole Oceanographic Institution and Jean-Louis Michel of IFREMER had located the wreck. At first I thought that the discovery might spoil some of the allure. Part of the spell seemed to depend on the great ship, still hauntingly beautiful in her final moments, disappearing beneath the sea forever. But it soon became clear that the discovery actually added to the mystique. The magnificent photographs of the ghost-like bow had a haunting quality all their own. Later, the close-up pictures taken in the 1986 expedition each suggested a fresh vignette: an empty davit, an opened porthole, the crow's nest. And what little girl owned the doll's head that shows up so clearly in one of the shots taken near the stern?

Now these classic photographs have been gathered together in a volume of their own. Looking at them and reading the story of the expeditions, we can understand why Bob Ballard himself finally fell victim to the *Titanic*'s mystique. Initially the search was, for him, basically a professional challenge — a sort of diver's Mount Everest — but by the time he came up from his final dive, he felt differently:

> *A melancholy feeling of emptiness came over me. How could I be experiencing this sense of loss, I wondered? After all the* Titanic *was, in the final analysis, only a big wreck in deep water. Our mission had been a technological success. I should be feeling jubilation. Instead, I felt like a high-school senior saying goodbye to his steady girlfriend before heading off to college. I wanted to look to the future, but I couldn't help looking back.*

One feels the same way on turning the last page of this magnificent book. The mystique of the *Titanic* lives on.

CHAPTER 1

·······························

SEARCH FOR
A LEGEND

THE RESEARCH VESSEL *KNORR* HEAVED AND PLUNGED WITH the ocean swell as I leaned out over the bow railing, squinting into the blackness. I was bone tired — a combination of fatigue and the beginnings of despair. This was the fifth week of our search for the *Titanic*; only five more days to go, and still nothing. All we had seen so far was an endless seascape of ocean above and a barren, muddy bottom passing below. Did I expect to see the ghost of the *Titanic* coming at me through the dark? I thought of the *Titanic*'s lookout, Fred Fleet, nearing the end of his watch on a clear but moonless night. Suddenly he sees something dead ahead and coming fast. There is barely time to react…

Like that fateful April night 73 years ago, the August air was chilly — summer is fleeting in the North Atlantic — and the rail cold and wet to the touch. Through the cold steel I could feel the vibrations of the *Knorr*'s powerful engines as they drove the ship painstakingly forward at a speed of 1.5 knots.

Not for the first time, I reflected on the enormity of our mission: to locate a wreck two and half miles down in the middle of nowhere. It was far worse than looking for a needle in a haystack, and yet I'd often boasted that finding the *Titanic* would be easy — with the right equipment and manpower. On this expedition we had both. What had gone wrong?

Both my French co-leader, Jean-Louis Michel, and I had prepared carefully for our expedition to find the legendary wreck of the R.M.S. *Titanic*, sunk in 1912 with great loss of life. We had followed our plan faithfully. But now time was running out. Had we somehow missed the ship? Or were we looking in the wrong place?

By August 31, 1985, time had almost run out and still there was no sign of the Titanic.

I walked aft, alone with these thoughts, to the *Knorr*'s deserted fantail. A few feet away was the long inanimate shape of ANGUS, its white paint glowing faintly in the deck lights. Not very lively company, but we planned to use this sled-like assemblage of steel tubing and underwater still cameras to take beautiful pictures of the wreck — if we found it. Beyond ANGUS I could just barely make out the even more ghostly silhouette of the *Knorr*'s crane, used for launching and recovering ANGUS and its sibling *Argo* — a sled that took moving television pictures as it was pulled a few feet above the bottom of the ocean floor. In my current state of mind the crane resembled an arm bent at the elbow and ready to land a punch.

At this moment *Argo* was out of sight, trailing just above the seafloor at the end of a slender cable. With its high-tech video eyes, *Argo* was continuing our around-the-clock search for the *Titanic*. Meanwhile, I waited, ruefully reflecting on the vast gap between the glamorous stereotype of the underwater adventurer and the mind-numbing reality of our endless, often boring, search.

Only a few yards forward, a squat rectangle loomed in the darkness. This was the control van, the nerve center of our mission. All I had to do was walk over, open the door, and I'd enter a world of light, warmth, and companionship. Soft music would be playing on the tape deck and the day's shipboard gossip would be in the process of dissection. Since I wasn't there, there'd also probably be the inevitable griping. Morale was at its lowest ebb and some members of the team had even begun to question our search strategy…

What was it about the *Titanic* anyway? Why did she

....

still exert such a powerful spell over so many? I'd certainly caught the bug, and I was supposed to be a hard-headed scientist using the sunken ship as an excuse to test some fancy new equipment. But long ago the *Titanic* had ceased to be just another shipwreck.

In the popular imagination the events of the night of April 14, 1912, have distilled themselves into a powerful morality play about overweening pride leading inevitably to a tragic fall. A great passenger ship, the largest and most luxurious yet built, sets out on her maiden voyage. She is widely believed to be "unsinkable" — although her builders and owners never make such a claim — and there are not enough lifeboats. Aboard are gathered a glittering array of the wealthy set of England and America, the celebrities of an age that worshiped old money and blue blood. In command is a veteran captain whose lack of self-doubt epitomizes his rich passengers' confidence in the world they control. Despite a number of warnings of ice ahead, he does not slow down and takes only the minimum precautions. He has made this passage countless times before and, besides, there is often ice in April.

The ship hits an iceberg at full speed, a glancing blow but a fatal one, and begins to sink. The passengers are at first simply curious, turning the event into a diversion from shipboard routine. But as the ship begins to show a pronounced tilt at the bow and a slight but definite list to starboard they begin, reluctantly, to enter the lifeboats, many of which leave not even half full. Less than three hours later, the great ship has vanished beneath the freezing water of the North Atlantic. Of the more than 2,200 passengers and crew on board, only 705 are saved.

Somehow the world will never again seem quite so certain and controllable.

As I stood there on the *Knorr*'s stern, somewhere not far from where the real *Titanic* sank, not the one of legend and half-truth, I pondered the enduring fascination of this ship. I wondered what we would find in the blackness and crushing pressure below. What condition would the wreck be in if we located it? What changes would the deep sea have wrought over the years? Had the *Titanic* sunk in one piece like many other wrecks? It seemed probable. Was she lying intact on the bottom after falling two and a half miles, having been subjected to incredible underwater pressures, and hitting the bottom at considerable speed? There was every reason to expect that she was. Would the Grand Banks Earthquake of 1929 have unleashed an avalanche that left her buried beneath tons of mud, never to be found? I fervently hoped not.

I'd dreamed of sending my soon-to-be-completed seeing-eye robot vehicle down the *Titanic*'s Grand Staircase. What would be left of this once-magnificent structure? Would the 1912 Renault car still be sitting in the hold, waiting to take a spin along Fifth Avenue, or would its tires have been eaten away by underwater organisms, and the gleaming metal of its body corroded into unrecognizable junk? Would the wood paneling in the first-class lounge still show its careful craftsmanship? And a darker thought: would there be human remains?

These questions would all be academic, though, if we didn't find the ship. I shivered and started toward my cabin. Five more days and then we'd be heading home — either as heroes or losers. Maybe the *Titanic* really was a cursed ship and our expedition, despite its high-tech excellence, would be only the latest to fall victim to her spell.

So much had been invested in this effort: so many years, so much money, so much labor. If we failed, no doubt many of my scientific colleagues would mutter about grandstanding and straying away from the proper precincts of science. And I would have to put a brave face on things, reminding the press that the official purpose of the trip was to test our new deep-sea visual-imaging technology. The *Titanic* was merely incidental. The tests had gone well.

But I would be bluffing. As I walked through the darkened lab, past the constantly jabbering sonar printout, by the deserted galley, and up the stairs to my cabin, I knew that sleep wouldn't come easily. Too many questions were waiting to be answered.

WHAT HAPPENED THAT NIGHT

IN THE WIRELESS ROOM ABOARD THE ROYAL MAIL SHIP *Titanic* — on the fifth day of her maiden transatlantic voyage — Jack Phillips was busy dealing with the day's radio traffic, most of it private messages to and from the passengers on board. In 1912, wireless was a relative novelty — many ships still traveled without it — and Phillips and his junior, Harold Bride, as employees of the British Marconi Company, were not part of the established shipboard chain of command and followed no routine procedure in the delivery of messages to the bridge.

At 9:00 that Sunday morning, April 14, the wireless room received a message from the Cunard liner *Caronia* reporting "bergs, growlers, and field ice at 42°N, from 49° to 51°W." This was not the first ice warning the ship had picked up during the trip and it would not be the last. When he had a moment Bride took the message to the bridge, where it was probably received by Fourth Officer Joseph G. Boxhall. In all likelihood Boxhall noted the position on the ship's chart.

The officers on the bridge paid little attention to this information. Ice was not unknown in this part of the Atlantic during April crossings, and they were confident they would have no trouble spotting an iceberg in time. Indeed, the sea was calm, the weather cool and sunny and, besides, what danger could a few bits of ice pose to their magnificent new ship?

Elsewhere on board passengers went about the leisurely pursuits of a typical transatlantic passage — reading, writing letters, strolling along the promenade decks, chatting with old friends or new acquaintances, or reclining with a cup of broth and a biscuit in a sunny deck chair. Since it was Sunday, divine services were held. The first-class

This side view of the Titanic *was shot from the tender embarking passengers at Queenstown. At the very top is Captain Smith, looking down from the starboard wing of the bridge, photographed here for the last time.*

service, at 10:30 A.M. in the first-class dining saloon, was presided over by the redoubtable Captain Edward J. Smith. At the age of 62, Smith was to retire after taking the *Titanic* on her maiden voyage — a fitting end to a sterling career with the White Star Line. To this assemblage of the rich and titled, the dignified and self-confident Smith must have seemed the perfect pastor.

The first-class passengers on board the *Titanic* represented the cream of Anglo-American society of the day. The wealthiest among them was indubitably 47-year-old Colonel John Jacob Astor, great-grandson of the wealthy fur trader, who had extended the family's wealth through real estate acquisitions — especially hotels. Astor had recently been the center of scandal when he was divorced by his wife and had then married an 18-year-old girl from New York. He and his now-pregnant bride, Madeleine, were returning from a long winter trip in Egypt and Europe where they'd been hiding out of the range of reporters.

Playboy scion of the American mining and smelting family, Benjamin Guggenheim was also on board. So were Isidor Straus and his wife, Ida. He was the owner of Macy's, the world's largest department store. The list of the very wealthy was rounded out by the presence of George Widener of Philadelphia, along with his wife and 27-year-old son Harry. The Widener family had made their huge fortune building streetcars.

Besides these super-rich, there were many other merely wealthy people on the *Titanic*'s maiden voyage: for instance, Mr. Arthur Ryerson, steel magnate; John B. Thayer, second vice-president of the Pennsylvania Railroad; Charles M. Hays, president of the Canadian Grand Trunk

Railway; and Harry Molson of the Montreal banking and brewing dynasty. Among the representatives of the British upper classes were Sir Cosmo and Lady Duff Gordon; he was a British peer and she was a successful dress designer with stores in Paris and New York.

In addition to the very wealthy, the ship was well stocked with prominent personages. Among these were Major Archibald Butt, President Taft's military aide and a close friend of Theodore Roosevelt, returning to Washington after a leave of absence, and William T. Stead, renowned British spiritualist, editor, and political reformer who was traveling to New York to attend a peace rally.

The roll call of the rich and famous might have been even more impressive had some prominent people not canceled their tickets. Financier J. P. Morgan, whose shipping trust owned the *Titanic*, was too ill to take the trip. Alfred G. Vanderbilt and his wife decided at the last moment not to sail, but were too late to retrieve their luggage or their personal servant; both went down with the ship. And Lord Pirrie, chairman of Harland & Wolff shipbuilders in Belfast, who had built the *Titanic*, canceled because of poor health. In his place sailed Thomas Andrews, the company's managing director.

While the wealthy brought retinues of maids and manservants and mountains of luggage, most members of the crew earned such tiny salaries that it would have taken years to save the money for a single deluxe first-class ticket. In fact, the *Titanic* was a kind of floating layer cake, composed of a cross-section of the society of the day. The bottom layer was made up of the most lowly manual laborers toiling away in the heat and grime of the boiler

Lord Pirrie of Harland & Wolff and J. Bruce Ismay of the White Star Line inspect the Titanic *before her launching on May 31, 1911.*

rooms and engine rooms located just above the keel. The next layer consisted of steerage or third-class passengers — a polyglot mixture hoping to make a fresh start in the New World. After that came the middle classes — teachers, merchants, professionals of moderate means — in second class. Then finally, the icing on the cake: the rich and the titled.

The ship that carried these passengers was absolutely the last word in floating luxury — with its opulent public rooms and splendid private staterooms. The finest quarters were the two first-class suites on B Deck, a full 50 feet in length, which included private promenade decks with half-timbered walls echoing the Elizabethan period. First-class cabins were decorated in various periods and styles from Louis Quinze to Queen Anne. Many of the public rooms were paneled in wood. There were elevators (for both first and second class); a gymnasium (with the latest in exercise equipment); a Turkish bath and swimming pool; an à la carte restaurant (as well as the usual dining rooms); the Café Parisien, a replica of a sidewalk café where the younger set gathered; and the most lavish Grand Staircase afloat. It added up to quite a conspicuous display.

Even the third-class compartments were impressive by the standards of the day, and the ship itself, as her name boastfully indicated, was indeed the biggest afloat. She displaced 52,310 long tons, was 882 feet, 9 inches long overall, 94 feet wide at her widest point (the hull itself reached a maximum breadth of 92.5 feet), and 175 feet tall from the keel to the top of her four funnels. Put another way, she was as tall as an 11-story building and a sixth of a mile long. It was no wonder that the more than 1,300 passengers felt there was nothing that would threaten their safety.

At 11:40 A.M., the wireless room received a message from the Dutch liner *Noordam*, reporting "much ice" in about the same position as the *Caronia* earlier that morning. There was no evidence this message ever reached the bridge.

Around 1:30 P.M., Captain Smith was on his way to lunch when he ran into J. Bruce Ismay, president of the White Star Line, on the Promenade Deck. They stopped for a minute to chat about the performance of the new ship on her maiden voyage. Between noon Saturday and noon Sunday, the *Titanic* had made 546 miles — her best day so far. The next day, they were planning to bring her up to full speed for a short test to see what she was capable of, perhaps as much as 23 knots. The ship was performing well and to make matters even better, the fire that had been smoldering in the forward coal bunker of boiler room No. 5 had finally been put out the previous day. Perhaps they also commented on the weather, which remained unusually calm. Before Smith and Ismay parted, the captain handed him a wireless message recently received from the steamer *Baltic*: "Greek steamer *Athinai* reports passing icebergs and large quantities of field ice today in latitude 41°51'N, longitude 49°52'W… Wish you and *Titanic* all success." That put the ice field about 250 miles ahead of the *Titanic*. Ismay casually put it in his pocket. Later that afternoon Ismay would wave the message at two prominent passengers, Mrs. Arthur Ryerson and Mrs. John B. Thayer. It was as if Ismay were

An ice warning from the German steamer Amerika *that the* Titanic *received and dutifully relayed onward.*

Second-class passengers strolling on the starboard Boat Deck while the Titanic *is anchored off Queenstown.*

reinforcing just how great and powerful the ship was. Despite the ice warning already received, Captain Smith and Bruce Ismay, the two most important men on the ship, remained unconcerned. Yet another ice warning, this one intercepted from the liner *Amerika*, was received at 1:45 P.M., but was not sent to the bridge.

The daylight hours passed uneventfully. There were no rigid routines, no organized recreational activities. Even though it was Sunday, some passengers played cards in the first-class smoking room. As the day unfolded, the sound of a bugle announced lunch, then dinner. In the late afternoon, the temperature had begun dropping rapidly. On instructions from Captain Smith, the ship altered course slightly to the south, perhaps to avoid the ice ahead. Darkness approached.

Around 7:30 P.M. in the à la carte restaurant, Mr. and Mrs. George D. Widener were hosting a dinner party in honor of Captain Smith. The guest list included a select group of the more prominent Americans on board — most representing the high society of Philadelphia. As well as the Wideners' son Harry, there were Mr. and Mrs. John B. Thayer; wealthy Philadelphians Mr. and Mrs. William Carter, who were bringing over a 25-horsepower Renault car (for which they would later claim damages of $5,000); and finally, Major Butt.

While the captain sat at dinner, Junior Marconi Operator Harold Bride delivered yet another ice warning to the bridge. It was from the steamer *Californian*, well ahead of the *Titanic*, and on a course slightly to the north. The *Californian*'s master, Captain Stanley Lord, reported passing three large icebergs three miles to the south. The message was never given to Captain Smith.

Around 9 P.M., Captain Smith excused himself from dinner and went to the bridge where Second Officer Charles Herbert Lightoller was on duty — the 6-to-10 P.M. watch. He and Lightoller discussed the changing weather conditions — it was possible the drop in temperature indicated they were entering a region of ice and both were aware that some ice was ahead. They were also both aware that bergs could be very difficult to see on a clear, calm, moonless night with no wind or swell to cause surf. Lightoller informed Smith that with the temperature continuing to drop, he'd ordered the forward forecastle hatch closed so that the glow from inside wouldn't interfere with the lookouts in the crow's nest above it. At 9:20, Captain Smith retired for the night, leaving Lightoller with these words: "If it becomes at all doubtful, let me know at once. I shall be just inside." Ten minutes later, Lightoller had Sixth Officer Moody tell the lookouts in the crow's nest to "keep a sharp lookout for ice, particularly small ice and growlers." It was customary, at that time, for ships to travel at full speed until a berg was actually sighted, so it probably never entered Smith's mind to reduce speed on such a clear night. The sea was so calm, in fact, and reflected the starlight in such a way, that the horizon itself was difficult to discern. One sailor, a veteran of 26 years at sea, later said that he had never seen the ocean so flat.

At this point, apart from the slight alteration of course to the south, the closing of the forecastle hatch, and the warning in the crow's nest, the officers of the *Titanic* had taken no precautionary measures to deal with the hazards ahead. It was common practice to rely on lookouts and they seemed confident in their ship's ability to avoid a collision. Because of the lack of coordination between the bridge and the wireless room and the absence of any standard procedure for dealing with ice warnings, they seem to have been under the impression that the main body of ice lay to the north of their path. In the words of Walter Lord, "The result was a complacency, an almost arrogant casualness, that permeated the bridge."

Two more ice messages were received by the *Titanic* that night. None of the surviving officers remembered either of them making it to the bridge. The first one, which arrived in the wireless room at 9:40 P.M., might well have galvanized Lightoller into some sort of action. "From *Mesaba* to *Titanic*. In latitude 42°N to 41°25', longitude 49°W to longitude 50° saw large icebergs, also field ice, weather good, clear." This ice was quite clearly directly ahead of the *Titanic*'s present course.

In the Marconi room, Harold Bride had now retired for a much-needed nap — between the two operators they kept the wireless operating 24 hours a day — and Jack Phillips was busy trying to wade through the commercial traffic. The nearest North American shore station at Cape Race on the southeastern tip of Newfoundland had come in range and messages that had piled up all day could now be sent. In fact, Phillips was now so busy he brushed off the final ice warning altogether. It was the *Californian* again, still ahead but now stopped in field ice on a course a mere 19 miles north of the *Titanic*'s line of travel. Her position was now so close to theirs that the message literally blasted in his ears. Irritated by the interruption, he cut off the sender with the words: "Shut up, shut up, I am busy. I am working Cape Race."

Altogether, the day's seven ice warnings indicated a huge field of ice some 78 miles long directly ahead of the *Titanic*.

In the crow's nest, lookouts Fred Fleet and Reginald Lee had passed an uneventful watch. It was now 11:40 P.M. In another 20 minutes they would be relieved and would head below, perhaps for a hot drink, before hopping into warm bunks. The sea was still flat calm, but the air was now bitterly cold. A few minutes earlier, they'd noted what looked like a slight haze extending a couple of miles to either side and dead ahead. But they were without binoculars, which had

Frederick Fleet, the ship's lookout who spotted the iceberg that sank the Titanic.

been misplaced before the ship left Southampton.

Suddenly, Fleet caught sight of something directly in the *Titanic*'s path. In a few seconds it grew larger. Automatically he rang the warning bell three times to alert the bridge, then picked up the phone.

Sixth Officer Moody, the junior officer on watch under First Officer Murdoch, who had relieved Lightoller at 10 P.M., picked up the receiver and calmly asked, "What did you see?"

"Iceberg right ahead," replied Fleet.

The *Titanic*'s officers were experienced seamen. When Moody relayed the news, Murdoch reacted immediately. He moved quickly over to the telegraph and ordered the engines stopped, then reversed, at the same time telling Quartermaster Robert Hitchens to turn the wheel "hard-a-starboard," which would have the effect of turning the ship to port. Murdoch then pulled the lever to close the doors to the watertight compartments in the bottom of the ship. Hitchens spun the wheel as far as it would go. At the last moment the ship veered slightly to port.

It was too late. A head-on collision had been averted but the ship rushed forward, hitting the iceberg a glancing blow along its starboard bow. At the bridge level it seemed as if the ship might have escaped unscathed. Several tons of ice fell into the forward Well Deck as it passed, but the ship only shuddered and glided on. A few minutes later, she came to a stop.

Most passengers aboard the *Titanic* were unaware the ship had hit anything, let alone been fatally wounded. Because the air was so biting, most were inside and some had already turned in for the night. The Wideners' dinner party was finally winding down. The ladies had already retired to their cabins and the men had gathered for an after-dinner cigar in the first-class smoking room on A Deck, where a few other small groups were enjoying a nightcap before calling it a day. They heard a faint grinding jar. A couple of people jumped to their feet and ran out on the deck in time to see the iceberg vanishing astern. They were soon joined by others, curious to know what had happened. When they heard it was just an iceberg, they drifted back to their games, their drinks, or headed to their cabins to bed. When other passengers heard about all the ice in the forward Well Deck, they lightheartedly made plans for snowballing matches the following morning.

Lawrence Beesley, a young science teacher, was reading in his second-class cabin when "there came what seemed to me nothing more than the extra heave of the engines and more than usually obvious dancing motion of the mattress on which I sat. Nothing more than that — no sound of a crash or anything else: no sense of shock, no jar that felt like one heavy body meeting another." Divining nothing out the ordinary in this, Beesley returned to his reading. His first intimation that something was wrong was when, a few moments later, the engines stopped dead.

Second Officer Lightoller was just drifting off to sleep when he felt "a sudden vibrating jar run through the ship. Up to this moment she had been steaming with such a pronounced lack of vibration that this sudden break in the steady running was all the more noticeable. Not that it was by any means a violent concussion, but just a distinct and unpleasant break in the monotony of her motion."

A number of other passengers and crew felt the gentle jar as the iceberg brushed by and described it in various ways: like rolling over "a thousand marbles"; "as though somebody had drawn a giant finger along the side of the ship"; "a disquieting ripping sound like a piece of cloth being torn."

Down at the very bottom of the ship, the collision was perceived very differently. Second Engineer J. H. Hesketh was in the forwardmost boiler room (No. 6) when the STOP sign lit up on the boiler-room indicator. Barely had he given the order to "shut all dampers," thereby shutting off the flow of air to the fires, when there was a noise like "a big gun going off" — someone else compared it to "the roar of thunder." Hesketh and leading stoker Frederick Barrett were immediately hit by a jet of icy water. The combination of noise and the shock of cold water was enough to send them both running aft through the short tunnel to boiler room No. 5 just before the watertight door glided shut. The remaining men in No. 6 raked out the fires before clambering up the ladders to the relative safety of E Deck.

Twenty minutes after the collision, Captain Edward J. Smith knew the worst. He and Thomas Andrews, chief among the ship's designers, had just completed a rapid tour belowdecks to assess the damage. The mail room was filling with water and sacks of mail were floating about. The forepeak tank was breached as were the three forward holds and boiler room No. 6.

The *Titanic*'s hull was divided by 15 transverse watertight bulkheads into 16 "watertight" compartments. She was designed to float with any two of these compartments breached. In addition, she would survive if all of the first four were flooded — but not the first five. The critical compartment was boiler room No. 6. With these first five compartments breached, water would eventually fill them and overflow into the compartments aft, one by one. And the *Titanic* would inevitably sink. Andrews estimated the ship would be gone in an hour — an hour and a half at the most.

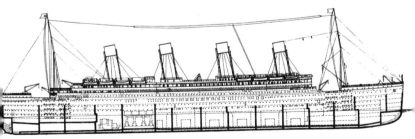

The Titanic *was divided by 15 transverse bulkheads into 16 compartments that were said to be watertight because the bulkheads extended well above the waterline.*

Captain Smith had no time to ponder the mistakes that had led to this disaster. Because he was a man of action, his thoughts turned to the orderly evacuation of his ship and the business of keeping her afloat as long as possible. This was his first real crisis in a long and remarkably uneventful career. Undoubtedly, he wrestled with the reality that the ship had lifeboats for barely half the estimated 2,200 on board. Incredibly, the *Titanic* actually carried *more* lifeboats than British Board of Trade regulations of the day required. Given her tonnage, she need only have had lifeboat space for 962. The actual lifeboat capacity was 1,178. Captain Smith knew that more than 1,000 people — assuming every lifeboat went away full — would be left on the ship. He would have to proceed carefully to delay the inevitable panic. Later, as he stood on the bridge, he would have time to contemplate what had gone wrong as he prepared to go down with his ship.

At 12:05 A.M., the squash court, 32 feet above the keel, was awash. Smith ordered Chief Officer Henry Wilde to uncover the lifeboats. Fourth Officer Boxhall was sent to wake Second Officer Lightoller, Third Officer Herbert Pitman and Fifth Officer Lowe. Then the captain walked aft along the port side of the Boat Deck to the wireless room — a distance of about 20 yards — to personally give instructions to Phillips and Bride to send out the standard CQD distress call. Later that night, Bride decided to try out the new distress signal, SOS, which was just coming into use. And the *Titanic* sent out one of the first SOSes from a ship in distress. Her position, as worked out by Boxhall, was 41°46'N, 50°14'W.

Not far away, about 12:15 A.M., aboard the Leyland

At about 12:05 A.M. wireless operators Jack Phillips (left) and Harold Bride (right) began sending the standard distress call, CQD. Later Bride would try out the new signal, SOS.

liner *Californian*, Wireless Operator Cyril Evans had retired for the night shortly after getting that soon-to-be-famous brush-off from Jack Phillips aboard the *Titanic* and only minutes before the first distress call was sent. Third Officer Charles Groves had just finished his watch and had stopped by the wireless room. He liked playing around with the set — maybe he could raise the ship whose lights he could see coming up from the southeast. To him she appeared to be a passenger liner about ten miles away. But with Evans gone he couldn't get the receiver to work. After fiddling with the dials, he headed for his cabin several minutes before the *Titanic* sent out her first distress call.

On the bridge of the *Titanic* a little after midnight, Fourth Officer Boxhall observed the lights of a steamer seemingly about five miles distant and pointed it out to Captain Smith, who gave him permission to send up distress signals. Boxhall then instructed Quartermaster George Rowe to begin firing white rockets, which he proceeded to do at about five-minute intervals. The first rocket went up at about 12:45. In the wireless room, Bride and Phillips feverishly continued to send out their distress signal. Although numerous ships heard and responded to their calls, the closest vessel they had been able to reach was the Cunarder *Carpathia* under the command of Arthur Rostron about 58 miles southeast of the *Titanic*'s position. Captain Rostron was incredulous at the news, but nonetheless turned his ship full steam toward the *Titanic* and raced to the rescue.

At approximately the same time, Second Officer Stone, alone on duty on the *Californian*'s bridge, observed a white rocket bursting above the strange ship to the south. Attempts to contact it by Morse lamp had been futile and no one wanted to wake up Evans, who as the only wireless operator on board worked an all-day shift from 7 A.M. to 11 P.M. The first rocket was followed at several-minute intervals by more white rockets — five in all. Stone called Captain Stanley Lord on the speaking tube. The captain had gone to lie down in the chart room but asked to be informed if the strange ship came any closer. Lord asked if the rockets were private signals and, when Stone replied that he didn't know, instructed him to attempt once again to raise the stranger by Morse lamp.

Stone was again unsuccessful. He and Apprentice Gibson, who had joined him on the bridge, now watched as three more rockets were fired, the last of these at 1:40 A.M. Around 2 A.M., the anonymous ship appeared to be sailing away to the southwest. Stone sent Gibson below to wake up the captain and bring him up to date. Lord again asked what color the rockets were and told his officer to continue signaling with the Morse lamp. Sometime between 2:00 and 2:20, the mysterious ship disappeared completely.

On board the *Titanic*, almost an hour after the collision, the seriousness of the situation had still not sunk in for the majority of passengers. By 12:30, Captain Smith had instructed his officer to start loading the lifeboats — women and children first. Most of first class was now on the Boat Deck wearing lifebelts as the stewards had instructed them, but despite what Beesley described as the thunderous "roar and hiss of escaping steam from the boilers," and even though the ship was slightly down at the bow and was beginning to show a discernible list to starboard, many people remained reluctant to exchange the seeming safety of the ship for the apparent risk of the tiny lifeboats. The ship's band added to a kind of party atmosphere from their position just inside the Boat Deck entrance to the Grand Staircase (they'd started playing in the first-class lounge) where they continued to play a medley of lively tunes.

Both First Officer Murdoch, in charge of the starboard side, and Second Officer Lightoller, looking after the port side, were having trouble persuading people to enter the boats. No later than 12:45, and quite probably earlier, the first boat was lowered — starboard boat No. 7. Although it had a capacity of 65 people, it left with only 28 aboard, among them artist's model Dorothy Gibson and several men from first class.

Below, in the steerage decks of the ship, there was

considerably more confusion and alarm. Most third-class passengers had so far failed to get abovedecks; others had reached the Poop Deck — third-class space — or were milling about the forward Well Deck. Most of those who made it onto the Boat Deck had done so either by circumventing the barriers between third and first class — or breaking them down. The White Star Line would later deny that any favoritism had been shown to first-class passengers, but the naked statistics told a different story.

By 12:55 A.M. — with the ship distinctly down at the bow — the first port-side boat, No. 6, was sent on its way. Denver socialite Margaret "Molly" Brown, who had been walking away from the Boat Deck, was picked up and dropped unceremoniously into the less than half-full boat as it was lowered with only 28 people aboard. When Lightoller realized that there was only one crewman — Quartermaster Hitchens — in the boat, he let Arthur Peuchen, a middle-aged manufacturing chemist and skilled yachtsman from Toronto, slide down the fall to join him. Back on the starboard side, boat No. 5 was lowered with 41 people aboard, then No. 3, with only 32 — 11 of them members of the ship's crew. By 1:10, the second port-side boat, No. 8, carrying only 39 people, was finally lowered away. Since there weren't enough crewmen, the Countess of Rothes boldly took the tiller.

Of all the boats launched that night the most controversial was undoubtedly starboard boat No. 1. Although it had a capacity of 40, it left the ship with only 12 aboard, including Sir Cosmo and Lady Duff Gordon, their private secretary Miss L. M. Francatelli, and two American men. The remaining seven were members of the crew. Later, this

Bandleader Wallace Hartley and his musicians played lively ragtime tunes while the boats were being lowered. None of them survived.

boat — and many of the others that were less than full — would fail to return to pick up people dying in the water.

The band played on as the bow sank farther. With the firing of the distress rockets, the milling passengers began to realize that the *Titanic* was in genuine trouble. On the Boat Deck, there were numerous touching scenes as husband bade farewell to wife and children, then helped them into a waiting boat. Many women were reluctant to leave their husbands and some refused. The best-known story that has survived is that of Mrs. Ida Straus, wife of the owner of Macy's department store. At one point she almost got into boat No. 8. Then she changed her mind and said to her husband, "We have been living together for many years. Where you go, I go." Calmly, the two of them sat down in a couple of deck chairs and watched and waited.

As the slant in the deck grew steeper and more alarming, the boats began to go away more fully loaded — but seldom full. A number of male passengers behaved as if nothing at all was amiss. Archibald Gracie observed a scene in the first-class smoking room on A Deck: "There all alone by themselves, seated around a table, were four men, three of whom were personally well known to me, Major Butt, Clarence Moore and Frank Millet. All four seemed perfectly oblivious of what was taking place on the decks outside." Then there was Ben Guggenheim who, having realized the ship was sinking, went below to his cabin and exchanged his lifebelt and warm sweater for evening clothes. When he reappeared on deck, he declared that if he was going to perish he wanted to die like a gentleman.

Below in the engine room, Chief Engineer William Bell and a few crewmen kept the steam up in boiler rooms No. 2 and No. 3 so that the lights on the ship would remain lit and, more important, so there would be power to keep the pumps going. Anyone who wandered into the deserted first-class dining saloon would have seen the lights still burning brightly.

By 1:30 A.M., the bow was well down and the list had shifted heavily to port. People found it hard to keep their balance, and signs of panic began to appear. As port-side boat 14 was lowered, a group of passengers rushed to the rails and threatened to jump in. The boat was already loaded with 40 people. Inside the boat, Fifth Officer Harold Lowe fired two shots to warn the crowd on deck away and the boat reached the water safely.

In the Marconi room, the wireless operators were still at their posts — but the tenor of their distress calls was becoming increasingly desperate. At 1:25 A.M.: "We are putting the women off in the boats." At 1:35 A.M.: "Engine room getting flooded." At 1:45 A.M.: "Engine room full up to boilers," meaning several of the boiler rooms had flooded.

By 1:40, most of the forward boats had gotten away and collapsible (canvas lifeboat) C had been fitted onto the davits for starboard boat No. 1. This part of the deck was now fairly deserted as the majority of passengers had moved toward the stern area, which was already beginning to lift out of the water. Chief Officer Wilde's call for women and children got no further response and he ordered the well-fitted boat lowered away. As it left the deck, William E. Carter and Bruce Ismay, the latter having assisted in the loading of passengers since the first lifeboat was uncovered, stepped into the boat. Ismay would later be pilloried for this perceived act of cowardice.

Over on the port side, things had proceeded more slowly with the forward boats under Lightoller's charge. He had followed his orders to the letter and been much more strict than First Officer Murdoch about not letting men into the partly full boats. He made no exception for Colonel John Jacob Astor. At 1:55, Astor assisted his young wife into boat No. 4 and then requested permission to join her. Lightoller replied, "No sir. No men are allowed in these boats until the women are loaded first." Astor asked what boat number it was — Lightoller thought he planned to lodge a complaint — then watched as the boat dropped away only two-thirds full. Astor went off to await his end like a gentleman. His body was later recovered, identified by the letters "J.J.A." on the back of the collar. Other prominent passengers in No. 4 included Mrs. Arthur Ryerson, Mrs. George Widener, and Mrs. John B. Thayer. The Thayers' son Jack had been separated from his parents for some time. He would jump for it at the last moment.

By 2:05 A.M., the forward Well Deck was deeply awash, the sea only ten feet below A Deck and, except for collapsibles A and B, only one boat was left — collapsible D fitted on the davits of port boat No. 2. More than 1,500 people remained on the sinking ship and Second Officer Lightoller was taking no chances. He ordered his crew to lock arms and form a ring around the boat, allowing only women and children to come through. Collapsible D (capacity 47) left the ship with 44 people. Now Lightoller and several other crewmen climbed onto the roof of the officers' quarters to attempt to free collapsible B, but they had little success as the ship's tilt grew steeper. Meanwhile, Murdoch and Moody were faring somewhat better on the starboard side with collapsible A, which they managed to get down from the roof and attach to the davits where lifeboat No. 1 and then collapsible C had been launched. But before they

This 1912 drawing, showing the lifeboats being lowered, puts the distance from the Boat Deck to the water at 75 feet. In reality, the distance was a still considerable 60 feet.

could load it, it was off the deck and floated free.

As Walter Lord described the scene in *A Night to Remember*, "With the boats all gone, a curious calm came over the *Titanic*. The excitement and confusion were over and the hundreds left behind stood quietly on the upper decks. They seemed to cluster inboard, trying to keep as far away from the rail as possible." Captain Smith, who seems to have been a curiously passive figure throughout the final hours of his ship, made his way to the wireless room and told the operators they had done their duty. "Now it's every man for himself." Quietly, he walked around giving various crew members the same message. Then he headed back toward the bridge.

There were conflicting eyewitness reports about Smith's final words and final actions. But given his character and pride, it seems likely that he went down with his vessel stoically.

Probably the last glimpse anyone had of the *Titanic*'s designer, Thomas Andrews, was of him standing alone in the first-class smoking room, staring into space. (Although one witness recalled later seeing Andrews on deck, helping with the boat loading.)

Archibald Gracie was one of the unlucky ones left on the ship once all the boats were gone. "It was about this time, fifteen minutes after the launching of the last lifeboat on the port side, that I heard a noise that spread consternation among us all. This was no less than the water striking the bridge and gurgling up the hatchway forward." Gracie and his old friend J. Clinch Smith considered heading in the direction of the bridge to try to help those attempting to free collapsible A, but thought better of it and headed for the stern. "We had taken but a few steps in the direction indicated when there arose before us from the decks below, a mass of humanity several lines deep, covering the Boat Deck, facing us, and completely blocking our passage toward the stern." These were steerage passengers who had been languishing belowdecks. As the water surged over the bridge, Gracie managed to climb up the starboard roof of the officers' quarters where a wave washed over him. "Before I could get to my feet I was in a whirlpool of water, swirling round and round, as I still tried to cling to the railing as the ship plunged to the depths below. Down, down I went: it seemed a great distance." He swam underwater away from the ship, surfaced and safely reached collapsible B, which had floated free upside down as the ship sank.

Moments before Gracie was engulfed, young Jack Thayer stood at the ship's rail until the water was only a few feet below and then jumped. He was sucked down in the icy water as he swam for his life — in a direction he hoped was away from the ship. When he finally surfaced, gasping for air and numbed by the water, the ship was perhaps 40 feet away and there was no sign of his friend Milton Long, who'd jumped seconds before. Thayer never saw him again. The ship's lights, which had burned almost until the end, had blinked once and gone out (according to Beesley). Now Thayer watched in fascination — almost oblivious to the killing cold — as the practically unsinkable ship went into its final death throes. It was now 2:18 A.M.

"The ship seemed to be surrounded with a glare, and stood out of the night as though she were on fire… The water was over the base of the first funnel. The mass of

Boat No. 14 approaches the Carpathia *with collapsible D, the last lifeboat launched from the* Titanic, *in tow.*

people on board were surging back, always back toward the floating stern. The rumble and roar continued, with even louder distinct wrenchings and tearings of boilers and engines from their beds. Suddenly the whole superstructure of the ship appeared to split, well forward to midship, and bow or buckle upwards. The second funnel, large enough for two automobiles to pass through abreast, seemed to be lifted off, emitting a cloud of sparks. It looked as if it would fall on top of me. It missed me by only twenty or thirty feet. The suction of it drew me down and down struggling and swimming, practically spent."

When Thayer surfaced he found that, miraculously, he'd come up against the overturned collapsible lifeboat B. Several men were already clinging to the upturned bottom of the boat. They helped Jack up to safety. He had a ring-side view of the last moments of the *Titanic* as she disappeared beneath the still waters.

"Her deck was turned slightly toward us. We could see groups of the almost fifteen hundred people aboard, clinging in clusters or bunches, like swarming bees; only to fall in masses, pairs or singly, as the great part of the ship, two hundred and fifty feet of it, rose into the sky, till it reached a sixty-five or seventy degree angle. Here it seemed to pause, and just hung, for what felt like minutes. Gradually she turned her deck away from us, as though to hide from our sight the awful spectacle."

During these final moments, the overturned collapsible was being sucked toward the ship and the men on her were desperately trying to row her away. "I looked upwards — we were right under the three enormous propellers. For an instant, I thought they were sure to come right down on top of us. Then, with the deadened noise of the bursting of her last few gallant bulkheads, she slid quietly away from us into the sea."

That was the end of the greatest ship the world had yet seen. Scattered over the sea were lifeboats, many of them partially filled. Almost immediately, the silent night was punctuated with the calls of floating survivors, growing in number and anguish until in Thayer's words they became "a long continuous wailing chant." Long before dawn the wailing had stopped.

The people who shivered in the drifting lifeboats, waiting for dawn, waiting for rescue, were the last people to see the R.M.S. *Titanic* for more than 73 years.

....

THE QUEST BEGINS

I'VE OFTEN BEEN ASKED WHEN THE DESIRE TO FIND AND FILM the *Titanic* first entered my mind. The precise answer to that is difficult to give. Certainly I'd known about the ship for many years before it ever occurred to me to go looking for her. You can't live your whole life as closely entwined with the sea as I have and not know the outline of her tragic story. As much as anything, however, it was the scientific challenge of actually visiting and filming the *Titanic* that first captivated me. And yet the *Titanic* also appealed to a romantic part of my personality — the underwater adventurer, the submarine cowboy. My childhood idols were imaginary explorers at the technological frontiers of science — people like Jules Verne's Captain Nemo and his *Nautilus*.

As long as I can remember I've been enthralled by the sea. But I've always been more interested in what goes on underneath the waves than on the surface. To me the surface of the ocean is beautiful but ultimately boring. As a boy walking along a California beach, I always found things the ocean washed up on the shore more interesting than the crashing surf. I was fascinated by the marine life you could discover in tidal pools. As a teenager, I became a scuba diver rather than a surfer and began to discover the world just beneath the surface. As an adult scientist, I began to go deeper still. But I wasn't particularly interested in shipwrecks. Up to the time the *Titanic* entered my head, the only wreck I'd had anything to do with was a sailboat I had helped a friend salvage and raise.

Still, I had no doubt that finding the *Titanic* would be a pioneering feat; and that visiting her and filming her at such a great depth would extend the known limits of undersea exploration. But I was not yet under her spell. She was simply a big wreck, down deep, out of reach of the technology then available when I moved from California to the Woods Hole Oceanographic Institution in Woods Hole, Massachusetts, in 1967 as a young scientist and ensign in the U.S. Navy.

Shortly after my arrival I joined the legendary Boston Sea Rovers, one of the oldest diving clubs in the world, whose history goes back to the days before Jacques Cousteau invented the aqualung. The people I met at the club meetings talked about wrecks all the time and they began to infect me with their enthusiasm for exploring these archaeological treasures of the deep. The Sea Rovers' members represented an incredible spectrum of humanity, where lawyers and surgeons mixed with stevedores and gas jockeys, all of them united in their love of the sea and the thrill of exploring it. In the late sixties, the club was still in its heyday and its annual get-togethers attracted many of the biggest names in the underwater world, people who walked in the same rarefied circles as Jacques Cousteau. One of these was Jacques Picard, son of Auguste, the Swiss balloonist who really invented deep diving. Jacques had continued his father's work in the U.S. and French bathyscaphes *Trieste* and *Archimède*. Another was Captain George Bond, the Navy physician whose research into the physiological effects of scuba diving had led to the development of the Navy diving tables, now used by every diver. Bond had pioneered "saturation" diving, the technique that allows human beings to work below depths of 100 feet for hours or even days, but to go through the process of "decompression" only once. These gatherings were also attended by some of the finest underwater photographers and filmmakers in the business, people like Stan Waterman and Peter Gimbel, who filmed *Blue Water, White Death*.

I was young and completely in awe of these heroes of the underwater world, impressed not only with their professional achievements but with their skill as popularizers. Their adventures beneath the sea were breathtaking and so was their ability to communicate their exploits to the public. Stan and the others would sometimes speak about the *Titanic*, dreaming out loud of what it would be like to dive down and swim along her stately decks — and soon I caught the bug.

But in my early days at Woods Hole I was hardly in a position to realize such a dream. I was young and my scientific reputation was barely in the making. Woods Hole, however, was a good place to be to make it.

The Woods Hole Oceanographic Institution was then and remains one of the two most important American institutions in the field. Our main rival is the Scripps Institute of Oceanography in La Jolla, California (close to home and where I'd always assumed I'd end up). During the sixties, Woods Hole geophysicists had helped gather important information about the ocean floor and the movement of the earth's crust. The Institution had grown with the boom in oceanography that happened when the space program was in its heyday, a time when there was talk of "wet NASA" concepts for the conquest of the oceans. In those days, oceanographers as well as astronauts appeared on the cover of *Time* magazine.

But to visitors, Woods Hole then as now must have seemed an unlikely place for such intensive scientific activity. It remains by all appearances a sleepy New England town with a winter population of barely more than a thousand people, perched on a splendid natural

An aerial view of Woods Hole, Massachusetts, showing the Institution docks and the original administration building.

harbor at the southwesternmost point of Cape Cod. In the distance you can see the waters of Nantucket Sound and the island of Martha's Vineyard and in the summer the tourists outnumber the locals as cars line up for the ferry boats.

The Woods Hole Oceanographic Institution (WHOI), referred to as "Whooey" by local residents, was started in 1930 by a few oceanographers who wanted a quiet place to work in the summer. It is dispersed over many acres throughout the town and on a nearby estate. For the most part, its buildings blend into the surrounding architecture, half-hidden by the foliage of century-old trees. On the surface, there's little about the Institution to dispel the town's image of a rural backwater, but since its founding the Institution has grown into a very sophisticated place.

It's a unique American phenomenon — a blend of cloistered academe and competitive free enterprise. Every tenured Woods Hole scientist is, in a sense, an independent entrepreneur operating under the Woods Hole banner. Woods Hole gives them the credibility of a respected name in ocean science. But they must go and raise the money to pay their own salaries and the salaries of those who work for them. The scientists with vision and ambition eventually gather around them a scientific "company" that can be either a large and complex organization or a small and relatively simple one.

Woods Hole is organized along the lines of a federal system with a weak and loosely defined central government existing primarily to serve a group of strong individual "states" — often in fierce competition with each other — each ruled by its chief scientist. The management of the

Institution — the central government — takes its cut of each state's annual income, but otherwise leaves them pretty much alone — unless it thinks they are doing something to hurt the image of the Institution or making promises they can't keep.

The first time I remember seriously thinking about going after the *Titanic* was in 1973. By then I had left the Navy and, as a junior scientist at Woods Hole, I was a brash 31-year-old member of the Alvin Group. *Alvin* is a small three-man submarine named after one of its early advocates — Al Vine — and the Alvin Group was then moving into the forefront of underwater research technology. Built in 1964, the sub had been developed as a tool in underwater scientific exploration. Its range was limited, however, by its HY-100 steel hull, permitting it to dive only to about 6,000 feet, far less than the average depth of the deep ocean (about 12,000 feet or two and a half miles).

In those days, oceanography was rapidly moving from a rather primitive science to a high-tech, high-profile grouping of disciplines. In the forefront of the research that was developing the revolutionary theory of plate tectonics were the geophysicists with their fancy sonar equipment and deep-drilling ships. (Plate tectonics explains the phenomenon of continental drift — the fact that the earth's crust is divided into moving plates that carry the continents about with them.) These geophysicists were radically changing the way we viewed our living planet. They had already mapped the broad contours of the Mid-Ocean Ridge and vast areas of the ocean floor.

But I was a geologist, not a geophysicist. I have always had a strong bias toward observation and direct experience and so had naturally gravitated to geology, which is a visual, hands-on science. Geophysicists, by contrast, are abstract scientists who love equations and abstruse theories, but in general don't like to get their hands dirty. One of their favorite tools is sonar; they prefer to bounce sound waves off the ocean's bottom rather than go down and look at it firsthand. There has long been competition between these two schools of earth science, even on land or in outer space.

In the early 1970s, the underwater geologists like me were somewhat in eclipse. We were pretty much stuck in the shallow waters of the continental shelves while the geophysicists pondered global questions. *Alvin* was out of the action. It couldn't dive to the deep parts of the ocean where the tectonic plates were actually drifting apart. In fact, the geophysicists sneered at us geologists, dismissing *Alvin* as an expensive toy. It was too difficult to see underwater, they said. Sonar was the better way.

But in 1973, *Alvin*'s steel hull was replaced with one made of a titanium alloy. *Alvin*'s new hull would double the sub's maximum depth to 13,000 feet, sufficient to dive to the crest of the Mid-Atlantic Ridge — and, incidentally, just enough to reach the ocean floor in the region where the *Titanic* had sunk. Finally, the geologists in the Alvin Group could compete with the geophysicists.

With the changes to *Alvin*, it would become the only modern submersible capable of reaching the *Titanic*. The only other manned submersibles that could go that deep were the bathyscaphes *Archimède* and *Trieste II*, but by comparison with *Alvin* these were primitive machines, big, unreliable, difficult to maintain and awkward to maneuver. Essentially they were underwater elevators. By contrast, *Alvin* was a tiny submarine with all the flexibility that that implies.

The *Alvin* conversion program was called Project Titanus. Titanium, Titanus, *Titanic*: perhaps I was struck then by the closeness of those three words. Perhaps the talk of the *Titanic* I'd heard over the years — especially from the redoubtable Sea Rovers — had been working away in my unconscious. Whatever the reason, the *Titanic* now began to dominate my thinking. It became routine for me to imagine myself directing *Alvin* to a soft landing on the *Titanic*'s bow or exploring the famous gash made by the iceberg.

As part of the Alvin Group, I could combine primary research with my appetite for technological challenge and adventure. Diving to great depths in a tiny sub and seeing the features on the ocean floor with my own eyes seemed the only way to practice oceanography.

But at the same time, I began to dream of ways to improve our ability to see so far below the surface. I was already convinced that the best way to do this was with deep-towed vehicles mounted with special cameras and lights, eventually to be supplemented by remotely controlled robots. Among other things, such a system would save the enormous amount of time spent getting to and from the ocean floor in manned submersibles. But I also knew it would be hard to sell my dream directly, with the geophysicists still holding sway. So in 1973, the *Titanic* appealed to me not just as an adventure but as a means to fund the development of much better and revolutionary deep-sea visual-imaging technology. For the first seven years of my quest, from 1973 until 1980, this was in essence the approach I took. I thought that the prospect of searching for and finding this legendary ship might attract the money needed to develop the very means required to find and film her. But having the idea and getting the money are two quite different things. And I would see all of my *Titanic* proposals turned down over the next few years.

During the years I was trying to raise money for a *Titanic* expedition, I was busy continuing the basic work in marine geology that earned me a Ph.D. in 1974, thereafter keeping me on Woods Hole's tenure track. In 1973 and 1974, I was part of Project Famous, the joint French and American expedition sent out to explore the Mid-Atlantic Ridge. This ridge is a mammoth mountain range running

With Woods Hole scientist Dr. Wilfred B. Bryan during the Project Famous expedition in 1974.

down the middle of the Atlantic Ocean and part of an even larger undersea range called the Mid-Ocean Ridge, which extends for 40,000 miles around the world. In 1973, I dove with French scientists in the French bathyscaphe *Archimède*. In 1974, *Alvin*, with its new titanium hull, joined *Archimède* and the French submersible *Cyana* as we continued our investigations. In the ensuing years, I made descents of 20,000 feet in the Cayman Trough, studied underwater oases of life in the Galápagos Rift — including giant tube worms and clams — a submarine ecosystem based on chemical rather than solar energy, and discovered on the East Pacific Rise the amazing "black smokers," hydrothermal vents that belch mineral-rich fluids hot enough to melt lead.

The second year of Project Famous, 1974, was also a test voyage for ANGUS (Acoustically Navigated Geological Underwater Survey), a by-product of the acoustical tracking system developed for *Alvin*. This tracking system, which would be critical in our search for the *Titanic*, allowed those in the sub and those on the surface to know exactly where *Alvin* was. Once we had the tracking system, it meant that any object equipped with a small sonar interrogation beacon could be precisely tracked underwater. So the Famous group developed ANGUS as an additional underwater tool.

The name is pretty impressive, but ANGUS was a homely fellow. In fact, its nickname soon became "the dope on a rope." In 1974, it consisted of a heavy-duty steel sled mounted with black-and-white cameras, which was towed on the end of a long trawl wire over the area we wanted to explore, its down-looking cameras snapping

Our deep-towed sled ANGUS *(Acoustically Navigated Geological Underwater Survey) in the late '70s.*

away. The result was thousands of photographs adding up to a mosaic of the ocean floor — a visual survey.

ANGUS was fine up to a point. But before you could see what ANGUS had seen, you had to wait until the sled was back on deck, and the film removed and developed. For instance, it wouldn't be very efficient for actually finding the *Titanic*. By the time the film was processed the wreck could be far behind the search vessel and would have to be found again. Even as early as 1974, I knew that another generation of deep-towed vehicles needed to be developed — one that would give us real-time visual presence on the ocean floor, something I came to call "telepresence." I didn't then have a name for the piece of hardware I would develop — but when it finally was built, it would be known as *Argo*.

At the same time as I was exploring the potential of ANGUS for underwater mapping, I was working on more sophisticated techniques for taking pictures underwater. My collaborators in this effort were *National Geographic* and especially Emory Kristof — the fine *Geographic* photographer I'd met in 1974 during Project Famous. Before long, each time we went to sea, we had not only color film, but an on-board film-processing van. For a time Emory also came to share my dream of finding the *Titanic*.

Once I'd completed my Ph.D., my position at Woods Hole became somewhat more secure. But I was still viewed as an upstart by many of my older and more established colleagues and my interest in finding the *Titanic* was looked upon by some as unscientific and inappropriate for someone working at an institution devoted primarily to pure science. Nonetheless, my desire to locate the sunken ship continued to grow even as I continued to add to my scientific credentials.

Looking back now, I'd have to say that 1977 was a pivotal year in my *Titanic* quest. It was the year of the *Alcoa Seaprobe* misadventure and the year I met Bill Tantum of the Titanic Historical Society.

As word circulated that I was interested in finding the *Titanic*, people began to come out of the woodwork. There was an outfit called Big Events that wrote to me in 1977. One of their big successes had been buying up old cables from the Golden Gate Bridge, chopping them into small pieces and selling them as souvenirs. I soon discovered that their goal for the *Titanic* was to turn her into paperweights. Our preliminary negotiations didn't last long. But before they were over, Big Events had introduced me to Bill Tantum — whom they were also trying to involve in their project.

When I met him, William H. Tantum IV was known as "Mr. *Titanic*" to buffs all over North America. As his wife, Anne, puts it now, "He really lived and died for the *Titanic.*" In fact, Bill had first become interested in the ship in 1937 at the tender age of seven when he took a vacation cruise with his father on the Canadian Pacific steamer *Duchess of Athol*. During that voyage, the passenger ship collided with the Danish collier *Maine*, which sank. Fortunately the *Duchess* sustained only minor damage, but

Bill Tantum and I give a presentation to a potential sponsor of our Titanic *expedition.*

the mishap led the passengers to talk about earlier steamship tragedies. And, for the first time, young Bill heard the names *Empress of Ireland* (sunk in the St. Lawrence in 1914 with great loss of life), the *Lusitania* (sunk off the coast of Ireland in 1915, also with great loss of life), and the *Titanic*.

I doubt few alive knew more about the *Titanic*. Gradually, largely through his influence, the ship became much more than something to find in deep water. It became a fascinating chapter in human history. He let me browse through his collection of books and memorabilia — and he talked. Bill loved to talk and I used to love to sit and listen to him. He knew the *Titanic* story cold. And he knew its heart. As I listened to Bill, I began to understand the full dimensions of the tragedy and to acquire some of his passion for the ship. As he recreated the *Titanic's* final hours, she began to take on a personality — to develop a soul. Pretty soon I could picture Captain Smith joking with the wireless operators as the ship was sinking or visualize Colonel Gracie huffing and puffing along the sloping Boat Deck in a vain but gallant search for the missing Mrs. Candee.

Bill was a born comedian and a wonderful morale booster. He was always making you laugh until you cried, always had a new joke or a funny story to tell — even though he himself was in poor health and had been for many years. When I met him, he'd been working with Jacques Cousteau finding the *Britannic*, the *Titanic's* short-lived sister vessel, which had been converted to a hospital ship and sunk by a German torpedo or mine in the Aegean in 1916.

Over the next few years until he died, he was my

friend and cheerleader. When I got depressed or discouraged, he always seemed to be on the other end of the phone with words of encouragement. He never lost faith in me. Today, his wife swears that from the first time we met he was sure I would be the one to find the *Titanic*. There are certainly many times I myself doubted it.

In the spring of 1977, I started to negotiate with Alcoa Aluminum regarding the use of their advanced salvage ship, the *Alcoa Seaprobe*, to search for the *Titanic*. But Alcoa was one step ahead of me. Negotiations were already under way to give the ship to Woods Hole. Even though these negotiations eventually fizzled out, the news galvanized my plans. I began to study the ship in detail.

The *Seaprobe*, brainchild of Scripps' ocean engineer Willard Bascom, was essentially a drill ship — with a big drilling derrick placed amidships — which used a conventional drill pipe not to drill but to lower a heavy pod down to the bottom of the ocean. The pod was a rectangular box that contained various sensing instruments for conducting a search, including a side-looking sonar and both video and still cameras. The pod on the pipe had to be lowered in sections 60 feet long. Once one section had been lowered, the next one had to be screwed into place and the whole pipe lowered until another section could be attached — an annoyingly slow process. A wire strapped to the pipe communicated between the pod and the surface.

When something was found on the bottom, the pod was raised and replaced with a claw, which was then lowered back down to grapple the object and laboriously raise it again to the surface, 60 feet at a time. The drill pipe was capable of a quarter of a million pounds of lift.

The ship and its rig represented a bold step forward in deep-sea technology, but it was far from ideal for my purposes. What I really needed was a system towed on a flexible cable that could be raised and lowered with relative ease, but the *Seaprobe* would have to do.

I had to convince Woods Hole to support my venture. I argued that if the *Seaprobe* found the *Titanic,* our Institution would emerge in a relatively short period of time with the most advanced deep-sea search-and-mapping system in the world, a system that could then be used for scientific work. Dr. Paul Fye, then director, was sympathetic and, while the Institution's directorate was split, I was at least given the green light for a rigorous series of sea trials. Officially, these were to evaluate the potential value of the *Seaprobe* to the Institution. They would also prove whether I had what I needed for the *Titanic.*

I began borrowing sophisticated equipment: from Westinghouse, a side-scan sonar (a sonar we would attach to the pod and that could acoustically "see" objects on both sides); from the Naval Research Lab (NRL), a deep-towed magnetometer (an instrument towed on a long cable near the ocean floor that would measure the magnetic field of any object picked up by the sonar, allowing us to disqualify immediately anything the sonar found that wasn't made of metal); from the Navy, the LIBEC imaging system (a sophisticated black-and-white underwater still-camera system), developed by NRL's Bucky Buchanan; from Benthos, underwater cameras; and from *National Geographic*, additional filming equipment. The cameras and sonar would be mounted in the pod, the magnetometer on a boom. At the same time, I began approaching potential sponsors for the *Titanic* project, including Alcoa itself.

On the historical front, Bill Tantum and I began to tackle in earnest the problem of where the *Titanic* was really located and to speculate on what condition she would likely be in. If our sea trials were successful, I hoped that sometime in 1978 I could go after the ship for real. So Bill and I reviewed the historical data base and then I developed a search plan. I concluded that the *Titanic* was inside an area of 100 square nautical miles and estimated that the search would take 10–12 days. *Years* would have been more like it.

The basic historical facts were not in dispute. The *Titanic*'s official CQD or distress position was 41°46'N, 50°14'W, worked out by Fourth Officer Boxhall, who was generally considered to be an excellent navigator. But there was good evidence to suggest Boxhall was wrong. Captain Rostron on the *Carpathia*, steaming at full speed from the southeast in response to the *Titanic*'s distress call, reached the lifeboats well before he should have, which suggested the sinking was southeast of the official position.

In light of the variables, it would not have been all that surprising if Boxhall had made a mistake. His position was reached by dead reckoning — estimating the distance traveled from the last reliable navigational fix at sunset by simply extrapolating from estimated speed and direction of travel. But celestial navigation was itself notoriously inaccurate and dead reckoning only added to the imprecision. Furthermore, Boxhall knew nothing about the ocean currents, and if the ship had been traveling slightly more slowly than he thought, his final position

....

could easily be ten miles off — possibly even more.

We were confident the *Titanic* wasn't west of the CQD position, but we had to come up with a search area big enough to be sure the wreck was somewhere inside it. In fact, Bill Tantum had figured out where the *Titanic* ought to be and the spot he'd marked on my map was remarkably close to where we actually found her. His guess was 50°01'W, 41°40'N, about three and a half miles west and slightly south of the wreck.

By the beginning of October 1977, everything was ready for our sea trials. Sadly, Bill Tantum's failing health prevented him from going on the trip, but Emory Kristof was aboard — by now a familiar face on our expeditions — assigned by *National Geographic* to work with us on developing our deep-sea photography.

The *Seaprobe* may not have been the ideal ship for the job, but it appealed strongly to my romantic side — the Captain Nemo in my make-up. There was a big hole in the center of the vessel for the drill pipe to be lowered through and a tall derrick dominating the superstructure. At the base of the derrick — above the huge, cold, cavernous room where technicians worked on the pod — roughnecks assembled or disassembled the pipe during raisings and lowerings, while the water in the big salt "moon pool" sloshed about. To one side, behind plate glass giving a panoramic view of this noisy scene of clanking machinery and cursing humanity, was the control center — all clean and quiet, warm and bright, and filled with gleaming racks of science equipment.

The *Alcoa Seaprobe* set sail from Woods Hole right on schedule — just like the *Titanic* on her maiden voyage. And

The Alcoa Seaprobe *with its tall drilling derrick.*

like the *Titanic*, a few days out of port, disaster struck. The drill crew had worked hard all during the preceding day lowering our vehicle pod with its expensive equipment 60 feet at a time, 3,000 feet into the sea. Finally, we were only 60 feet above the ocean floor and the exhausted drill crew turned in for the night, while I prepared for the long hours needed to test our borrowed Westinghouse sonar. None of us knew as night descended that a fatal mistake had been made. Just before we sailed, our drilling superintendent had walked off the job and the remaining crew was unaware of a special reinforced section of pipe that was meant to be wedged into place during any towing operation.

At about two in the morning, after practically everyone on board had gone to bed, I was working in the control center with a skeleton crew of three, conducting a final sonar run in preparation for our first camera tests of the pod the next day. We were in that state of dream-like concentration that happens late at night when distractions are few. Except for the pinging of the sonar, only occasional scraps of conversation broke the silence.

Suddenly, there was a thunderous crash directly over our heads — it seemed as if the world was coming to an end. We rushed out of the room to be confronted by a grisly scene of disaster. The drill pipe had broken, and the huge counterweight perched high in the drilling derrick had dropped like a bomb over our heads. Three thousand

An overhead view of the "moon pool" through which our expensive equipment went crashing to the bottom.

feet of pipe weighing about 61,000 pounds plunged toward the ocean floor with enough impact to bury our vehicle full of expensive equipment forever. The severed communication cable dangling from the derrick cracked like a whiplash, spewing dangerous sparks. Someone ran to switch off the power; others went to peer down into the empty "moon pool" — as if they expected to see some sign of the vanished pipe. It was not only a terrible setback, but an enormous blow both to my reputation and my self-confidence.

I returned to Woods Hole with none of the borrowed hardware, apart from the magnetometer. Fortunately, Alcoa had an insurance policy that covered the lost $600,000 of borrowed equipment. But next time it would certainly be much harder to borrow things. I'd been riding high, always with the feeling that luck was smiling on me, overstepping my bounds — and suddenly I was brought back down to earth.

But I wasn't about to give up on the *Titanic* because of one major setback. Even if I'd had any thoughts about abandoning my quest, Bill Tantum wouldn't have let me hear the end of it. He was even more determined than I was that the *Titanic* would be found. Shortly after the *Seaprobe* debacle, he introduced me to a British filmmaker named Alan Ravenscroft, who was interested in making a documentary about the discovery, having already made a film about the *Titanic* tragedy. With the help of *National Geographic* executives and other friends, I began contacting a whole new group of potential funders, including the BBC, the major U.S. television networks, and Roy Disney.

In the aftermath of the *Seaprobe* accident, Woods

Hole began to distance itself from my *Titanic* project. Essentially, they told me not to actively pursue the *Titanic* under their banner. I was accustomed to raising money for my projects with the prestige and clout of the Institution behind me. Now this routine support was being denied.

I'm sure they assumed I'd simply fold up my tent and go back to basic science (something I'd never abandoned). Instead, I formed a company in partnership with Bill Tantum, Emory Kristof, and Alan Ravenscroft. It was called Seaonics International and it had a simple purpose: to raise money to build deep-towed visual-imaging vehicles and find the *Titanic*. Once I had the financial backing, I figured I could come back to Woods Hole management and present them with a fait accompli. Understandably, Woods Hole's new director, John Steele, wasn't too happy about this.

By May of 1978, I'd been turned down by all my major funding prospects except Roy Disney. He'd actually come out to Woods Hole and seemed genuinely impressed and interested. Then at the beginning of June, I got his decision: "Because of the enormous capital investment which you require immediately, it is simply not feasible for us to become involved." (We were asking for $1.5 million.) It was as if the *Seaprobe* pod had crashed to the ocean floor once more. I'll admit I was asking for a lot. I wanted someone to pay for the development of my underwater eyes and hands as well as funding the cost of the search expedition itself.

In 1979, with the *Titanic* still simmering, but definitely on the back burner, Emory Kristof and I had an opportunity to further develop advanced imaging systems underwater. Emory and his *National Geographic* colleagues,

This drawing was done in 1978 to show Roy Disney how we would explore the Titanic. *The underwater robot in the picture is not unlike the* Jason Junior *robotic vehicle we would eventually use in 1986.*

Pete Petrone and Al Chandler, had been instrumental in helping to develop new cameras and to design the color-film lab that now processed our ANGUS pictures right on board ship. Now, as we returned to the Galápagos Rift for another look at the deep-sea life we'd discovered in 1977, we brought with us the latest in solid-state imaging devices produced in the highly competitive world of television technology. We hoped this would give us high-contrast video pictures at great depth.

This pocket-size television camera was mounted outside *Alvin* on its movable arm used for picking up samples. And this time when we visited the hydrothermal vents, we were able to come back with spectacular color video footage that was the highlight of a *National Geographic* television special called *Dive to the Edge of Creation*. Even more memorable, that trip was the first time scientists in *Alvin* turned their backs to the viewports and watched the television monitors instead for a better view. I could now imagine the day when we would replace *Alvin* altogether with remote-controlled eyes in the deep.

During the years after the *Seaprobe* disaster, I continued to promote the *Titanic* project through Seaonics International with all the time and energy I could muster, but I was running out of steam. At one point, Seaonics was approached by a Texas oil millionaire named Jack Grimm who wanted to back a *Titanic* expedition. Emory Kristof negotiated with him briefly, but neither of us liked Grimm's style and the negotiations never got far. We'd had our fill of hustlers and promoters. Bill Tantum's enthusiasm never faded, but his health finally gave out. And it seemed that my dream was dying with him. Then I got the news that Jack Grimm had teamed up with the scientists at Scripps and Lamont-Doherty and that in the summer of 1980 they were going out to find the *Titanic*. The legendary Dr. Fred Spiess, whom I had come to regard as a sort of nemesis, would be in charge.

That pretty much knocked the wind out of me. Well, I thought, Fred could have the *Titanic*. It was time for me to attend to my own career. If I was finally going to get tenure, I had to get back to my writing. In June of 1979, I packed up my family and moved to California's Stanford University on sabbatical. It was a good place to work — and a good place to hide while I watched my dream realized by others. I had no doubt Fred Spiess and Bill Ryan of Lamont would find the ship and I didn't want to be anywhere close by when they did.

A year later, in early June of 1980, Bill Tantum died. Right up to the end, he'd continued to live and breathe the *Titanic* and the other great ships he loved so much. Only three weeks before the stroke that killed him, he'd traveled to Rimouski, Quebec, to speak at the opening of the *Empress of Ireland* museum. And apparently right to the end, he believed I'd find the *Titanic*. He had more faith than I did.

CHAPTER 4

....

WATCHING FROM THE SIDELINES

WHEN JACK GRIMM'S 1980 *TITANIC* EXPEDITION SET SAIL aboard the *H. J. W. Fay* from Port Everglades, Florida, on July 14, 1980, I was on the other side of the world. Collaborating once again with fine French oceanographers, I was aboard the oceanographic research ship *Le Suroit* near Easter Island and Pitcairn Island in the southern Pacific. It didn't escape my notice that nearby Pitcairn Island was where mutineers from HMS *Bounty* had escaped to hide out. I felt as though I'd done the same thing.

Jack Grimm, the brash Texas oilman known as Cadillac Jack for his extensive collection of vintage cars, had certainly gotten plenty of publicity. He'd pre-sold media rights to the story and was talking about salvaging valuable artifacts from the wreck, some of which he would consider donating to the Smithsonian Institution. The way he carried on you'd have thought he'd already found the *Titanic*.

Grimm was a curious combination of hard-nosed business acumen and naive schoolboy romanticism, a man of mercurial disposition given to quixotic quests. He had previously backed a number of eccentric enterprises including looking for a "hole" in the North Pole, Noah's Ark in Turkey, Scotland's Loch Ness Monster, and even the Abominable Snowman of Tibet. He was a man not satisfied with simply making money. He wanted to be remembered in the history books. This time, since he was looking for something that definitely existed, he had a much better chance of success.

Grimm was a risk taker, but he was certainly no fool. To lead his first *Titanic* expedition he hired Fred Spiess and Bill Ryan, two of the top oceanographers in the world. Spiess, a geophysicist, was the natural choice as chief scientist since he knew as much as anyone in the world about towing side-scan sonars over the ocean floor. He agreed to

Texas oilman Jack Grimm stands on the dock in Boston after his second expedition in 1981.

take part because a successful *Titanic* expedition would be a big boost to the cause of sonar technology — leading to a higher profile and more funding. Ryan's main interest was in developing and eventually owning an advanced undersea mapping technology. Thus the expedition was suited to their respective scientific agendas. And, as well, both men were attracted to the challenge of the search.

When I was studying to become an oceanographer, Fred Spiess was already at the height of a scientific career that had put him in the forefront of underwater science. A distinguished U.S. submariner in World War II, he'd subsequently earned his Ph.D. in nuclear physics, but then joined the Scripps Institute of Oceanography to get back to his first love, the ocean. He'd been there since 1952, since 1958 as head of the Marine Physical Laboratory, and he was in the forefront of developing technology to improve scientists' ability to accurately detect what is on the seafloor using sonar. And over the years he'd also helped the Navy find a number of sunken wrecks.

The oceanographic community is small and rather close-knit. As I worked at Woods Hole, I'd gotten to know Fred Spiess and a friendly rivalry had developed between me and this man about the age of my father. I'd been turned down by Spiess when I had applied to the Scripps graduate program in the mid-sixties, and I still wanted to prove he'd made the wrong decision. We'd been on joint expeditions, including the 1979 trip to the East Pacific Rise that had found the black smokers, and we'd talked informally over the years about combining forces to go after the *Titanic*. But I'd never been able to come up with the money.

Bill Ryan, of the Lamont-Doherty Geological Observatory

Fred Spiess of the Scripps Institute of Oceanography (left) and Bill Ryan of the Lamont-Doherty Geological Observatory.

in New York, had actually worked at Woods Hole early in his career and had since done important research that contributed to our understanding of the formation of submarine canyons and active geological processes in the deep sea. He is now one of the leading mappers of the deep ocean. Like Spiess, Ryan is a dedicated scientist with a strong interest in exploration technology.

Grimm's 1980 expedition was plagued by many problems — the most serious of which stemmed from the fact that he was not using proven Scripps technology, the Deep Tow. This was a deep-towed near-range side-scan sonar, much like the one the French would use in the first part of our 1985 expedition, which Spiess had developed in the early sixties. Over the years, he had refined it into a highly reliable mapping and search vehicle. But by early 1980, when the expedition was getting off the ground, Deep Tow had already been committed elsewhere for the summer — and it was still the only sonar around that could do the job. Instead, Bill Ryan convinced Grimm to fund the development of *Sea MARC I* — an intermediate-range sonar for large-area mapping, designed to explore geological features like submarine landslides and canyon systems.

Unfortunately, *Sea MARC I* was less than ideal for looking for the *Titanic*. In principle, it worked like all deep-towed side-looking sonars. As it was trailed 656 feet above the seafloor at the end of a long cable, it shone a "flashlight" out to either side, but instead of light waves, its illumination was produced by means of sound waves. Any object caught by the flashlight's beam cast a shadow and its characteristics were recorded when the sound waves bounced off the object and back to the vehicle.

Sea MARC's great advantage for a search of this sort was that it would cut a swath one and a half to three miles wide along the ocean floor, two and a half to five times the width of the Scripps sonar — so it could cover much more ground in the short time available. Its disadvantage was that its images would not be as high-resolution as Deep Tow's even though it was designed to be able to pick out a *Titanic*-sized object right to the edges of its range. But if bad weather was encountered, *Sea MARC*'s sonar records would be even fuzzier, as surface motion reduces the effectiveness of any deep-towed vehicle. Because it was covering such a wide area, a large object might therefore be lost in the "shadows" of more complex bottom terrain. To make things even dicier, Ryan would still be working out the kinks of this new and untested piece of equipment, even while the search was being conducted. In sum, *Sea MARC* might pass directly over the *Titanic* and not even see her.

The expedition was scheduled to reach the search area in late July. That gave Ryan roughly three months to design and build *Sea MARC* and work out any problems. Not surprisingly, when the ship left Florida they were still working on the equipment. It had its first test on the way out to the site, and last-minute hiccups led to a time-consuming delay in Bermuda. But, miraculously, Bill had it all working for the search, despite numerous operational wrinkles still to be ironed out.

Before the ship left port, Grimm did his best to turn the expedition into a publicity carnival. He arranged for a monkey by the name of Titan to go on the trip. According to William Hoffman, who wrote *Beyond Reach*, an account of Grimm's second expedition, "The monkey had been taught to point at a spot on the map indicating where the *Titanic* was. Grimm believed this was a remarkable accomplishment that would add immeasurably to the movie he was making out of the search. The scientists, especially the illustrious Dr. Spiess, thought the idea bizarre, insane, and circus-like, which could only detract from and hold up to ridicule what they regarded as a very serious endeavor. They laid down the law: 'It's either us or the monkey.' 'Fire the scientists,' was Grimm's reply. Saner heads prevailed. The monkey was left behind."

In 1980, they did no better than the monkey would have. Before setting out, the scientists had only concentrated on preparing for the scientific aspect of the expedition, while Grimm looked after the historical research. As Bill Ryan recalls it, they set out with only one working hypothesis: that the *Titanic* had sunk east of the ice barrier that the *Californian* had stopped in for the night. When the scientists discovered this lack of historical preparation, they hastily attempted to rectify matters on the way out to the site.

Their basic search strategy was to first investigate the area in the vicinity of the *Titanic*'s distress or CQD position. If they found nothing there, they would survey a much larger area concentrating on a rectangle just east of the CQD position bounded by 41°40'N to 41°50'N and 50°00'W to 50°10'W. This region is bisected from northeast to southwest by a submarine valley with many tributaries, which the scientists christened Titanic Canyon.

Following their plan, the *Titanic*'s official distress position was investigated and nothing was found. Then they began to run a series of north-south lines, which surveyed wide swaths of the ocean floor with the *Sea MARC* side-looking sonar, carefully overlapping one line with the next. This technique is known as "mowing the lawn," a tedious and relentless back-and-forth process. In the meantime, the weather was getting worse and the *Fay* proved less than adequate for the task. On a number of occasions time was lost because she could only make way downwind and was going too fast to trail *Sea MARC* at the right depth. According to Fred Spiess, 30 to 50 percent of the time on site in 1980 was wasted due to either bad weather or equipment problems.

On August 2, only a day and a half into the search, disaster struck. *Sea MARC*'s fiberglass tailfin ripped off during a high-speed turn, taking the magnetometer to the depths with it. The loss of the magnetometer — which would have shown up any magnetic signature characteristic of large metal objects like a steel-hulled ship — combined with Sea MARC's teething pains, made the remainder of the 1980 expedition something like searching in the dark with one eye closed and the other one squinting. However, Ryan's sonar was soon repaired and went on to survey an area of roughly 500 nautical square miles and to identify 14 widely scattered sonar targets — including several that corresponded in size to the *Titanic*'s hull.

Throughout the 1980 search, Spiess and Ryan were not only dogged by bad weather and equipment problems, but also by Grimm's public relations pronouncements on shore. At one point, he actually led the press to believe that the *Titanic* had been found. When those on board the *Fay* heard the news report, there was laughter and incredulity. Naturally, when they sailed into Boston on August 21, Grimm wanted the scientists to back up his claim. After the *Fay* docked, there was something of a confrontation in the ship's lab. Grimm wanted the scientists to say that they'd found the ship — that one of those 14 sonar targets was the *Titanic*. As careful professionals Spiess and Ryan were having none of this. There was a long, tense argument, at the end of which the wording of a noncommittal press communiqué was agreed to. All Grimm had to show for his money were some questionable maybes.

Jack Grimm's second *Titanic* expedition departed from Woods Hole on June 28, 1981, and there were crowds of people to see off his ship, the research vessel *Gyre*. Although Woods Hole was the port of departure, it wasn't meant as a deliberate snub (it was simply that the *Gyre*'s preceding charter was held by Woods Hole scientists) but it felt as

The research vessel Gyre *leaving Woods Hole Harbor on June 28, 1981.*

though Grimm was rubbing salt into the wound of my disappointment. And in 1981, he seemed assured of success.

This time, Grimm himself was on board along with both Fred Spiess and Bill Ryan, but now the searching sonar would be the Scripps Deep Tow. (Ryan also brought with him an underwater imaging unit, the Deep Sea Color Video System, which would be used to photograph the wreck. He had deployed it only once in 1980 — on the way home after the search — and was eager to try it on the ship itself.)

After 1980, Grimm and the scientists had been more thorough about their historical homework. And this homework led them to the correct ultimate conclusion. They hypothesized that Fourth Officer Boxhall had made a mistake in calculating the distress position because he'd failed to properly take into account the retarding of the ship's local time as it moved west. This, they thought, could mean the real position was as much as eight miles farther east. Indeed, from the position of the ice floe, as reported by the *Californian* and later the *Mount Temple*, they concluded that the *Titanic* might be as far east as 50°03'W. They pondered the speed at which the *Carpathia* had arrived on the scene and figured that the lifeboats could not have been farther north than 40°45'N. They thought the *Titanic* hit the iceberg no farther eastward than longitude 50°00'W and that she could have drifted a maximum of four miles before sinking.

Their final conclusion, once they'd analyzed the data, was that there was a "high probability" the *Titanic* wasn't west of longitude 50°20'W (the *Titanic*'s CQD position was 50°14'W) and that it wasn't east of 49°55'W. In addition, they figured that the ship couldn't be north of 41°55'N or south of 41°35'N.

As it turned out, the *Titanic* was within this rectangle — barely. In 1981 they were too busy going over old ground. If they'd followed their own conclusions and searched thoroughly east of 50°W, they would undoubtedly have found the ship. As it was, Deep Tow passed within a mile and a half of the wreck, a distance well outside the range of its sonar.

Hoffman provides a nice summing-up of the two fundamental assumptions underlying Grimm's 1980 search strategy: "Because of the extensive search conducted in 1980 and location of fourteen possible targets, the 1981 search operated on the assumption that the *Titanic* was more or less intact but acoustically obscured by nearby geological features." In other words, they thought they hadn't found her in 1980 because she was hidden in the shadow of some natural feature. This time, the more precise images of the Deep Tow would see into all these shadows and find the ship. Hoffman adds, "The scientists knew fairly well where the *Titanic* had to be, unless the ship's navigation was so poor that her SOS position was in error by more than ten miles. It seemed impossible since that implied corresponding errors for other ships as well." Both assumptions were wrong. And they led Grimm to spend most of his time investigating Titanic Canyon and its tributaries, the underwater feature that would mesmerize us as well in 1985.

Once again bad weather hampered the search, but the Deep Tow did a thorough job of covering *Sea MARC*'s tracks. One by one the sonar targets were eliminated — natural features every one.

After three weeks, they had not spotted even a sign of debris and Grimm was growing desperate. As the final hours of their time on site approached, the ship's winch broke, requiring recovery of the Deep Tow and apparently scotching further search efforts. While the winch was being frantically repaired, Grimm managed to wheedle the ship's owners into giving him ten more hours on site before the *Gyre* had to head home. By this time, the Deep Tow transponders — the underwater acoustic beacons that anchor its navigation — had been recovered. But Ryan was willing to put his video vehicle in the water for an eleventh-hour effort.

The Deep Sea Color Video System wasn't designed as a search instrument and Ryan knew the odds were one in a billion, but he figured it was a great opportunity to test his still-new equipment under difficult conditions. So they started by taking one last run down Titanic Canyon and then went east until it was time to head home.

This is a part of the story I'm particularly fond of because Ryan's camera vehicle was a piece of video hardware, not a sonar. So it was a visual search that found Grimm's "propeller." The Deep Sea Color Video doesn't show high-quality images in real time. What you see is a fuzzy black-and-white image on the shipboard TV screen while the high-quality color video is recorded and stored down below and can't be viewed until the vehicle is recovered. The vehicle is equipped with a microphone. So you get a color movie with underwater sound.

It wasn't until the *Gyre* was steaming back to Boston, as the crew gathered to watch the footage, that Grimm, Spiess, and Ryan could see clearly what Ryan's vehicle had seen. The surprise came in the last 30 minutes of the video — a point at which the ship had left Titanic Canyon and was moving east toward the area where the lifeboats had been picked up. As Hoffman describes it, "From a sea of empty life, just rushing water, stunningly it was there. It looked to be the twenty-six tons a *Titanic* propeller would weigh. The television coverage was so impressive because what was captured appeared suddenly, a colossus right before the eyes, and then it was gone." Accompanying this image was a metallic scraping sound picked up by the microphone. This could have been the frame of the vehicle hitting a large rock formation — or hitting the metal hull of the *Titanic*'s stern looming above. (Since the video vehicle lacked a magnetometer, there was no way of knowing.) But the camera showed no image of what it was scraping against, only the "propeller," which looked as if it was suspended in the water from above.

Spiess and Ryan of course balked at positive identification. The pictures weren't clear enough and there was no magnetic reading to reinforce the visual image. In fact, the area had been covered by the *Sea MARC* sonar in 1980 and by Deep Tow plus magnetometer in 1981, with no indication of the ship. But the professional sailors on board, including the ship's captain (and many who saw the video later) all agreed the fuzzy television image looked like a propeller and that it was the right size and general shape. The scientists remained dubious, but Grimm was completely convinced and told the world he'd found the *Titanic*.

The media dutifully reported his claim and the networks aired his video footage, but with mounting skepticism. Like the boy who cried wolf, Grimm was beginning to lose his credibility. For the second year, he was convinced he had found the wreck, but his scientists weren't. It wasn't long before the whole subject disappeared from the news pages.

It took Jack Grimm two years to raise the funds to take another look at his "propeller." This time, he would have only a handful of days on the site — but he figured that was all he needed. He believed it was simply a question of sailing out to his "propeller" and filming it attached to the hull of the *Titanic*. His expedition had been organized on short notice and Fred Spiess was committed to other projects, so only Bill Ryan was with Grimm aboard the research vessel *Robert D. Conrad* when it departed from Halifax in July of 1983. By the time they reached the "propeller" position, the weather was turning from bad to worse — 30- to 40-knot winds and 15- to 30-foot seas.

Their plan was to check out the "propeller" with Ryan's sonar and, if that didn't work out, to continue their search to the east — east of 50°W, into an area they hadn't looked into since 1980 — and then into virgin territory. But the sonar showed nothing even close to the *Titanic*'s proportions at the "propeller" site, and the weather was deteriorating further.

In the time remaining, Ryan began his eastward search, hoping the weather would permit him to put in two north-south swaths that would extend the Sea MARC coverage about six miles to the east. At the end of a long day, he went to bed, assuming that when he awoke the next morning a lot of new territory would have been covered. But while he was asleep, Grimm ordered the watch to turn the ship around and take one more pass over his "propeller": he just couldn't believe the *Titanic* wasn't there. By the time that pass was complete, the weather had worsened and gale-force winds made further sonar search impossible. A couple of last-ditch out-of-control camera runs over the "propeller" site yielded nothing, and Grimm headed home knowing only that if a propeller was down there, it wasn't attached to any wreck.

Jack Grimm had been both foolish and, contrary to his reputation, unlucky. According to Bill Ryan, over the course of all three expeditions — more than 40 days on site — Grimm enjoyed only one day with winds less than force 4 (13–18 MPH).

Jack Grimm's three expeditions didn't find the *Titanic*, but they were of some use to underwater science. Bill Ryan developed and tested his large-area mapping

....

sonar and showed some of the potential of visual imaging in the deep ocean. In fact, *Sea MARC* actually passed within range of the *Titanic* several times. However, the *Titanic* did not stand out on the sonar record due to the fact the sonar was not working properly. Spiess and his Deep Tow gathered the most precise data yet on the seafloor in the area, including Titanic Canyon.

I think Grimm's failure can be ascribed to four basic problems. First, he didn't put enough faith in the scientists he'd hired. Second, he didn't go out with a thorough enough idea of where he should be looking. Third, he didn't stick to a basic search strategy, but kept going back to "targets" that fascinated him. Fourth, he wasn't at sea long enough on any one occasion to expand his search area once he didn't find the ship where he thought it should be. So, against all odds, the *Titanic* was still waiting to be found. I would soon be in a position to again take up the challenge myself.

JASON AND THE ARGONAUTS

IN 1980, WITH BILL TANTUM'S DEATH AND JACK GRIMM OFF looking for the *Titanic*, I turned to the U.S. Navy to fund the development of the deep-sea visual-imaging technology I'd dreamed about — a dream that now carried the name *Argo/Jason*. After my year at Stanford — and the publication of several papers on hydrothermal vents — Woods Hole had granted me tenure. Now I could concentrate on bringing to fruition the concept that I'd been refining over the years. *Argo/Jason* was to be a remotely controlled deep-towed deep-sea video vehicle combined with a swimming robot on a long cable-leash. I had chosen the name *Argo* as a reference to Jason and his mythological ship the *Argo*, which sailed in search of the Golden Fleece in the ancient Greek legend. It seemed appropriate for what I hoped would become the cutting edge in deep-sea research.

That fall, I concluded that the Office of Naval Research (ONR) was the best bet to back my vision. ONR has a tradition of taking chances on individuals as much as research programs. I also knew the Navy had until now overlooked the importance of visual imaging underwater and that my approach held great promise, not only for research and exploration, but for use in submarine warfare.

As I conceived it then, *Argo* was to be an unmanned submersible loaded with video cameras, towed above the ocean bottom at the end of a long fiber-optic cable by a mother ship cruising along at one or two knots. The ship's terrain-mapping, multiple-beam sonar would pave the way for *Argo* — surveying the area and digitizing the gathered data to produce a three-dimensional map. *Argo* itself would have two sonar systems — a forward-looking one to detect any obstacles in its path and a side-looking sonar to investigate bottom geology. It would also be equipped with five video cameras, giving the operators on the surface

A side view of Argo *beginning a descent.*

a panoramic view of the ocean floor. When the scientists spotted something interesting, they would then be able to activate the robot *Jason*, while *Argo* hovered stationary above the bottom. *Jason* would be attached to *Argo* on a tether and equipped with lights and stereo cameras and its own propulsion system, allowing it to roam into riskier places and gather specimens from the ocean floor or take close-up color images.

After my return to Woods Hole, I continued to work with Emory Kristof on developing underwater photographing technology. In early 1981, testing a prototype SIT camera on the Caribbean island of St. Croix, we took the largest underwater images ever seen, three-quarters of an acre in size. (SIT stands for Silicon Intensified Target; the technology was originally developed for sniper scopes used in the Vietnam War. It magnifies available natural light 10,000 times, making it possible to literally see in the dark.) The Navy was impressed with our results, but not with the fact we were unable to explain how we achieved them. Up until this point we'd proceeded largely by intuition. In order to maintain Navy funding, I would have to come up with a much more scientific approach to the problem.

While Emory went on to other photographic pursuits, I turned to the group of imaging engineers I had been gathering at Woods Hole — the nucleus of my newly formed Deep Submergence Laboratory (DSL). They were eager to take over where Emory had left off and, unlike Emory and me, they could explain exactly what they were doing. They would develop *Argo* and *Jason* step by step, testing it every inch of the way. My Navy sponsors felt much more at ease with this traditional approach.

The genesis of DSL was the ANGUS group, which I had formed and led during the latter half of the 1970s while I continued to dive in *Alvin*. At one stage, I'd spent more time in *Alvin* than any other scientist, as well as more time on the deep-ocean floor than any other researcher using deep submersibles. If I was going to challenge the future of manned submersibles in the deep sea, at least I couldn't be accused of doing so from a position of ignorance.

My philosophy in building DSL was to create a family atmosphere — similar to the one I'd experienced as part of the Alvin Group in the early seventies. In carrying out this philosophy the essential rule is that the team does the hiring and firing, not you. In this way they feel responsible for the strengths or shortcomings of an individual member.

One of the key people we hired for DSL was Stu Harris, the man who would be *Argo*'s chief designer. With a master's degree in electrical engineering and a strong background in visual-imaging systems, Stu was ideal for the role. The first person he picked to join the *Argo* team was Bob Squires, an expert in video-imaging software. A later addition to Stu's team was Tom Dettweiler, an excellent seagoing engineer who had already worked with a deep-towed vehicle system similar in many ways to *Argo* and had at-sea expertise in side-scan sonars and television search systems.

If the *Argo* team in some ways represented the brains of the Deep Submergence Lab, then the "techies" were its soul. Of these, the most vivid character was (and is) Earl Young, a crusty veteran of my ANGUS team, an irascible old salt and superb seaman. Earl is a true intuitive techie — he feels his way to the heart of a problem and then fixes things with a hammer and a hack saw. Many times, when the engineers on board are seasick or shaking their heads over a design problem, Earl and his buddies Emile Bergeron and Tom Crook are out on the rolling and freezing deck in the middle of the night, working coolly under fire and getting the job done.

The building years were 1980 to 1984 — both of a team and a new deep-sea exploration vehicle. By the time Jack Grimm came home empty-handed in the summer of 1983, the Deep Submergence Laboratory was at full strength and *Argo* was becoming a reality. (*Jason* was then still on the drawing board.) It now seemed a perfectly logical suggestion to test *Argo* in the area where the *Titanic* went down, or better, on the *Titanic* itself.

After all the years of dreaming of going to look for the ship, coming achingly close, then seeing my hopes dashed, it suddenly all came together. Early in 1984, the Navy agreed to fund a three-week test for the summer of 1985. Tight, but I knew we would have *Argo* ready in time.

I knew my team was the best, but 100 square miles of rugged deep-sea terrain is a big piece of real estate and three weeks just didn't seem enough time to ensure that I'd find the ship. (Grimm had several weeks and had failed to find it.) So as soon as I knew our 1985 expedition had been approved, I hopped on an airplane to Paris and the headquarters of IFREMER, the French National Institute of Oceanography. The French could almost always be counted on to join ranks with us, particularly when high technology was involved. Besides, having worked so well with them in the past, and knowing their predilection for underwater adventure, I was sure they'd want to get in on the action.

I'd known IFREMER's number-two man, Claude Riffaud, since the planning for Project Famous, which he had supervised from the French side. Jean Jarry, an engineer with whom I'd worked closely during the Famous expedition, had moved out of field operations at Brest into a position of responsibility at head office. He was bound to be interested. Then there was Jean-Louis Michel, another compatriot from Project Famous days, still working as a field engineer. Jean-Louis now had a fancy new side-looking sonar called SAR (for *sonar acoustique remorqué*) that was as good or better than the Scripps Deep Tow.

When I arrived in Paris, Claude Riffaud hosted a dinner at his apartment. In a relaxed atmosphere of wine and good food, I explained my plan to find the *Titanic* and then film it with *Argo* and ANGUS. Was IFREMER willing to participate in a co-expedition? With our combined resources — which meant both more time and technology — I was sure we would find the ship. It would be a great moment in the history of international scientific cooperation and a glorious scientific accomplishment. By the time dinner was over, I was sure IFREMER would go along. And indeed they did.

Jean Jarry would be the French project leader. Jean-Louis Michel — who would co-lead the expedition at sea with me — and I began to formulate a plan. The lion's share of the spadework would be done by the French, because my part of the expedition was not officially to look for the *Titanic* but to test a new piece of equipment, *Argo*. While I would be going out under the Woods Hole banner, the Institution was not backing me officially in

Jean Jarry, the leader of the French phase of the 1985 search.

any way. By contrast, the *Titanic* was an official goal for IFREMER, who saw it not only as a chance to demonstrate their equipment and expertise but as a potential source of revenue. There would undoubtedly be books and documentary films that would result if the ship were found.

The French agreed to recheck the weather patterns in the area to determine the optimum schedule: we knew the North Atlantic weather was unpredictable at the best of times and had badly hampered Grimm's expeditions. One of my major jobs was to research the nature of the bottom topography, especially any canyons that would make our efforts more difficult. (Canyons provide confusing echoes and large objects can get lost in the noise.) We already knew that water conditions at the *Titanic*'s depth were suitable for a visual search. (Years before, Bill Tantum had arranged to have the International Ice Patrol take Emory Kristof and two photographers out to check the bottom water.) Then there was the perennial question of where to search. Three previous attempts had been made by fine scientists using excellent equipment, but they had failed.

Bill Ryan at Lamont kindly showed Jean-Louis the *Sea MARC* records from 1980, but Fred Spiess was unwilling to release the 1981 Deep Tow data without Grimm's approval. Although we doubted the Deep Tow had missed anything, there was still that possibility. After all, the sea bottom in the area was complicated, especially around Titanic Canyon. And there was no guarantee the ship was still in one big piece, as Spiess and Ryan had assumed. Lacking the Deep Tow records, and seeing the poor quality of much of the *Sea MARC* data, we concluded we would have to go over the area covered by Spiess and Ryan just to be sure.

I concentrated my limited resources on finishing *Argo*, while IFREMER put money and man-hours into further historical research. Jean-Louis and I read and reread the various accounts of the disaster and pondered the conflicting information. When we had finished, we had come up with a 100-square-nautical-mile primary search area and a secondary search area of an additional 150 square nautical miles (which included part of the primary search area) mostly to the east.

At the Deep Submergence Laboratory, the spring of 1985 was a blur of action. As so often happens when you've got a tough deadline, things came down to the wire. Suppliers were late delivering key components. And I had to know the whole thing was working properly before we set out. The ship we would be using, the *Knorr*, was departing Woods Hole on another scientific expedition on June 17. *Argo* had to be ready by then.

Over the next five weeks the DSL Argonauts worked overtime — nights and weekends — as our deadline rapidly approached. The team spirit seldom waned; wives and children came to keep us company and held informal barbecues while we fine-tuned *Argo*, making last-minute adjustments to the telemetry system. At last everything was ready — except for the tow cable, which hadn't yet arrived. It would have to be shipped air freight to the Azores where our team would board *Knorr* in early August. If the cable didn't make it, *Argo* would be useless.

Our expedition plan called for a two-phase operation. During phase one (approximately four weeks on site), the French ship *Le Suroit*, led by Jean-Louis Michel, would find the *Titanic* by conducting a systematic search of the selected area using his newly developed deep-towed SAR sonar. In phase two (about 12 days on site), aboard the American ship *Knorr*, we would use *Argo* to visually inspect the various sonar targets SAR had picked up. The one that turned out to be the *Titanic* would be documented with *Argo* and with ANGUS, our veteran underwater still-camera vehicle that had by now taken hundreds of thousands of pictures in the ocean depths.

On June 24, 1985, *Le Suroit* set out from Brest, France. After a short stopover in the Azores, it headed for the area where the *Titanic* went down. I would join the ship about halfway through the first phase of the expedition. I prayed the French wouldn't find the *Titanic* before I got there.

····································

DISCOVERY

IN THE GRIM STRETCH OF THE NORTHWEST ATLANTIC WHERE the *Titanic* foundered, there is only a handful of weeks when the elements are likely to be kind. This prime summer "weather window" lasts from about mid-July to mid-September, but even in midsummer terrible storms are possible — as Jack Grimm had the misfortune to find out. We knew that our decision to stretch these limits, and begin the search in late June, was a risky one. But given the size of the area we planned to search, it was a necessary gamble. Subtracting the time required to get to and from the search area — first for the French ship *Le Suroit*, then for the American ship *Knorr* — we would have barely five weeks to accomplish our missions. Five weeks not only to find the *Titanic*, but to bring back a detailed photographic record of the wreck for the waiting world.

On paper, the search seemed simple. Our strategy was set, our equipment was in place and operational, and, as I'd always said, finding the *Titanic* should be easier than actually getting her on film. Jack Grimm, Fred Spiess, and Bill Ryan hadn't found the task so simple, however; neither would Jean-Louis Michel aboard the French research vessel *Le Suroit*.

Jean-Louis and his French crew arrived on site July 5 to begin the first part of the sonar search. Meanwhile, I was busy off the Pacific coast of Mexico, doing a series of dives in *Alvin* and conducting preliminary tests on *Jason Junior*, a prototype of the *Jason* robot that would eventually become part of the *Argo* system. Finally, on July 22, I arrived on the French island of St. Pierre, just south of Newfoundland in the Gulf of St. Lawrence, where, after two weeks of searching, *Le Suroit* had come to resupply.

So far the French had found nothing. They had covered a fair bit of ground, but had been hampered by a stronger-than-expected current. The expedition had barely begun and we were already behind schedule.

With me as I boarded the French ship were three other Americans who made up the documentation team that would immortalize our mission if it became a success. Bill Lange, the youngest of the three, was from Woods Hole. Eager to learn and excited to be on the trip, he would be a combination of aide de camp and apprentice to the two veterans — Ralph White, whom I had hired to help document the expedition on 16-mm film, and my old partner Emory Kristof, *National Geographic*'s renowned still photographer.

I'd wanted Emory on the trip not just because he's one of the best and someone I'd worked with many times before, but because I felt he'd earned a piece of the discovery, given our previous *Titanic* collaboration.

When we walked on board *Le Suroit*, we entered a foreign country. For Kristof, White, and Lange, it must have seemed as though they had landed on another planet. None of them spoke French and they were consigned to quarters in a separate container on the stern. As a result, they kept pretty much to themselves, playing cards, listening to music, reading — and waiting for something to happen.

The first thing that strikes you on board a French oceanographic vessel is the importance of food. The smell of food is everywhere, the rich odors of meat and garlic pervade the ship, and mealtimes are the central and rather formal ritual of shipboard existence. Apparently as much as a third of a total expedition budget is spent on food. It was certainly all very civilized, but the general atmosphere was too restricted for my liking.

Le Suroit was also very cramped. With about 50 people on board, it was almost impossible to find a private space, particularly in bad weather. I was forever banging my head or my knees and it was all I could do to get four feet of work space. Even the sleeping accommodations were crowded and the bathroom facilities inadequate. It was like living in a floating college dorm.

Thank God for Jean-Louis. Having spent a year at Woods Hole, he now spoke quite fluent English — with a charming Maurice Chevalier accent — and he was an old and good friend. With him on board, I found it easier to ignore the cramped formality of this foreign ship and concentrate on the task at hand: finding the *Titanic*.

As *Le Suroit* put out to sea, I must confess I was having some mixed feelings. I was hoping the French would find the *Titanic* and I was hoping they wouldn't. If they failed, that would leave very little time for the American phase of the expedition to both locate the wreck and photograph it. But it was only human for me to want to be the one to find the ship. This is not to say that Jean-Louis and I didn't share the power and the responsibility of command. We were a team and he consulted me on every decision he made, but as long as we were on a French ship Jean-Louis had the final word. Later, our roles would be reversed.

Jean-Louis and I had always worked together well, something that may seem surprising to outsiders because we couldn't be more different. He is a very quiet person, very private, and very serious, the epitome of the professional engineer — dedicated, meticulous, and methodical to the point of stubbornness, extremely cautious, and with a quiet sense of humor. He's also cool under pressure.

By contrast, I'm always joking around; sometimes this gets me into trouble or I make a fool of myself. But the main difference is that whereas Jean-Louis is careful and conservative, I'm a risk taker. Because we respect one another's strengths, which complement each other, we make a perfect combination: together we take calculated risks.

By the time *Le Suroit* arrived back in the area where the *Titanic* foundered, only 17 days remained to finish the sonar search. With good weather, it still might be possible. In order for his strategy to work, Jean-Louis had to know, within 30 to 50 feet or so, where his sonar SAR was as it was towed 12,500 feet beneath the support ship and only 600 feet above the ocean floor.

SAR was Jean-Louis' baby — he had designed and built

Jean-Louis Michel and his baby, the SAR sonar system.

it — and it was quite a beautiful child, resembling a spiffy red torpedo. Employing the latest in signal-processing technology, it was France's latest entry in the deep-towed, side-scan sonar business. Its shadow graphs, even better than those of the Scripps Deep Tow, were of such excellent quality that they resembled black-and-white photographs of the seafloor — visual pictures taken with sound waves. It was quite amazing. But for the search to work, SAR had to be towed with precision back and forth across the ocean floor so that nothing could escape its acute sense of hearing. It was the same laborious process, known as "mowing the lawn," that Spiess and Ryan had used.

The process was a bit like towing a kite on a two-and-a-half-mile string. *Le Suroit*'s movements along the surface ultimately determined the path SAR followed. *Le Suroit*'s position could be plotted precisely with the help of an extensive net of acoustical transponders — rather like the sonic equivalent of a radio beacon — that had been positioned on the ocean floor at the beginning of the French search. Every ten seconds or so, *Le Suroit* would send out an acoustic signal from her "tow fish," a small instrument she towed just beneath the surface. When each transponder heard this signal, it would respond by sending out its own unique sound. SAR would also chime in at regular intervals and these alternating "conversations" with the fixed transponders, first from *Le Suroit* and then from the moving deep-towed vehicle, allowed those on board to know almost exactly where both *Le Suroit* and SAR were at any time.

When SAR showed up a possible target it would be cross-checked with the record produced by the magnetometer, which measured the magnetic field, towed behind the "torpedo." We expected to see numerous sonar targets in the search area that might look like the *Titanic*, but only the *Titanic* would also have the magnetic signature of a large metallic ship — or so we hoped.

In good weather, the kite flyer (*Le Suroit*) could keep the string taut and fly the kite (SAR) along a straight underwater path. But, as Jack Grimm had discovered, bad weather or strong currents at the surface made "mowing the lawn" much more difficult. Each swath cut by this acoustical lawnmower was about 1,000 meters wide. However, since a side-looking sonar towed close to the bottom casts a "shadow," it could well miss the *Titanic* if she were hidden in one of the canyons or gullies traversing the search area. To be certain as possible that he too hadn't missed it, Jean-Louis had to run each new line slightly overlapping the first.

We picked up the search exactly where Jean-Louis had left off and for the first couple of days the weather held. We had a two- to-three-knot current to contend with, which made things slow enough. But then the weather turned and a series of storm fronts crossed over us, bouncing our ship around like a cork in a churning whirlpool. Having spent a great deal of my life in ships, I have always been amused when the weatherman reports that a "storm has gone harmlessly out to sea." I'd love to take one of those land-bound meteorologists out on one of our tiny vessels to experience one of those "harmless" storms.

Life aboard *Le Suroit* became quite unpleasant during bad weather. The already cramped spaces became even more claustrophobic. Outside, the decks were awash with waves breaking over the sides, often getting us cold and wet. It was rough, tough, thoroughly unpleasant seagoing, made worse by our impatience to get back to work.

Each time the weather worsened, Jean-Louis gallantly maintained the search until it simply became impossible to control SAR's path across the bottom, or to know where SAR was, or worse, until we were in danger of losing the vehicle altogether. Then he was forced to recover his sonar and ride out the heavy seas, with more precious time lost. Grimm's bad luck seemed to have returned to curse the French, but Jean-Louis never lost his cool, never abandoned the search strategy he had decided on. If he was worried or depressed, he never showed it.

In 1929, 17 years after the *Titanic* had sunk, the area 314 miles to the northwest had experienced a massive tremor known as the Grand Banks Earthquake, which broke numerous transatlantic cables and triggered massive mudslides. What if the mudslides had extended to the *Titanic* site and the ship was buried? Throughout the rest of our quest this thought would come back to haunt me: perhaps there was nothing there for us to find.

For the next week *Le Suroit* continued her patient sonar search, but as the first week gave way to the second and the second to the third — with still nothing to show for our efforts — you could feel the sadness envelop the ship. SAR had performed magnificently in the face of considerable adversity, "mowing the lawn" over 70 percent of the search area Jean-Louis and I had initially decided on. The SAR data base was a work of technological art collected by a master in his trade and it had told us where the *Titanic* wasn't. But I could see that despite SAR's accomplishments Jean-Louis was deeply disappointed. He had failed to corner our quarry. Now it would be up to an American ship and an American team to carry on our search.

On August 6, in the late morning, when it finally came time to recover SAR for good and head back to port, a hush seemed to fall over *Le Suroit*. The cramped and crowded ship suddenly seemed empty as people tried to find a quiet corner to reflect on failure. The day was gloomy, cool, and overcast, and I remember walking out on the starboard side and back toward the fantail where SAR was moored, its work now done. I looked out at the choppy sea overcast with gray. Suddenly the sky cracked open, the sun's rays streaming down, and out of nowhere a beautiful rainbow arced in the distance. I may spend most of my time being a rational scientist, but as a sailor I'm also a little superstitious. Perhaps the rainbow was an omen of better things to come.

On August 12, four days and many connecting flights after leaving *Le Suroit* in St. Pierre, Jean-Louis and I arrived in Ponta Delgada, Azores, in the middle of the Atlantic. Waiting for us was the U.S. oceanographic research ship *Knorr* and the American science team from Woods Hole's Deep Submergence Laboratory. Emory Kristof and Ralph White would catch up with us before we sailed. And *Argo*'s crucial tow cable had arrived by air just in time.

After the cramped quarters and somewhat stifling formality of the French ship, walking on board the *Knorr* was a little like going from boarding school to a country club. The *Knorr* has graceful lines, spacious quarters, and possesses a special cycloidal propulsion system that gives her maximum stability and maneuverability in bad weather. The *Knorr*'s two cycloids are like giant egg beaters — one under the bow and one under the stern. As a result, the ship can go backward or forward with equal ease, turn on a dime, or hold an optimum stationary position in a heavy sea. She was the last word in seagoing technology.

Knorr was the perfect ship for the job at hand — with one glaring exception. There was no suitable room on

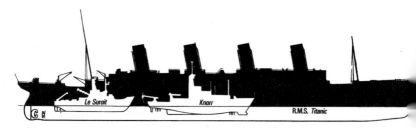

Silhouettes of the Titanic, Le Suroit, *and the* Knorr *show their comparative sizes.*

board to serve as a command center. I'd sailed on the *Knorr* for 12 years and I knew that in her main lab I could never achieve the atmosphere of intense concentration I wanted during our search. The ship's main corridor runs through her center. During a voyage, the traffic down that corridor is constant and distracting.

That was why, when I boarded the *Knorr* in the Azores, an alien object sat on her starboard afterdeck. It was a large rectangle, measuring 18 by 20 feet, composed of two portable shipping containers connected together like a mobile home. This was the *Argo*/ANGUS control van, mission control for the American phase of the expedition. Diagonally and aft across the deck from the van, on the port side, sat a third container — the photo-processing van where still photos would be developed. And sitting on the fantail, moored securely to the deck, were the white steel sleds of *Argo* and ANGUS, each about 15 feet long. Otherwise, the main piece of deck equipment was the take-up drum, just aft of the control van near the starboard rail. The cable ran from there up to the cable traction unit on the roof of the lab, where an electric winch paid out the line or hauled it in. From the roof of the lab, the cable fed back across the fantail to an A-frame — positioned over the starboard rail just aft of the take-up drum — and thence down into the water.

The architects of the *Knorr* had presciently provided space for the van by shifting the ship's superstructure to the port side, leaving a big deck area to starboard. Even with all this stuff taking up space, there was still room for a game of touch football. Weather permitting, this fantail deck would become the social center aboard the *Knorr,* the place where people would congregate off-duty to have a beer, talk, and relax, while still being able to follow any action on deck.

Walking from the fantail inside the superstructure, you entered the main lab, which we would mainly use for data-processing. If you continued down the main corridor that ran through the center of the ship, you'd pass the hospital, then the main dining galley, where the officers and science party ate. Beyond that was the kitchen and then the crew's galley.

The next two decks consisted mostly of sleeping quarters. The second deck also had a wet lab, a library, and a radio room. Forward on the third deck were the cabins for the chief scientist and the captain. On the fourth level was a bridge, the preserve of Captain Richard Bowen. I'd sailed with Captain Bowen before and knew him to be an excellent skipper. I was glad he was on board.

Added to the perfect ship was the ideal team — old ANGUS hands like Earl Young, Emile Bergeron, Tom Crook, Steve Gegg, and Martin Bowen; and the *Argo* specialists, including *Argo*'s designer, Stu Harris, and his engineers Tom Dettweiler and Bob Squires. They were backed up by navigators, data processors, and sonar operators making — with me — 25 in all. This team was drawn mainly from the family that I had assembled at DSL.

For the American phase of the search, Jean-Louis Michel would be joined by two other representatives of IFREMER, Jean Jarry and Bernard Pillaud. Jarry, now usually stuck in IFREMER's Paris head office, was looking forward to this brief return to the front lines. Bernard, a French Navy officer on loan to IFREMER, was experienced in the operation of cycloidal ships like the *Knorr*. They would certainly bring added professionalism to our venture.

As we headed across the Atlantic, there was time to finally nail down our last-ditch search strategy — in the event a visual search of Titanic Canyon (and the sonar targets identified by SAR and the Grimm expeditions) yielded no sign of the ship. The French had taken the traditional approach to underwater searches — sonar. Given the equipment at hand and my own background as a visual scientist, I intended to do something radically different — a visual search using *Argo*.

The new strategy was based on my long experience of looking for lost objects in the sea. Ever since 1964, when Woods Hole got into the diving business with *Alvin*, the phone had rung at least once a year with someone who wanted our help. The calls have run the gamut from the H-bomb lost off Spain in that same year (which *Alvin* found), to the Korean Airlines jet shot down by the Soviets in 1984 (for which *Alvin* was unavailable). Although these were gloomy missions, they had taught us a tremendous amount about how objects behave as they plunge to the bottom of the deep sea.

Whatever the type of wreck, all experience some degree of fragmentation as they sink. In shallow water, where the fall is short, fragments land on the seafloor pretty well directly below where they sank. In deep water, however, where the fall to the bottom takes much longer, the ocean currents have an opportunity to disperse them: the heavier the object, the more direct its downward path; but the lightest fragments will fall slowly in the underwater currents like leaves blown from a tree. The result is a long comet of debris along the ocean bottom, with the heaviest objects at the "windward" end of the field. At normal ocean depths of about two and a half miles — the depth to which the *Titanic* sank — with average currents of slightly over one knot, we have found these debris fields to be typically a half mile to one mile in length or longer.

It was with this knowledge that I made what turned out to be a crucial decision. In the next phase of the search — if more searching was needed — we would look for the *Titanic*'s debris field, not the *Titanic*. With this as our target, a visual search made more sense than a sonar search, since a sonar cannot distinguish a small man-made object lying on the bottom from natural debris, but a camera can.

As we steamed out toward the search area, I met in my cabin with Jean-Louis and the other Frenchmen to discuss this new strategy. While a visual search was alien to their way of thinking, they could see it was the only way we could cover the remaining ground with *Argo* in the time available. We all knew that time was running out.

Jean-Louis and I now discussed expanding the original primary search area. We were both convinced that we had now searched farther west than the *Titanic* could possibly have been. The secondary search area we'd identified was to the east of our initial one, but now we decided to extend it even farther east than originally planned. Perhaps the *Titanic* had been traveling much more slowly than her captain thought. Perhaps the current that night was even stronger than we had calculated. The southern boundary of our new search area was simpler to come up with — the position where the lifeboats were found. These were in effect the lightest pieces of *Titanic* debris — they didn't sink at all, but simply drifted south with the current.

From the *Californian*'s logbook, we had been able to calculate the speed and direction of her drift that night. That ship had encountered the ice field at 10:32 on the evening of April 14, 1912, and had drifted until 6:00 the next morning, a distance of five nautical miles. Hence the current was 0.7 knots to the south-southeast. So the *Titanic* had to be north of where her lifeboats were found.

The current had also provided another crucial clue. If the lifeboats had drifted south, so must have the underwater debris. Therefore, the *Titanic* and her debris field should lie to the north of the lifeboats along a roughly north-south line extending approximately one mile in length and with the lightest debris at the southern end. This meant we would run our search pattern in east-west lines to intersect the debris field at right angles.

All that remained was to decide where in the expanded area to begin. Our analysis of the historical data gave us a bull's-eye: a spot where the *Titanic* should be if all our assumptions were correct. But the one thing we knew for certain was that the *Titanic* wasn't in that exact spot (SAR had already checked there). And, in fact, one of the rules I always follow is never to start at the bull's-eye. I always make a search area large enough so that the target must be inside it and then start at the edge. The obvious choice was to start at the southern end of the area near where the first of the *Titanic*'s lifeboats was picked up by the *Carpathia*.

Our strategy was now set. To save time, we would run our lines one mile apart. If we missed the wreck on the first set of passes, we would come back with runs halfway between our first set of lines, meaning we would have surveyed the bottom at half-mile intervals. In this way, we could cover ground much more quickly. But first, we would take one last look at Titanic Canyon and the various sonar targets to make sure Jean-Louis hadn't missed anything in its nooks and crannies.

Our decision to go back over the canyon, despite the fact that SAR had yielded nothing conclusive, was a combination of the canyon's geology and emotional pull. It is by far the most dramatic underwater feature in the area and canyons have a habit of collecting debris, something like a big vacuum cleaner. If the wreck had settled somewhere in the canyon's vicinity, over the years some of its pieces might have flowed into the canyon. In that case, surely *Argo* would find some visual evidence of the *Titanic.*

As we neared Titanic Canyon, life on board the *Knorr* had settled into a fairly predictable routine. In contrast to *Le Suroit,* the atmosphere was informal and relaxed and meals were casual affairs. In their spare time, people were often seen reading the various *Titanic* books on board or watching one of the two *Titanic* movies, *A Night to Remember* and *Raise the Titanic,* on the VCR. Some people played cards; others fished for squid or dolphin, or tried to catch occasional sharks that invariably trailed the ship.

At dusk, people would gather on the fantail to relax and unwind. They'd lounge in deck chairs and have a few bottles of Sagres, a Portuguese beer bought in quantity in the Azores, and watch the sunset. When the weather was warm, people splashed in our "swimming pool" to take the heat off the day. (It was actually an enclosed area on the stern filled with water.) During these evening rituals,

A picnic on the fantail. Left to right: Emile Bergeron, Cathy Offinger, and Bernard Pillaud.

a casual observer would have had trouble guessing the seriousness of our mission or the high professionalism of those on board. But our real work was to come.

Early on the evening of August 24, we arrived in the vicinity of Titanic Canyon. We now had 12 days to go. Miraculously, the sea was flat calm. It was as if old King Neptune had said, "Here it is, it's yours." Calm weather makes seasoned mariners nervous. It's like pitching a no-hitter in baseball. You don't talk about it, you just watch it happen. At sea, there's a superstition that whistling brings storms. That evening nobody was whistling aboard the *Knorr*.

Satellites in orbit far above the earth gave us our position — so much more precise than the celestial fixes on which the *Titanic* and all other vessels depended back in 1912. I stood alone in the darkened chart room (the shades were pulled to eliminate glare) on the ship's bridge just aft of the helm, in the eerie glow of the red lights (used on all ships after dark because they don't affect night vision) and reflected once again on the *Titanic's* endless fascination. Surely her remains lay somewhere within a few miles?

At 7 P.M. local time, Captain Bowen slowed the *Knorr's* mighty engines, declutched the aft cycloid, and reduced speed to four knots. The stern cycloid makes a lot of noise and we needed to be able to hear well underwater in order to pick up the signal from the acoustic transponder that *Le Suroit* had left behind. Over the next 18 hours, we worked steadily, and by early afternoon the next day, August 25, our transponder net had been meshed with our U.S. Navy map of the canyon. *Le Suroit's* network and ours had become one. Now the hunt could begin in earnest.

People were pouring into the control van to man their

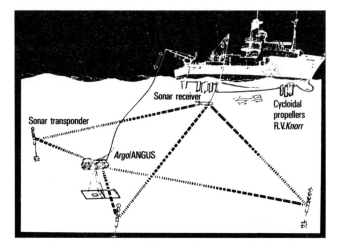

A small sonar receiver and transmitter towed below the Knorr *"talks" to the transponders and to* Argo *or* ANGUS.

stations. *Argo* was ready to dive. Whenever *Argo* was flying
and the search was on, all shipboard operations were
concentrated in our control van. Inside was a chart table
and a desk set back from several banks of TV monitors.
Every piece of information relevant to the search appeared
on one of those screens. Every function related to the
search could be carried out in that room.

I thought of the control van as the bridge of an imaginary submarine, its huge television monitors like windows
in the sea. When I stepped into the van, I could dive to the
bottom of the ocean with none of the peril and discomfort
of real submarines like *Alvin* — and with no time limits.

From my position at the plotting table in the center of
the van, I could observe every member of the seven-man
crew of each successive watch during *Argo* operations.
(ANGUS, having fewer instruments, operated with a much
smaller contingent of three.) Because there were three
watches, three different people were thus assigned to each of
the seven jobs. Directly forward of me and to the left was the
"flyer," the person operating the winch that controlled *Argo*'s
cable. His responsibility was to fly *Argo* at an optimum
distance from the bottom (altitude) and, above all, never to
crash. My three flyers were my most experienced technicians,
Earl Young, Martin Bowen, and Emile Bergeron.

In front of the flyer and slightly to the right sat the
navigator. His (or her) job was to know where *Argo* and
Knorr were at all times. My three trusty hands there were
Steve Gegg, Tom Crook, and Cathy Offinger.

To the immediate right of the navigator sat the driver,
the person actually steering the ship and controlling her
speed. If we found the *Titanic*, that hot seat would belong

to Captain Bowen, but during most of our straight-line search runs the job would be handed by a member of the regular watch. The steering mechanism reminded me of video game controls — two small levers with round black balls on top. One controlled the stern cycloid propeller and one the bow cycloid. For most of the expedition the three drivers were the watch leaders, Jean-Louis Michel, Jean Jarry, and Bernard Pillaud, who would mainly concentrate on driving the ship in tandem with the flyer. But if tactical decisions not covered by my instructions had to be made, they would make them — or wake me to consult. When the driver and the flyer worked well together — and the best at it were Jean-Louis Michel and Earl Young — then we could cover the maximum amount of ground.

To the right of the driver was the work station for the *Argo* engineers — Stu Harris, Tom Dettweiler, or Bob Squires, who wrote *Argo*'s complex software. Stu, as *Argo*'s chief architect, was probably the most important member of our whole science team. If something went wrong, he'd be the one to figure out the problem, or find the right man to fix it. He's a steady anchor when tension rises, very good for morale. But he's a reluctant seagoer; throughout the whole cruise he wore a circular sea patch behind his ear, which steadily dispersed medicine through his pores to prevent seasickness.

Behind the *Argo* engineer sat our sonar operator. Lt. George Rey of the U.S. Navy was with us on a temporary duty assignment from the Submarine Development Group One, the Navy's center of expertise on deep submergence in San Diego, California. One of his two alternates was Terry Snyder from the Klein sonar company, which had manufactured *Argo*'s side-scan. Between them these two had seen thousands of sonar blobs and smudges and had become masters at guessing what a shadow might be. The third sonar operator was Jim Saint, on loan from Colmek, the company in Utah that had manufactured *Argo*'s sensitive cameras and helped build its telemetry system.

The members of the documentation team also stood watch: Bill Lange, Emory Kristof, and Ralph White.

The final member of each watch, moving between work stations — mostly from navigator to *Argo* engineer to plotting table — was the data logger, either Sharon Callahan, Georgina Baker, or Lisa Schwarz. Their job was to maintain the "war map" resting on the chart table, a topographic map of the search area that already showed where SAR had been and now showed *Argo*'s proposed tracklines. As *Argo* inched along, the data loggers gathered information from the work stations and laid out on this map the actual sonar and visual coverage. In turn they gave the navigator and driver the tracking information as it was required.

The last member of the team was unattached to any particular watch but was often in the van. This was Dana Yoerger, a freshly minted Ph.D. in robotics from MIT, and the future father of *Jason*. He was along to smell and taste what the slogging was like in the trenches of oceanographic research. Since he wasn't needed on watch, he spent most of his time rewriting *Argo*'s tracking software, which was in desperate need of revision.

Whenever I walked into the control van, I could look at the map and see the order of battle at a glance. As chief scientist of the *Knorr* expedition, I didn't stand a watch,

Dana Yoerger, the future father of Jason, *and sonar operator Lt. George Rey of the U.S. Navy.*

but I could almost always be found in mission control when not asleep. My job was to be where the action was, whether at two in the morning or two in the afternoon; sleep would come when I got it. As long as the search was routine and no sign of wreckage appeared, I would have lots of time for rest and contemplation. When I was in the van, I'd be at the large chart table in the center of the room, which gave me a bird's-eye view of things as they unfolded. Or I would circulate from work station to work station for a close-up view of one aspect of the search.

During the watch, there was usually music playing — everything from reggae to Ravel — and often the van would be filled with the smell of fresh buttered popcorn brought in from the galley. When the weather grew cold and wet, as it would later in the voyage, the van was a haven of warmth and camaraderie. You could always find a place to "hide" in the back — close to the action but out of the way. When it was hot, as it had been for much of the trip to date, the van's four air conditioners kept the temperature cool. The only real problem was the amount of cigarette smoke. As many as half the members of any watch were smokers, and sometimes the cloud got so dense that I had to ration cigarette time in order not to overload the air-circulation system — and the lungs of non-smokers.

On our first launch on the afternoon of August 25, Earl Young was flying *Argo*, wearing a hard hat turned backwards on his head and cursing colorfully at the slightest irritant. Of the old salts aboard, Earl was the saltiest. Although I'd long ago nicknamed him Grumpy for his unfailingly sour demeanor and constant critical commentary, I couldn't think of a better man to have at the controls. We'd been through quite a few wars together and he'd never once broken ranks, no matter how rough the seas, late the hours, or challenging the task.

Now I watched Earl as he got ready, clutching the winch controls and checking the altimeter, which measured *Argo*'s height above the bottom, then glancing at the screen that would show the underwater scene viewed by *Argo*'s forward-looking camera. Should something suddenly appear on the screen, it was Grumpy's job to bail out fast, reeling in *Argo*'s 0.68-inch-thick cable quickly enough to lift the vehicle above any obstacle. He was a veteran of several crashes with *Argo*'s sibling, ANGUS, but now he had the advantage of real-time eyes underwater. He could see what he was doing with *Argo*, whereas ANGUS flies blind with only a down-looking sonar to guide it.

Now Earl jammed the control lever forward, paying out cable, and *Argo* began the first serious descent of its brief career. It had worked fine in test lowerings; but this one was for real. On Earl's right, Tom Crook, the navigator, watched his monitors to make sure *Argo* was in the right place. Tom is another Woods Hole old-timer — our all-time navigational expert at sea and a steady hand at the controls.

So far the launch was picture perfect. But no sooner had we begun to relax than Stu Harris, at the *Argo* work station, reported technical problems. Evidently a ground had shorted out *Argo*'s telemetry system — the television monitors in the van were washed with static. That meant *Argo* would have to return to the surface...

A short time later, with the white sled back on deck outside the van, its engineers swarmed over it like worker bees pampering a queen. Within 22 minutes *Argo* was on its way back to the bottom. Everyone on board knew we hadn't a minute to waste.

The beginning of a highly technical expedition is always plagued with problems. When the expedition is also inaugurating a completely new piece of hardware like *Argo*, these problems tend to multiply. New or not, no instrument system as complex as this could have been immune to the steady pounding of waves against the

Knorr's hull and the constant vibration caused by the engines during the long trip out from the Azores. As well, there's the ever-present salt and humidity, which love to wreak havoc on electronics, laying down a corrosive layer of salt on our circuit boards. In expeditions such as this one, the question is not whether we will have equipment problems but when and how many.

One hour and 40 minutes later, *Argo*'s altimeters finally sensed bottom 100 feet below it. At the winch control, Earl now slowed *Argo*'s descent and the watch tensed for our first look at the bottom. A few minutes later, at 3:30 P.M., the seafloor came into view on our black-and-white monitors with *Argo* hovering at 50 feet. Bottom depth was 12,690 feet from the surface. The faint tracks of deep-sea slugs, or holothurians, appeared, etched in the mud. Otherwise nothing…

For the next several hours, we explored a region a few miles to the east of the canyon, the watch team settling down into a routine set to the rhythm and tune of *Argo*'s instruments: pings sent out by the navigation system, *Argo*'s sonar, and the ship's echo sounder; the hard-copy recorder singing out a line of data. The smell of buttered popcorn filled the van and the mood was one of relaxed concentration. After the long slow trip out to the site, finally we were getting down to business.

With the help of the sonar, we investigated a number of "bomb craters" I knew from previous experience could have been made by the impact of heavy pieces of *Titanic* wreckage. Most of them were empty, but in one we saw a huge glacial boulder. It would be a wonderful irony, I mused, if this boulder had come loose from the very iceberg that had sunk our quarry, jogged loose by a *Titanic* collision of ice and steel. Apart from these craters, the cameras revealed only a gently rolling countryside consisting of hills of muddy sediment.

Over the next two days, as the clock ticked relentlessly onward, we investigated the various sonar targets identified by the Grimm expeditions and by SAR. Jean-Louis and I knew we were grasping at straws, but we felt we had to definitely eliminate all possible targets in the canyon and vicinity before starting a new search effort. Three of Grimm's sonar and magnetometer targets held particular interest. One was the "propeller" site. Another was one we nicknamed "Ryan's Madness" after Bill Ryan of Lamont, who had identified it. The third was dubbed "Spiess's Obsession" in honor of Fred Spiess. This one had really mesmerized him. During Grimm's 1981 expedition he'd come back to it again and again.

I didn't know it then, but Grimm had played a trick on us. The position of the "propeller" site we checked so carefully was wrong. Grimm had deliberately falsified its location on the map of the search area published in his book *Beyond Reach*. Furthermore, none of Grimm's legitimate sonar targets showed up anything of interest, just glacial droppings and canyon outcroppings. The canyon and its tributaries were clean.

In the process of touring the canyon itself, we had gone on a fascinating slalom ride, glimpsing beautifully worn outcrops of canyon fill as we zigzagged back and forth. The carved walls were reminiscent of the Grand Canyon, etched layers that told a long and complex story of deposition, erosion, and redeposition. Near the southern limit of our search, the canyon bottom became rough as numerous gullies cut into the slopes, reminding me of the badlands of South Dakota. Before we called it quits, we actually continued well south of the southern limit of our search area, guessing that over the years debris might have been transported far from the the actual wreck. No such luck, but *Argo* had reached a major milestone, exceeding for the first time *Alvin*'s diving depth of 13,000 feet. Years before, I had explored similar underwater valleys off the coast of New England inside the cramped and cold quarters of our submarine *Alvin*. Now here I was sitting in a comfortable chair, drinking a Coke Classic and eating a warm piece of pie, with the strains of a Willie Nelson tape filling the van, while the submarine landscape rolled by. Now *this* was exploring.

By late morning on August 27, almost exactly two days after we began our tour of Titanic Canyon, *Argo* was back on the fantail, having eliminated all possible sonar and magnetic targets from past expeditions. Nine days to go and the crunch had come. Suddenly the ocean was huge and self-doubt began to loom large. Was the *Titanic* really in our carefully plotted search area? If so, surely some evidence of her debris would have shown up in the canyon. Were we looking in the wrong place?

Now I began to feel a rising panic — and others on board seemed to be feeling it too: the tension increased and the atmosphere became almost frantic. This thing was harder to crack than we'd allowed ourselves to believe.

Jean-Louis, as usual, showed no sign he was worried. Perhaps it was easier for him because it wasn't his ship, but if we didn't find the *Titanic* it would be a shared failure.

Nonetheless, the visual search strategy was my brainchild. If it worked, I'd look pretty smart. If not...

At 1:40 P.M. on the 27th, after recovering, repairing, and relaunching a malfunctioning transponder, we were under way to the east, into the unexplored waters of our expanded search area. A small wedge at the eastern edge of the primary search quadrant had been previously missed by SAR due to the current, so the new area slightly overlapped the old to include this missed portion. If we came up empty, we could always return to the canyon for one more try. It was still difficult to let go of the idea that the *Titanic* was in that canyon somewhere.

During our short ten-mile transit to the southeast, the *Knorr*'s engineering department made a number of repairs to *Argo*'s large winch system. I didn't want anything to hold us up, and during the last lowering we had noticed that the take-up drum, which stored *Argo*'s expensive conducting cable as it was winched in, was slowly shifting off its axis. If that continued uncorrected, we might lose *Argo* and with it all chance of finding the *Titanic*.

By mid-afternoon, we were ready to position a new transponder network that would enable us to know where we were as we conducted this final search. With less than nine full days left, I decided on a shortcut. Instead of the three groups of three transponders that would ensure ideal navigation, I elected to put in only one group of three, forming a triangle in the middle of the remaining search quadrant. This would save a lot of time, but would make tracking poor to the north and south as distance from this net increased. The visual search strategy, which didn't require precise overlapping lines, permitted me to take this risk. I hoped it would work.

By 1:44 A.M. the next morning, we had surveyed the new transponder net into place and we were in position just south of where the *Carpathia* had retrieved the first lifeboats. We were ready to launch *Argo* into unknown waters.

As the little white sled with its jaunty tailfin slid beneath the gentle Atlantic swells, I contemplated what lay ahead. So far we had been blessed with almost perfect weather and in the darkness of the early morning hours it was cool, but calm. The area to be covered was about 100 square miles. This meant it would require ten to twelve east-west passes a mile apart. If all went well, I figured this process should take up five to six of our remaining eight and a half days. If we didn't find the ship by then, there would be time for only a partial doubling back between these lines.

Two and a half miles below us, the water was markedly clearer than in the canyon, making it possible to fly *Argo* at a higher altitude and for us to see farther out to the side. The extra width wasn't critical to our current mission, but it demonstrated how useful *Argo* would be on future scientific expeditions. What was important to us here was *Argo*'s ability to send continuous real-time television pictures of the ocean bottom to the van for instant analysis, playback, and response. The first thing *Argo* showed us, however, was a bottom of narrowly spaced sand ripples, large sand waves, and sand dunes. Jean-Louis, who was in the van for the lowering, remarked that it reminded him of a beach in Brittany — an empty beach, unfortunately.

By this point in our voyage, the three watches had each assumed a distinct personality and two of the three had already earned nicknames. Jean-Louis Michel's watch — midnight to 4 A.M. and noon to 4 P.M. — had christened itself with characteristic bravado "The Watch of Quiet Excellence." They were also occasionally known as "Harris's Heroes," after Stu Harris, *Argo*'s technical wizard. Their excellence stemmed from the fact that taciturn Jean-Louis at the helm and grumpy Earl on the winch control had developed into the most competent team at getting the most out of *Argo*. Since Jean-Louis had relinquished overall command for the American portion of the expedition, I had made sure he had the best watch. For some reason, the midnight watch always seems to be the one where things happen.

In 12,500 feet of water, it was impossible to tow *Argo* at high speeds because of the water friction that built up around the long cable running up to the surface. At only 0.68 inches in diameter this cable may not seem like much, but over two and a half miles that adds up to a lot of surface area. The faster Jean-Louis or one of his French colleagues drove the boat, the more *Argo* had a tendency to "kite" higher in the water and out of viewing range. We had counteracted this to some degree by making *Argo* heavier. As a result it towed closely behind the ship — the cable all but vertical — making it much easier to maneuver ship and underwater sled in tandem, especially during the turn at the end of each pass. Having *Argo* almost straight below us also made it easier to know where the sled was. The problem was that a heavier *Argo* put more strain on the cable and the whole winch apparatus.

Towing *Argo* became a balancing act between maximizing speed over the bottom while not exceeding the highest viewing altitude. Jean-Louis and Earl performed the job like veteran tightrope walkers. As the kiting action began to lift *Argo* off the bottom, Earl would pay out more cable. As Earl ran out of cable, Jean-Louis would stall the ship's forward progress, either by using the forward cycloids or by bringing the bow slightly into the wind. As the *Knorr* slowed and *Argo* began falling, Earl would take in cable to prevent the vehicle from crashing to the bottom. This went on, hour after hour, day after day.

It was an *Argo* mishap that earned the 8 A.M.-to-noon/ 8 P.M.-to-midnight watch its nickname, "The Crash Crew," and almost proved fatal to the entire expedition. After breakfast on August 28, we'd enjoyed another beautiful sunrise on the fantail as we neared the end of line number one. I was back in the control van as we prepared to execute what would become a routine maneuver — turning the ship to the north to begin the next line a mile away. Bernard Pillaud was driving the ship and Martin Bowen was on the winch controls. Martin, no relative of Captain Bowen, is the Deep Submergence Laboratory's specialist in remotely controlled robots, a marine biologist turned techie and an ANGUS veteran. He was the man who would drive *Jason Junior* on his maiden voyage the following year. For him, flying *Argo* was second nature.

A shorter tether would make the turn easier to execute, so Bernard stalled the ship, causing *Argo* to descend toward the bottom, and Martin began taking in cable. But he wasn't fast enough — *Argo* was heading for a crash landing. Instinctively, Martin threw the winch lever forward and the traction unit, perched on the deck over the main lab, began to send the cable toward the take-up drum 15 feet down on the starboard deck. He'd done the right thing, but the repairs just made to the take-up drum unexpectedly slowed down its turning. At this reduced speed of take-up, it couldn't keep pace with the amount of cable being fed to it. Martin glanced at the television screen (which monitored the cable as it runs from the traction unit to the take-up drum) only to see a large loop of cable forming — across the ship's main passageway. If someone were to walk down that passage as the loop went tight, it would cut him in half.

I was at the plotting table with my back to the work stations, pondering the next line, when I heard Martin yell. I spun around, took one look at Martin's face, and bolted out the door. Meanwhile Martin reversed the control lever to pay out *Argo* cable and take up the slack, but this only compounded the problem. As I emerged from the van, I watched helplessly as the now-limp cable jumped off the traction unit and started to wind around the winch axle. Then, as the axle began to eat the cable in half, it stalled, automatically shutting down the system. By the time I'd galloped up the ladder to the traction unit, I could see we had a disaster on our hands. The cable couldn't go forward or back and would soon be under enormous pressure. Only quick work would save *Argo*.

The stall had probably saved the cable from breaking, but back in the van Martin could no longer control *Argo*'s depth and the sled fell relentlessly toward the bottom. Out on the upper deck I could see that the winch axle had completely eaten through the cable's strong exterior armor; that meant if we speeded up the ship to kite *Argo* off the bottom, the cable would break and *Argo* would be lost for good. Our only hope was to let *Argo* crash and drag along the bottom while we desperately tried to solve our winch problem.

To make a bad situation worse, the ship was now at the very farthest point from our transponder net, making navigation shaky at best. Since we didn't have good tracking, we couldn't tell exactly where the ship was relative to *Argo*, which had now dug into the soft bottom and was acting like an anchor — on a very fragile chain. Any move in the wrong direction would increase tension and snap the damaged cable. I decided to let the ship drift while we attempted to salvage the situation. Fortunately, the seas were calm and the wind slight.

The cable's tension held at 17,000 pounds while Earl Young, *Knorr* bosun Jerry Cotter, the ship's deck crew and I went madly to work. If the tension increased to 20,000 pounds, the cable was in doubt; at 25,000 it would snap for sure; I had heard too many stories of cables parting under tension and dismembering or decapitating anyone in the way. Of all the things we did during the entire 1985 *Titanic* expedition, this was the most dangerous.

As we worked against the clock, everyone was on full alert. Occasionally, a terse comment or command punctuated the silence: "I need a knife"; "Get me line"; "Watch the tension"; "Be careful! Be careful!" Covered in grease, our knuckles bleeding, we all knew this was a desperate race against time.

In a frantic 20 minutes, we rigged a scaffolding on the stern beneath the damaged piece of cable, spliced in an attach point below the damage, and transferred the tension to a temporary line we'd fastened to a post on the fantail deck. The damaged section was now free of tension and at last we could breathe a partial sigh of relief — *Argo* could now be recovered, but seemingly for the last time. Even if we could figure a way to fly *Argo* again, it would be blind — the cable's innards must by now have been irretrievably damaged.

Back in the control van, Bernard and Martin were taking it pretty hard. But the accident could have happened on any watch: no one had foreseen the problem that would result from the repairs to the take-up drum. Around me, the other members of the watch weren't talking; the van was uncomfortably silent. We were all a bit in shock, looking the end of our expedition square in the face after

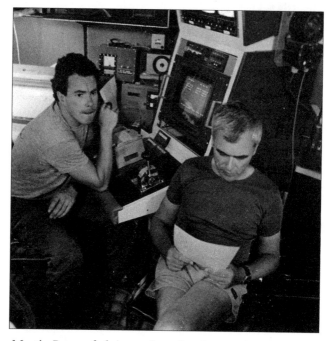

Martin Bowen feels pretty low after the near loss of Argo *as Jean Jarry checks the logbook.*

completing only one line of our visual search.

Then, like a clemency call from the governor moments before an execution, we were granted a reprieve. Stu Harris had joined us in the van and decided to turn *Argo*'s power back on to assess the damage. As the *Knorr* increased speed, *Argo* broke free of the bottom. The television pictures were suddenly crystal clear! The cable armor had been cut, but the cable's innards were fine. Quickly, we studied the cable meter readings and the depth charts of the search area. A second reprieve: our search pattern would slowly but continuously move us into shallower water as we worked our way up the continental rise toward the Grand Banks. We wouldn't be able to pay out cable to maximize our speed, but we would be able to continue the search.

So that was how the 8-to-12 watch came to be known as "The Crash Crew." Since they were generally a pretty quiet group, the name stuck. Fortunately, however, they did nothing further during the search to warrant their nickname.

A little after midnight, in the early morning of August 29 as we were traveling the third line, words like "boring" began to enter the logs kept at the various work stations. The routine inside the van had become numbing, hour after hour staring at video images of flat bottom mud, occasionally interrupted by a sea-slug track or a boulder crater. After an hour or so staring at a video monitor or sonar readout, your eyes get sore, your mind begins to wander, you start to go squirrelly and something has to give. Occasionally, I entered the van to discover the watch members out of their chairs and boogeying to loud reggae music. As the days wore on, people concocted some elaborate practical jokes to relieve the tedium.

The wildest watch, and the focus for much of these carryings on, was the 4 A.M.-to-8 A.M. There's nothing like getting up in the middle of the night to start work, and from the beginning this watch had been a little bit crazy. One time, they marched into the van at four in the morning in a neat little line whistling the tune the dwarfs sang in *Snow White and the Seven Dwarfs* — "Heigh-ho, heigh-ho, it's off to work we go." Stunts like this earned them their nickname, "The Zoo Crew."

Despite such antics, by August 30 as we reached the middle of line number five, morale was beginning to plummet. To boredom was now added a turn in the weather as wind and seas began to build. As we steamed north to begin line six, *Argo*'s cable got tangled in the second cable towing the small "fish" that talked to the transponders. Valuable time slipped away as the "fish" was recovered and the knots untied. Our concentration and dedication appeared to be slipping with only six days to go.

Not surprisingly, the first serious rumbles of discontent came from the most obstreperous watch, the Zoo Crew, and the epicenter was my old friend Emory Kristof. Understandably, Emory was getting impatient with the way things were going. And he was probably getting tired of being a watch flunkie. Emory likes to be a parachute commando, not a foot soldier. He and his sidekick Ralph White had lots of time to formulate their own theories about where the *Titanic* was and what it would look like on sonar, and indeed, for several days, new theories about

Launching the small "fish" that communicated with our transponders and with ANGUS *and* Argo.

where to look for the *Titanic* had been rattling around the control van. People who knew nothing about the *Titanic* before stepping on board the *Knorr* had been reading the various historical accounts sitting on the plotting table and they had become instant armchair experts.

During the 4-to-8 watch on the evening of August 30, as the Zoo Crew conducted the sixth pass over the search area, Jean-Louis and I suddenly found ourselves faced with a minor rebellion in the ranks. *Argo*'s sonar had found a target that seemed to correspond in size and signal intensity to the main wreckage of the *Titanic* — or so the Zoo Crew thought. Jean-Louis and I were quite certain it was nothing more than the crest of high sandwaves. We'd become quite familiar with how these looked on SAR's sonar and we were also quite familiar with how the *Titanic* should look on a shadow graph. We knew this definitely wasn't it.

....

But as morale dropped and boredom became unbearable, sonar targets began to grow in size and importance. Emory demanded rather forcefully that we abandon our carefully conceived search pattern and go check this one out. Others in the van seemed to think this was a good idea. But checking it out would take valuable time, time that might mean the difference between finding the *Titanic* and not.

What we were faced with was hardly a mutiny, but it was nonetheless a serious challenge to authority that might open a Pandora's box of other problems with every new sonar target growing in importance. There seems to be a point in almost every expedition when this happens and it was happening to us now. I knew that fast, decisive action was required.

Seeing that the possibility for rational discussion had passed, I asked Jean-Louis to join me outside to discuss a plan of action. We stood outside the fantail and talked it over. The early evening air was cool and the damp wind cut into our summer clothes — a sure sign the storm front was getting closer. We were more than halfway through the search area and still no visual sign of wreckage. Our own faith was at its lowest ebb. Perhaps Kristof and the gang were right.

We shook off these doubts and agreed on a compromise we felt would nip the "mutiny" in the bud. We decided to double back and run a line between numbers five and six. (Our original plan was that if we didn't find the *Titanic* during our first series of passes we'd double back between the original lines — so this would be a line we might have to run regardless.) Then we'd continue with the search pattern exactly as planned.

Jean-Louis and I re-entered the van. Without saying anything, I walked over to the watch navigator, Steve Gegg, and gave him the new plan. That accomplished, and with no further words exchanged, Jean-Louis and I started to leave the van. At that moment, Emory approached with fire in his eyes and gruffly asked me what I was going to do. "Ask the navigator," was my reply. I followed Jean-Louis out the door.

Line seven proved eventless. The mystery targets were indeed sand dunes. And that was the last hint of rebellion on board.

At lunchtime on August 31, after a minor delay to make some adjustments to *Argo*, we began the eighth pass. The weather was getting steadily worse and the sea was beginning to build; it seemed only a matter of time before the storm hit. Evening came and still nothing. All was quiet in the ranks and I had begun to face defeat. In only five days we would have to head home. Alone in my cabin after dinner, I washed my face and stared into the mirror. The specially designed *Titanic* patch — a gift from Jean-Louis Michel — sewn on the breast of my blue jumpsuit stared back at me. Each member of the scientific party had proudly sewn on one of these as we had sailed out of the Azores. That now seemed light-years away. Could it have been less than three weeks ago?

Whatever happened I knew I'd still be wearing the patch when we sailed into our home port at Woods Hole. Right then, however, I hoped our return would be under cover of darkness.

I went back to the control van, where the Crash Crew had just come on watch. Line nine was now in progress. Maybe Martin and Bernard would redeem their earlier humiliation and be the ones to spot the first sign of wreckage. But I doubted it. Wearily, I laid out the next line on the plotting table so navigator Cathy Offinger would know which course to follow when it came time to begin line ten. Our coverage of the new search area was now nearly complete. I noted that line nine would take us directly to the northeastern limit of previous SAR coverage, overlapping the portion they had missed — that sliver of bottom one mile wide and five miles long.

I stayed in the van until the midnight watch change. Jean-Louis and the other members of the Watch of Quiet Excellence came tumbling in, still rubbing their eyes and holding warm cups of coffee, breaking the quiet mood with a sudden infusion of noise and energy. With the changing of the guard, seven separate and simultaneous conversations filled the command center as the outgoing member of each station reported status to his replacement. The pleasant hubbub was occasionally punctuated by calls coming in over the speakers hooked up to the bridge, all underscored with the never-ending background noise of printers printing and sonars pinging. Then, after ten or fifteen minutes, the old watch was gone and the new watch settled down to work. This was always the quietest time of all — before the music and gossip returned. So began the graveyard shift of September 1, 1985.

During his watch, Jean-Louis was to continue line nine until *Argo* crossed over into the area already covered by SAR and then head north one mile to begin line ten, which

The graveyard shift — the Watch of Quiet Excellence — goes quietly about its work. Bottom to top: Jean-Louis Michel, Tom Crook, and Steve Gegg.

should happen not long before the watch changed at 4 A.M. Since the injury to *Argo*'s cable, Jean-Louis and Earl had maintained their reputation as the master flyers who covered more ground than the other watches — they had simply changed their style, speeding the ship up (and paying out the full length of undamaged cable) until *Argo* kited to maximum viewing height, then slowing it down again.

With Jean-Louis in charge and Harris's Heroes in the van, I knew *Argo* was in good hands. Now it was time for me to take a break. But before I left, I heard Billy Lange make his nightly forecast. The last couple of nights he'd taken to predicting exactly when the *Titanic* would be found. He'd pick a spot on the chart and estimate when *Argo* would be there. Tonight, he said, they would find the ship between 2 and 2:30. The *Titanic* sank at 2:20 A.M. Lange was getting superstitious, I thought, but I hoped against hope that tonight he would be right. As I left the van, "I Heard It Through the Grapevine" played softly on the stereo.

Back in my cabin, propped up in my bunk in warm flannel pajamas, I picked up Chuck Yeager's autobiography. As I began to read, my mind soon left the ocean depths and was soaring into the stratosphere.

Unbeknownst to me, a drama was beginning to play itself out in the control van below. About 12 minutes before 1 A.M., Bill Lange turned to Stu Harris and said, "What are we going to do to keep ourselves awake tonight?" All they'd seen so far was more mud, endless miles of bland, featureless bottom. Stu didn't answer. His eyes were glued to the *Argo* monitor. He had seen a new kind of image. "There's something," he said simply, as he pointed to the TV screen. Suddenly, every member of the sleepy watch become alive and alert, but no one could believe that it wasn't just another false alarm, or a practical joke. Had Zoo Crew fever infected the Watch of Quiet Excellence?

But no. Stu switched *Argo*'s camera from forward-looking camera to down-looking and a few seconds later, Bill Lange exclaimed, "Wreckage!" And sure enough, there on the video screen were the unmistakable images of things man-made. A few seconds later, Stu added his exultant note: "Bingo!" and then the van echoed with a chorus: "Yeah!" followed by shrieks and war whoops.

Moments later, Lieutenant Rey on the sonar reported, "I'm getting a hard contact." For a few minutes there was nothing more to see save for a few small glacial boulders.

Had they been seeing things after all? A discussion started as to whether they should go wake Ralph White so he could start filming. Then, at two minutes to one, more small definite debris fragments began to appear. They decided to go get Ralph.

After the long, tedious, fruitless search and yesterday's minor mutiny, no one wanted to drag me out of the sack on a false alarm. Nothing is more embarrassing than to become a member of the "I Saw a Flare Club." Bill Lange was the first to suggest that "Someone should go get Bob," but no one made a move. By four minutes past one, everyone in the van had become convinced something was up, but as all sorts of wreckage streamed past, no one wanted to leave. Now Stu Harris said, "Let's go get Bob," but still there were no volunteers. Ironically, the ship's cook, who had never before ventured into the van, now wandered in. He sure had picked a hell of a moment to take his first peek. The van crew immediately pressed him into service and sent him up to rouse me.

While the cook headed aft and up to my quarters, something new appeared amid the unrecognizable wreckage passing on the the video screen. It was perfectly circular… "A boiler?" someone mused. "It's a boiler!" Bill Lange sang out. Now there could be absolutely no doubt. But Jean-Louis still wouldn't believe what his eyes were telling him. He opened the book containing a facsimile of the now-famous 1911 *Shipbuilder* article on the *Olympic* and the *Titanic* and turned to the page with the pictures of the boilers. He looked from page to screen and back again, repeating over and over, as if to convince himself, "Yes, it *ees* a boiler."

When the cook stuck his head through the door of my cabin, I was still busy breaking the sound barrier with Yeager. Finally, I'd gotten the *Titanic* out of my mind. "The guys think you should come down to the van," he said. It took a couple of seconds for the import of his words to penetrate, then I sprang out of my bunk, Yeager's book flying, pulled on my jumpsuit over my pajamas, and practically knocked the cook out of the way in my haste to get to the van. I must have run the three decks down and aft in about 30 seconds.

When I burst into the van, Stu informed me that *Argo* had just passed over a massive ship's boiler. The initial elation in the room had subsided to a simmer, but was still ready to boil over again. Quickly, they replayed the tape and sure enough I saw the image of a big ship's boiler — *Titanic*'s. I didn't yelp or shout. In fact, for a few seconds, I didn't say anything. Then, totally at a loss for words, I simply kept repeating in a quiet but incredulous voice, "God damn. God damn…"

I turned to Jean-Louis. The look in his eyes said everything. The *Titanic* had been found. We'd been right all along. Then he said softly, "It was not luck. We earned it."

Our hunt was almost over. Somewhere very near us lay the R.M.S. *Titanic*.

Around us the van again erupted in whoops and shouts. I went around and congratulated the members of the watch, shaking hands, patting people on the back. But in the midst of my elation, I began to realize the danger we were in. Larger and larger pieces of wreckage were now passing under *Argo* and Earl had to winch in to avoid hitting them. We didn't yet know where the main wreck was. If large pieces of it were intact, they would loom up quite suddenly — too suddenly for even Grumpy to avoid. I cautioned the watch, "Be careful now about the altitude." But we were all so mesmerized by what we were seeing that it was some minutes before I converted the warning into a command.

As the images on the video screen grew more and more vivid — large pieces of twisted hull plating, portholes, a piece of railing turned on its side — for the first time since I had started on this quest 12 years before, the full human impact of the *Titanic*'s terrifying tragedy began to sink in. Here at the bottom of the ocean lay not only the graveyard of a great ship, but the only fitting monument to the more than 1,500 people who had perished when she went down. And we were the very first people in 73 years to come to this precise spot to pay our respects. Images from the night of the disaster — a story I now knew by heart — flashed through my mind with painful intensity.

At 1:13 A.M. — eight minutes after *Argo* passed over the boiler — I snapped out of my reverie and gave the order to raise *Argo* to its strobing altitude of 80 to 100 feet. I was being careful, but I didn't realize until later just how dangerous our situation was. Unwittingly, we were coming into the wreck at the worst spot. I would never have flown *Argo* through that place in the way that I did, knowing what I know now. It was as if we were towing our sled through downtown Manhattan after World War III. We were only about 12 feet above the *Titanic*'s deck.

Word had now spread through the ship and people were pouring into the van. The place was becoming a madhouse. With *Argo*'s running lights turned off, the newcomers saw not a real-time image of the bottom, but a series of snapshots taken every eight seconds — a sort of disco effect. By 1:25, we had crossed the debris field and I decided to pull *Argo* up. In this northwestern corner of our new search area, the tracking was poor. I wanted to put in a new transponder net before surveying the wreckage in detail. Besides, bedlam had erupted in the van — it was time for celebration before getting back to work — and people had started to pass around paper cups of Mateus wine purchased in the Azores. At least the stuff was bubbly. It was the closest we came to champagne.

I won't soon forget that scene of triumph and jubilation. Emory Kristof clapped me on the back and then went back to snapping pictures. Ralph White filmed furiously away. Jean-Louis grinned broadly. Everybody was talking at once, congratulating each other, while trying to pay attention to the job at hand.

Then, at the height of this victory celebration, our mood suddenly crashed as if *Argo* had again hit bottom. Someone — I don't remember who — pointed up to the twin clocks, one with Zulu (Greenwich time) and one with local time on it and said something like "Oh my God!" It was approaching 2 A.M. local time, very close to the exact hour of the *Titanic*'s sinking. That was all it took to break our mood. Here we were just catching our breaths at the peak of elation and suddenly we felt awkward, even sad. Part of our vulnerability may have been due to the fact that for the first time since the search had started we were without a purpose. All at once the professional was replaced by the human being. The van became quiet.

I said something like, "I don't know how you people

feel, and I don't want to impose my feelings on you all, but I know that in about 20 minutes I'm going out on the fantail. If anyone wants to join me, they're welcome. If not, that's okay." That was it. Then I walked out of the van.

I don't remember exactly what I did for the next 20 minutes. I just found a quiet corner to be alone with my thoughts. And I imagine a lot of others did the same. When I got to the fantail, quite a few people had gathered. I raised the Harland & Wolff flag, the emblem of the Belfast shipyard that had built the *Titanic*. I wasn't trying to be theatrical about it, it just seemed the right thing to do. The storm that had appeared to threaten us had passed by at a safe distance and the weather was beautiful: the sky was clear and filled with stars, the sea calm. Except for the moon, it was just like the night the *Titanic* went down. I spoke only a few words: "I really don't have much to say, but I thought we might just observe a few moments of silence."

It was one thing to have won — to have found the ship. It was another thing to be there. That was the spooky part. I could see the *Titanic* as she slipped nose first into the glassy water. Around me were the ghostly shapes of the lifeboats and the piercing shouts and screams of people freezing to death in the water.

Our little memorial service lasted five, maybe ten minutes. Then I just said, "Thank you all. Now let's get back to work."

CHAPTER 7

···································

TITANIC FOUND

AS DAWN BROKE ON THE COOL, GRAY MORNING OF SUNDAY, September 1, 1985, the *Knorr*'s radar told us our tiny vessel was surrounded by ships. Suddenly, a P-3 Orion submarine hunter thundered overhead, barely clearing the bridge as it tested its magnetometer on the *Knorr*. Moments later, a fighter bomber sporting a big red Canadian maple leaf flew past. All at once the sea and sky were alive with ships and airplanes. Did everyone in the world know that we had found the *Titanic*? As it turned out we had landed by pure chance in the middle of a NATO exercise: our discovery was not yet known to the world — or was it?

When I called Woods Hole to give them the good news, I was met with a jolt. The guard who answered the phone informed me that the press had been calling all morning wanting details of our *Titanic* discovery. Apparently, there'd been a story in the Sunday London *Observer*. If that was true, then the paper had gone to press at about the time we'd found the ship. Impossible. Or had someone been eavesdropping on our radio conversations between the van and the bridge?

I didn't have time to ponder the matter. Although the weather was still fairly calm, I could smell a storm on the way. Sure enough, our satellite readout had located an approaching storm front. We had barely four days before we were due to head back to Woods Hole, and a North Atlantic gale could cut seriously into that time, or put a premature end to our expedition.

In the short space remaining, I planned to get as many pictures of the wreck as possible. First, we launched more transponders, capturing the wreck firmly in our high-tech net. Then we mapped the debris field with *Argo*, avoiding the main wreckage and getting to know the lay of the land before we went in for a closer look. Ironically, the *Knorr's* old-fashioned echo sounder, which had been left running when the transponder net was surveyed into place, had located the main piece of the hull. With all this fancy equipment on board we had pinpointed the location of the *Titanic* with a run-of-the-mill fathometer, no better than on an ordinary deep-water fishing trawler.

A much more bitter irony became apparent when Jean-Louis and I examined how close *Le Suroit* had come to finding the wreck. On one of his very first passes Jean-Louis had come within less than 3,300 feet of the *Titanic*. The ship lay on the eastern edge of the primary search area — in that narrow wedge Jean-Louis had missed due to the strong current. His misfortune and my luck were intertwined. I tried to cheer him up, reminding him that ours was a partnership and that the glory would be shared. But he was inconsolable.

In the meantime, our reconnaissance runs over the debris field had taken too much time due to recurring tracking problems and I was beginning to feel desperate. But by early afternoon on September 2, as the storm drew closer and the winds began to build, I'd gathered enough information and screwed up enough courage to order our first *Argo* run over the major piece of wreckage we'd located. The risk I would be taking was brought forcibly home by the large profile of the *Titanic* that Jean-Louis had hung on the back wall of the van. It showed the ship's huge smokestacks and complex rigging, and was a constant reminder to me and everyone else of the dangers lurking below. If *Argo* got caught in wires or wreckage it would take a miracle to free it — likely we'd have to cut the cable and kiss a half-million dollars of new technology goodbye, not to mention the rest of the expedition.

Argo is launched on a video run over the Titanic's debris field.

Despite the delays, *Argo* had now added to our knowledge of the wreck site. It had explored large parts of the debris field and seen one of the ship's giant cranes lying on its side, the boom badly bent. It had crossed over a region of massive wreckage in the vicinity of our boiler — a tangled pile of twisted bulkheads and upturned hull plating. But we still didn't know what condition this main part of the wreck would be in — that major section we had so far stayed clear of. We still believed the ship could be in one piece — all the wreckage we'd seen could have been emptied from the interior of the ship after boilers and other heavy material had crashed through. (Many survivor eyewitnesses had described loud crashing noises when the ship had turned on end.) There still seemed a strong likelihood that some smokestacks remained upright and some rigging was still in place.

As we maneuvered the *Knorr* into position to make *Argo*'s first run across the main wreck, the word swiftly spread among the science party and a crowd began to gather in the back of the van. Not a word was spoken except for the terse dialogue between me and the watch crew. Appropriately, the *Titanic* discovery watch, Harris's Heroes, were at their post, with Captain Bowen's expert hands at the *Knorr*'s controls.

As *Argo* neared the bottom, I gave this command: "Flyer, stop at an altitude of 50 meters."

"Roger that." Earl Young was all business today. The flatness of his tone disguised the tension he and I were feeling as he stared at *Argo*'s fathometer, bouncing an echo straight down off the bottom.

"Sonar, tell me when you see anything."

"Roger that," replied Lt. Rey, ready for battle. His paper printout told him what *Argo*'s side-looking sonar saw to either side.

"*Argo* con, I want to begin the approach in high-altitude strobe mode."

"Roger that," Stu Harris returned softly. He was beginning to turn green from seasickness, but this was a moment he wasn't going to miss. Now his boy *Argo* could really show his stuff.

For our first approach, we would take as few chances as possible and come in at a safer high altitude. This meant using our high-power strobe flash, which concentrated our lighting energy into short, powerful bursts. In the flashes, *Argo* could see farther than in the continuous television mode, but our screen would only show snapshots every ten seconds.

In the driver's seat, Captain Bowen was clearly enjoying himself. During the search, he'd been mostly on the outside, usually holed up in his cabin with not much to do. Now his skill at handling the ship made him essential to our discovery mission.

"Flyer, keep your eyes peeled for a sudden change in altitude. Let it come up. It should stop at an altitude of 30 to 35 meters." My voice remained calm, but my hands were beginning to shake. In a few moments we'd know the worst.

At an altitude of 50 meters (164 feet), *Argo* was blind. It couldn't see bottom, so neither could we. Our video monitors were filled with the glare of strobe lights bouncing off tiny objects in the water. Too much submarine fog meant backscatter for *Argo*'s headlights, so we had to depend on *Argo*'s fathometer pinging directly off the bottom. It would tell us when we crossed over the *Titanic*. Flying at 50 meters, we should be safely above it. I held my breath...

Earl: "The altimeter is beginning to flicker."

Rey: "I have a massive object off to starboard on sonar; we're about to cross it."

Earl: "Altimeter has just jumped; the altitude is now 25 meters."

Me: "Hold; don't take in cable."

Argo was passing directly over the main hull of the *Titanic* — the Golden Fleece was within our grasp at last. Not a word in the van as faint objects flashed on the video screens. If we'd miscalculated I'd know it soon.

It was time to risk a closer look, to take the plunge.

"Shift to real-time mode. We're going down."

It was as if the crowd in the van, already holding its collective breath, inhaled further while, with the light touch of fingers on a keyboard, Stu Harris ordered *Argo* to turn on its incandescent lights and to again act like a normal television camera with very sensitive eyes.

"Flyer, down five meters."

"Roger that."

We were now dropping below the stack level of the *Titanic*. If the stacks were there — worse still, if the masts and rigging were still intact — we were in big trouble.

On the video screen I could see the dim shape of a hull: "It's the side of the ship. She's upright."

Lt. Rey immediately chimed in his sonar report: "I have what appears to be stacks off to the starboard on sonar. We are below them."

"Roger that," I responded. "Keep your eyes peeled." As if I needed to remind them.

Suddenly, out of the gloom, the Boat Deck of the ship came into view. We were on the port side looking at what appeared to be a stack opening — but the funnel was gone, the same forward funnel that had fallen into the water a few minutes before the ship sank, nearly hitting collapsible B, to which a handful of survivors — including Second Officer Lightoller, Colonel Gracie, and Marconi Operator Bride — had been clinging for dear life. Miraculously, its wash had pushed them clear of the hull just in time.

As we crossed over the center axis of the ship, we could see the flattened rectangular outline of the bridge. Was this where Captain Smith had stood stoically to the end? Thank God the cables were gone now.

Then I saw it, just off to the starboard side of the bridge — the unmistakable image of a boat davit; and suddenly it hit me square in the stomach. Empty davits: not enough lifeboats.

Before we knew it, *Argo* had safely passed out over the starboard bow railing and back into the featureless murk. All at once, the bottled-up excitement in the crowded van exploded. People were whooping, hugging, and dancing around while Jean-Louis and I stood quietly pondering the significance of the moment. In a few brief minutes, what our joint team of engineers had accomplished rivaled or surpassed all our previous underwater exploits. As the celebrations continued around us, Jean-Louis and I were almost in tears.

From start to finish our first look at the *Titanic* had lasted just under six minutes. Had the expedition ended then and there it would have been a great success. We now knew that the *Titanic* was upright and that a major portion of the

Jean-Louis uses a book containing a reproduction of the 1911 Shipbuilder *article about the* Olympic *and* Titanic *to identify parts of the wreck as we pass over it.*

ship appeared intact. As eyewitnesses at the time of the sinking had reported, the number 1 funnel was gone. There was still no reason to think the ship was not in one piece. We also knew the bow was facing slightly east of north, and we had established a safe viewing altitude, information we could use to make subsequent video runs over the ship and later to make more dangerous close-up runs with ANGUS.

I was ready to go back at the bow, but first it was time to clear the van. I needed my team as rested as possible for the next 64 hours, so I addressed the crowd: "Hey, we've got too many people up. Your butts are going to be dragging when your watch comes up. Let's get some of you back in the rack. This is a 24-hour operation." With a bit of good-humored grumbling, the reserve troops left the van and headed off to get some shut-eye — if they could calm down enough to do it. I wouldn't have had a hope of falling asleep, and there was no way I was going to miss a single run over the *Titanic*.

During the rest of that afternoon and evening, we only managed two more *Argo* passes over the wreck, our work increasingly hampered by the rising winds and seas, which gave the *Knorr*'s cycloids all they could handle. On the second of these subsequent *Argo* runs, as we moved aft from the area of the number 2 funnel — we still thought the funnel itself could be there because of a sonar image recorded on our first *Argo* approach — to where the stern half of the hull should have been, the deck began to plunge away from us and, as Earl lowered *Argo* to keep the hull in view, the video images faded into a confusing mass of twisted wreckage: turned-up windows, torn hull sections, razor-sharp edges of jagged steel. To our surprise and disappointment, the stern was gone. On the plotting table, we pinned a paper silhouette of the *Titanic* giving a plan, or overhead view, of the bow section, showing the wreck's compass orientation and its position in our transponder net. On the cutout we marked everything we knew about the *Titanic* up to that point: where the ship's bridge was, the position of the Grand Staircase opening, the number 1 funnel opening.

At the end of that pass, the rising seas had made handling *Argo* too difficult — at one point we'd crashed the sled into the hull — and I ordered a recovery. It was near 11:30 P.M. on September 2, nearly 24 hours since I'd last seen a bed. As the storm was reaching its absolute peak, with winds gusting to 35 knots, *Argo*'s crew, dressed in bright yellow foul-weather gear, spilled out of the warm control van and onto a dark, cold, wet, windy deck, the bitter salt spray slapping their faces. The scene was enacted in the garish glare of the *Knorr*'s floodlights, giving the whole thing a nightmarish, surreal quality. As the wind howled across the rolling deck, the yellow figures moved to their assigned positions as the officer on the bridge maneuvered the *Knorr*'s bow into the wind, using her tall superstructure as a partial windbreak. But nothing could stop the pitching and heaving of the ship.

Meanwhile, the *Argo* crew hung the large halter of black water-filled bumpers out beyond the starboard railing, ready to receive the sled. As *Argo* broke through the surface, it began to swing wildly in a magnified version of the *Knorr*'s heaving action. Now every second counted as ship's bosun Jerry Cotter shouted orders into the gale. The *Argo* crew — like bronco busters trying to put a saddle on a bucking horse — swiftly attached lines to the yawing sled. Then, at a sign from Jerry, the crane operator brought *Argo* toward the ship and crashing down into its rubber berth — tamed and docile at last.

It was mid-morning of Tuesday, September 3, and I had run out of patience. For ten painful hours I had waited for the storm to abate. I'd even spent a few futile and frustrating hours tying to catch some sleep in my constantly pitching cabin, but to no avail. Finally, I'd decided that if we couldn't work with *Argo*, at least we could lower ANGUS and get some still pictures of the debris field. ANGUS had worked in rougher seas than these. Anyway, the fear of losing ANGUS would take our minds off the rotten weather.

Through the afternoon and into the late evening of September 3, ANGUS's still cameras snapped off thousands of color pictures of the debris field. A few hours later, when Martin Bowen had developed the film, we discovered we had amassed a somber visual collection of artifacts — a chamber pot here, a bedspring there, a teacup over there, a silver serving platter, a multitude of wine bottles, even the white-painted headboard from a bed. And huge piles of unrecognizable wreckage.

By midnight, the storm front finally passed and the seas began to fall. Late that afternoon, we readied ourselves for our first ANGUS run over the main wreck. It was a nail-biter from start to finish — exhaustion and adrenaline competing for control of our weary bodies as Earl Young, Tom Crook, and Captain Bowen maneuvered our sightless "dope on a rope" back and forth over the *Titanic*'s decks. Each pass across the wreck was heart-stopping, not to mention stomach-turning. If slow maneuvers in a cycloidal ship in heavy seas don't make you sick, nothing will. Carefully, ever so carefully, Jean-Louis conducted the *Knorr* and ANGUS through four more runs, each one lasting about 30 minutes. As the fifth and final run came to an end, night had fallen for the last time on our *Titanic* mission. I ordered ANGUS recovered. If these pictures didn't come out, there was still time for one last go.

I wondered for a moment what a passing ship would have thought of our antics. There we were, this tiny vessel in the middle of nowhere, spinning around in circles for no apparent reason like a cat chasing its tail. They would surely have thought we had all gone mad.

Six hours later, madness seemed all too real a possibility.

All we had to show for ANGUS's first terrifying runs over the wreck were blurry images buried in a blue haze of backscatter. At least the cameras were working fine, but our passes had simply been too high, too cautious. I felt victory slipping away, my remaining energy seeping from my body.

Somewhere I found the resolve to continue. There was no way I was going to leave the *Titanic*'s resting place without trying one more time. We had until 7:30 A.M., when the remaining transponders would have to be recovered. Allowing one hour for lowering and one for recovering ANGUS, that meant a mere four and a half hours for our last attempt.

The final launching of ANGUS was a terror to behold. The wind and sea had picked up, again making it difficult to hold the *Knorr*'s head to wind. As soon as ANGUS's steel frame was freed from its moorings, it swung wildly despite the best efforts of the six-man ANGUS team, each man on a line threaded through block and tackle and attached to a 6,000-pound wrecking ball. Earl crawled out on ANGUS's frame to activate the cameras and strobes — a routine maneuver made hair-raising in such conditions. He had lashed himself securely to the ship, but, just in case, Martin Bowen was hanging on to his life-vest and Emile Bergeron on to Martin's. Then a bright flash lit up the sky as 1,500 watts of energy exploded through ANGUS's twin strobes. Satisfied the cameras were working, Earl gave the thumbs-down and ANGUS went crashing into the churning sea.

As we re-entered the control van and struggled out of our wet foul-weather gear, I could see that Jean-Louis had reached his physical limit. The look in his eyes told me that he wanted to keep fighting, but his eyelids simply

....

refused to stay open. "Get to bed," I told him. "There's no need for both of us to stay up." Reluctantly, but gratefully, he left the van.

I had to lie down or I would fall down, but I couldn't afford to leave my post. So, crawling on my hands and knees, I began to clear a small area beneath the chart table. From my prone position I could still talk to Earl on the winch, Tom Crook on navigation, and Captain Bowen on the ship controls. For our last desperate attempt we were down to a three-man ANGUS team under my command.

Now, even Earl was silent — one of the rare times I've known him to be at a loss for words. We both knew that what we were about to attempt was even crazier than the dangerous ANGUS launch just completed. I figured we now had to get our cameras within 23 feet of the *Titanic's* decks, but with the sea rising again the *Knorr* itself was now heaving up and down between 10 and 13 feet, and this motion would be transmitted down our 12,500 feet of cable to ANGUS. What the hell. If I was going to lose ANGUS, I couldn't think of a better time or place.

By the time we reached approach depth, almost all my strength was gone, so I draped myself over Earl's right shoulder and whispered commands in his ear. We certainly didn't look the part of a dashing suicide crew that night.

"Down to four meters," I croaked.

"Four meters?" Earl's question mark implied, Are you crazy?

"Four meters," I repeated.

For the next three hours hardly a word was spoken beyond whispered commands and quiet replies as we made pass after frighteningly close pass over the *Titanic*. The dim red glow of the night lights (which illuminated the van in tight moments like these) gave a ghoulish air to the stressed faces and bloodshot eyes of the ANGUS crew, already scruffy with four-day-old beards and haggard from lack of sleep. The usually imperturbable Earl Young gripped the winch controls so hard his knuckles were white, and it seemed as if the metal lever was about to ooze between his fingers. Outside, the wind rattled the walls of the van as the storm blew itself out. Inside, time became a sort of trance-like blur from which we were finally jolted at 5:56 A.M., when a simple message boomed over the bridge intercom: "You have to start up now."

Time and money had run out. Scientists were waiting back home to take the *Knorr* off on other scientific pursuits.

At 7:28 A.M., right on schedule, ANGUS was back on deck. There was no way I could sleep now, so I stood in the processing van and watched as Martin developed each 400-foot roll of film.

After several hours, the close quarters and the smell of the chemicals got to be too much, so I took a break out on deck. The wind had dropped, but the seas were still angry and the sky a grim overcast. Then out of the blue, a twin-engine, 12-passenger prop plane passed directly overhead. The plane was outfitted with special navigational antennae, clearly there for only one purpose: to determine our exact location. It crossed back and forth over us, first in one direction, then another. But whoever it was, he was out of luck, since we were recovering a transponder and a mile or more away from the *Titanic*. Probably Jack Grimm, I thought.

Moments later, Martin emerged from the photo lab to report that we had excellent color images — but I was too tired to feel much sense of triumph. My remaining energy was needed to take care of business. Immediately, I gave irreversible orders to recover the last transponder. As it rose swiftly back to the surface, our precise tracking net was destroyed for good. The *Titanic* was once again lost in the deep, but not too badly lost. During our short time on the scene, we had collected hundreds of satellite fixes. Returning to the *Titanic* and landing *Alvin* on her deck would be a piece of cake.

With our operations over, there was still one more job for me to do — deal with the media. Woods Hole had asked me to talk to as many reporters as possible and it seemed as if every print and television journalist in North America wanted a few words of wisdom from Dr. Ballard. I had expected people to be excited about our finding the *Titanic*, but never in my wildest dreams had I anticipated this level of excitement.

Punchy from lack of sleep, I stumbled up to the radio room and began conducting interviews. Most reporters wanted to know the condition of the ship and whether we'd seen any sign of human remains. I did my best to answer them all, but I was near the end of my tether. *Argo* and ANGUS had finished their work, the seas were finally subsiding, the *Knorr* was just about to head toward the shore, and I should have been in bed. But I managed to hang in there, until I talked to Tom Brokaw of the NBC *Nightly News*.

Just as I began to talk to Brokaw, I happened to glance out the porthole. Suddenly, I realized that the *Knorr* had

Our discovery of the Titanic *was front-page news around the world.*

finished recovering our final transponder and now was under way toward home. We were leaving the *Titanic* behind before I'd made my peace with her. Just as that moment Tom asked how I felt. Well, right then I felt terrible and it was all I could do to hold back the choking that rose in my throat. My resistance had gone and my emotions were quickly overwhelming me. Abruptly, I signed off and bolted from the radio room.

I went through the back of the lab so no one would see me and down into the now-empty fantail. The sun was just breaking through the clouds as I looked at the *Knorr*'s beautiful and peaceful wake streaming out toward the blue horizon. My emotions were mixed: there was a feeling of sadness and regret that we had come and gone so quickly and at the same time a warm satisfaction of having finally ended the *Titanic*'s long journey. I'm not a particularly religious person, but I suppose you could say this was a religious moment, similar perhaps to the impromptu memorial service held on the fantail the night of our discovery a mere four and half days ago. It was as if those who had perished aboard the *Titanic* could finally rest. That's how I felt.

For the last four and a half days, I had not managed a wink of sleep. Sleep. What a wonderful, blissful thought. I headed aft, through the main lab and up two sets of ladders toward my quarters. Then as I hobbled down the final passageway, I collapsed. My feet simply went out from underneath me and I found myself on the deck. Then I started to feel embarrassed. What if someone had observed the great Captain Nemo slump to the floor? Luckily the passageway was deserted. Carefully, I got back up and made it to my bunk.

Now, finally, I slept. When I awoke, it was nighttime and the good ship *Knorr* steamed quietly and steadily toward the tumult on the shore.

What should have been have been a pleasant trip home, with time for reflection and decompression, turned into a sour and disheartening experience. The bond of cooperation I'd built up over many years of working with French oceanographers seemed about to break.

Naively, I now realize, we had not agreed in advance on a set policy for releasing the news of our discovery to the waiting world, or the disposition of video footage and still images. We hadn't dreamed people would get so excited about our finding the ship, and we simply hadn't thought through all the ramifications of dealing with the news media while in the midst of a complex technical operation at sea in difficult conditions. It didn't help, either, that all of us were exhausted.

The trouble actually had begun on Sunday morning with the arrival of a helicopter from a Canadian television network that had provided funds to help cover the documentation budget of our expedition. The helicopter arrived with a news crew on board and asked if they could place the crew on board the *Knorr* to report firsthand on

A helicopter hovering over the Knorr *lowers a basket to pick up film and videotape of our discovery.*

this fast-breaking news event. I told them that was out of the question. We weren't giving exclusive access to anyone. But they could certainly have the "scoop" of filming us on site from the air. After all, they had earned it by being the only network to back us.

Jean-Louis, Jean Jarry, and I also saw the helicopter as an opportunity to regain some control over the news coverage of our own expedition, coverage that seemed to have gone bizarrely awry. The story in Sunday's London *Observer* had been followed by totally false news reports saying that we were actually salvaging the *Titanic* wreckage. Over the radio we'd even heard that protests against our supposed actions had been lodged with the United Nations. That had everyone on board upset. So we elected to use the Canadian helicopter as a courier to carry the first pictures of our discovery ashore. We chose the initial footage of the boiler and film of the jubilation in the van. These images would begin to tell the true story of finding the *Titanic*. As we watched the helicopter disappear into the gathering storm and returned to our *Argo* runs over the wreck, we were satisfied that our story would finally get told accurately.

The next thing I knew, Woods Hole was on the phone, not to congratulate us, but to complain about the apparent exclusive we'd given out. The images of our discovery had gone on air, but not all the big U.S. networks had them yet. Those who didn't were furious and threatened Woods Hole with lawsuits. Suddenly, a quiet scientific community in a remote corner of Cape Cod — with most people off enjoying the Labor Day weekend — was being subjected to unheard-of media pressure.

Immediately, I got on the phone to all concerned, explaining our position. News was news and the tapes we had sent ashore could be used by anyone. A scoop was one thing, but an exclusive was something entirely different. No one was to blame. Woods Hole was simply unprepared for the media onslaught, and this problem was aggravated by the fact that it was a holiday long weekend.

Now, as we sailed toward Woods Hole, my French colleagues and I concocted a careful scheme to show off some of our ANGUS pictures. There was frequent contact with IFREMER in Paris and with Woods Hole management. These were high-quality images and we wanted to be sure that they were released simultaneously to all North American television networks and to the French media.

On September 6, as we steamed home, another helicopter flew out to the *Knorr*, this one chartered by all three American TV networks. When it returned to Newfoundland, Bernard Pillaud and Steve Gegg went with it, carrying multiple copies of the ANGUS and *Argo* footage we'd agreed to release. One Frenchman and one American would make sure that this time our plan was carried out to the letter.

When the helicopter landed at St. John's Airport, a throng of reporters lay in wait as a handsome young American and a dashing Frenchman emerged. They must have looked a little like astronauts returning from a trip to the moon. How could Woods Hole and IFREMER withhold such important images from a waiting world? The media pressure proved too great and Woods Hole relented, releasing the material. That night, while Bernard was still flying across the Atlantic, French television viewers saw our newly minted *Titanic* images on their screens before

IFREMER could release them; they had been picked up from the American networks via satellite.

Quite understandably, IFREMER was furious at this apparent breach of our understanding, an anger compounded by the dawning realization of just how valuable these images were. I'd never had any plans to "sell" the news, but now Paris wanted to. Unfortunately, our earlier agreements did not make this point clear. So, as we headed toward a hero's welcome on the American shore, IFREMER and Woods Hole were locked in an unfortunate conflict over who owned the images from our *Titanic* expedition and how they would be used. Jean Jarry, who was IFREMER's head-office man on board, was caught in the middle — feeling the full pressure of his bosses back in Paris. My old friend Jean-Louis couldn't believe what was happening and spent most of this time in his cabin. I watched helplessly as all the good feelings of our voyage and 13 years of joint American and French cooperation seemed to slip away.

The low point of the trip home came when Emory Kristof decided he wanted a group picture of the victorious *Titanic* discoverers posed on the fantail with *Argo* and ANGUS in the background. By this stage none of us felt much like smiling, but at Kristof's insistence we reluctantly agreed. We made poor subjects, our forced smiles disguising the hurt underneath. Despite this setback, however, I wanted our homecoming to be a joint U.S./French celebration. And I spent two days polishing the brief remarks I would make to the waiting press.

What I would be able to say would be based on only partial knowledge of the state of the wreck. Careful analysis of the ANGUS footage over the next several months would reveal that a second large section of the hull rested roughly 2,000 feet to the south of the bow. This was the stern, but beyond that we knew little about its condition. We would also discover that all four funnels appeared to be gone. But the region of the tear on the bow section, and much of the larger debris field, remained a mystery, and we knew nothing about what lay between the bow and the stern. Only if we returned would we know the complete nature of the *Titanic*'s wreck.

On the clear, warm morning of September 9, 1985, as we steamed down Nantucket Sound, the *Knorr* was mobbed by helicopters, small planes, and pleasure craft running circles around us and blowing their horns. A boat had already delivered a small welcoming party — including Woods Hole director John Steele and two of his staff; Hugh O'Neill, representing the Secretary of the Navy; and my wife, Marjorie, and our two sons, Todd and Douglas. Having my family there was especially important to me. They had paid a tremendous price over the years during my long months away from home, but they'd never complained. Along with my parents, they have long been my most important rooting section.

As we turned the corner and entered the narrow channel leading to Woods Hole's marine facility, I couldn't believe my eyes. The dock was a mass of people filling every available inch of space. To the right, the networks had erected a wall of satellite antennae already sending their signals back to New York and around the world. In the middle of the dock was a makeshift platform bristling

A congratulatory banner hangs from the facade of the Bigelow Building, WHOI's original headquarters.

with television cameras and reporters — the media demanded and got the best view. Banners were flying, a band was playing, schoolchildren were hanging on to helium-filled balloons. As we neared our berth, a cannon boomed out a salute. It was as if the circus had come to town. In many ways it had.

I thought of the very different crowd that had met the *Carpathia* when she sailed into New York on the stormy evening of April 18, 1912, three and a half days after the tragedy. The offices of the White Star Line had been besieged by anxious crowds — many of them relatives of the passengers. Reporters had waited like sharks to prey on any survivors willing to sell their story. I pushed such thoughts away.

Since this was a celebration, I decided to give the people a little bit of a show. Climbing up to the bridge, I asked Captain Bowen to stop the *Knorr* less than 100 yards from the dock and to put his ship into a full 360-degree spin. (Few in the crowd knew of the *Knorr*'s unique propulsion system.) Then the captain brought his ship gently against the dock.

With the gangplank in position, proud wives and children streamed aboard for a hug and a kiss and a firsthand look at *Argo* and its control center, where every monitor was alive with images of the *Titanic*. Inside the van champagne corks exploded into the air.

Now it was time to meet the press. As Jean-Louis and I crossed the gangway to a waiting car, the reporters and cameramen jamming the makeshift platform started shouting for me to make some gesture — something the cameras could make immortal. Without thinking, I gave them the thumbs-up sign and stuck out my tongue — from hero to buffoon in ten seconds. That silly victory picture instantly flashed around the world still haunts me.

A few minutes later we entered the side door of the Woods Hole Oceanographic Institution's Redfield Auditorium to be met by a wall of cameras and a podium full of microphones. In that moment they looked threatening, like a mass of spears poised to strike. As I made my way toward my place on the platform amid popping flashbulbs, I remembered one of George C. Scott's lines in the movie *Patton*. In it, Patton says that whenever a victorious Roman general returned to Rome at the head of his army, riding in a chariot surrounded by slaves, a young man always stood at his side reminding him that fame and glory were fleeting.

Today, we were the main show in town. Tomorrow, the media circus would have moved to another event.

Jean-Louis went first, speaking so softly that the press strained to make out his words. Both of us were still exhausted, and the emotion of the moment was taking over. As always, however, his words were gracious and eloquent. Despite any feuding between our countries, ours was a friendship and a partnership that went back a long way.

He began by briefly recapping the search and discovery. Then he went on to speak of our expedition's teamwork. "Our results were not obtained easily. They are the product of highly skilled teams on both ships who worked in a closely coordinated matter. The French-American cooperation took root because of the inspiration of Bob Ballard

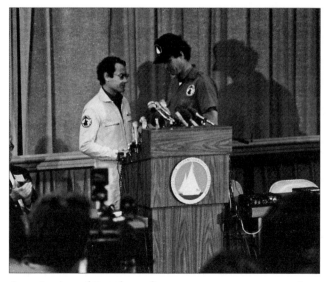

Jean-Louis and I at the podium as we prepare to meet the press in Woods Hole's Redfield Auditorium.

who made this discovery possible. Moreover, Dr. Ballard inspired among us all the idea that the success of the discovery must be assumed with the greatest respect and dignity befitting the *Titanic*. The endeavor between France and America has been technically and spiritually difficult, yet the R.M.S. *Titanic* site was explored with her dignity in mind at all times. We hope that the work in the deep ocean between France and America will continue."

Now it was my turn. I had given a thousand speeches in the past, but this one proved to be the most difficult to write or make, even though it would only take two minutes to say. I took a deep breath and began reading.

"This summer's joint expedition by the United States and France was a highly technical undertaking involving the finest technology of these two countries. In the field of deep submergence exploration, France and America are equal. But this summer's campaign was also the compassionate undertaking of two individuals who are human first and a Frenchman and an American second." I went on to talk of Jean-Louis' stature in his profession and the technical excellence of the SAR sonar system. I praised him as "a quiet and gentle man" with whom it had been a privilege to work.

"The *Titanic* lies in 13,000 feet of water on a gently sloping alpine-like countryside overlooking a small canyon below. Its bow faces north and the ship sits upright on the bottom. There is no light at this great depth and little life can be found. It is a quiet and peaceful and fitting place for the remains of this greatest of sea tragedies to rest. May it forever remain that way and may God bless these found souls."

I had already escaped with my family through a side

door and into a waiting Woods Hole car when I realized I hadn't said goodbye to Jean-Louis. Then I spotted him in the very crowd of reporters and photographers I'd hoped to escape. But I had no idea when I'd see him again. In a few hours, he'd be on a plane to France and, the next day, he'd be holding a press conference in Paris while I was doing the same thing at *National Geographic*'s Washington, D.C., headquarters.

I jumped out of the car into the sea of reporters, all of the them wanting a few pithy words for the nightly news. But Jean-Louis and I ignored them. The media buzz became a background blur and the only person I could see and hear was Jean-Louis. It was as if we were still out at sea, quietly talking on the fantail as we reconsidered the day's events or plotted some new twist in our search strategy. We swore to hang together, whatever happened, then shook hands and I fought my way back to the car. Soon I was racing away from this craziness.

I wondered then whether Jean-Louis and I would revisit the *Titanic* together. Whatever happened, nothing could take our accomplishment away from us.

CHAPTER 8

....

TOURING
THE TITANIC

WE RETURNED A YEAR LATER TO TAKE A CLOSER LOOK AT THE wreck, and this time finding the *Titanic* was easy. Our satellite fixes from the previous year meant we could simply sail the 900 miles straight from Woods Hole to the site — and that's exactly what we did, arriving in the early evening of July 12, 1986. And the luck that had smiled on us during 1985 seemed to be with us still: the weather was fine — the sea calm and the night clear — and spirits were high on board our new ship, the *Atlantis II*, as we launched the first of three transponder beacons that would form our tracking "net" around the wreck. With only 12 days on site, I didn't want to waste a single moment.

As the saying goes, what a difference a year makes — in both good ways and bad. This expedition, primarily funded by the U.S. Navy like last year's, was being undertaken with Woods Hole's full blessing and official support. Our technical goal was to demonstrate the capabilities of *Jason Junior* — the prototype of our remotely controlled underwater robot. And, with *JJ*'s help, we intended to come back with beautiful pictures of the exterior and interior of the ship — a comprehensive visual record of a legendary wreck.

Sadly, this year's *Titanic* expedition was being conducted without the French. After the disagreements arising from the 1985 expedition, relations between Woods Hole and IFREMER had hit rock bottom. But olive branches had been extended by both sides and, for a time, it even looked as though a French ship and a French sub (*Nautile*) would be joining us at the site. When I learned that the French hadn't been able to raise the funds for a second *Titanic* expedition, I invited Jean-Louis Michel, my co-leader in 1985, and long-time friend Claude Riffaud, who was now heading IFREMER's *Titanic* project, to come as my guests. Unfortunately, neither was able to make it.

The absence of Jean-Louis and his French colleagues not only struck a note of melancholy amid our generally high spirits, it introduced an additional element of risk. This year, we would explore the *Titanic* by manned submersible — my old friend *Alvin* — and without the French we would be diving without a back-up submarine in the event of trouble. As a result, we would be like astronauts landing on a distant planet millions of miles from home, with no hope of rescue should anything go wrong.

Captain Reuben Baker brought the *Atlantis II* about and began inching toward the spot beneath which the *Titanic* should lie, while I stood in the top lab just aft of the bridge and watched the sonar printout from the ship's echo sounder. Every second, a ping went out from the transducer attached to the ship's hull and, seconds later — like a shot fired into the Grand Canyon — a rapid succession of echoes came back from the bottom, setting off a corresponding succession of burn marks on a rotating drum of paper — a sonar picture. Minute by minute, the flat sediment-covered ocean floor took shape on the moving record. Then, suddenly, a faint second echo began to appear. An object was rising up toward us, too large to be an outcrop or other natural feature. We were directly over the wreck, its coordinates locked into our computer.

Our first dive to the *Titanic* started out in picture-perfect fashion. It was another gorgeous summer day with the sun already high in the sky. At 7 A.M., *Alvin* was rolled out of its hangar on the stern of the *Atlantis II* and positioned under the huge blue A-frame that loomed above

Alvin *is rolled out onto the* Atlantis II's *fantail to be readied for a launch at the beginning of our 1986 expedition.*

the fantail. This frame would lift *Alvin* from the deck and retrieve it from the water. *Alvin* and *JJ*'s support crews immediately went to work. Like a space launch, a careful sequence had to be followed, involving a lengthy series of safety checks — a thick pile of check-off forms were signed and countersigned: battery check, life-support system check, acoustic telephone check, sonar check, back-up battery check, and so on.

Four heavy weights were rolled out in their trolleys and attached to the sub's sides. Unlike conventional submarines, *Alvin* can't use air ballast tanks to control its buoyancy in deep water — the pressure is too great — so instead, it has a complex flotation system. Then three tubs containing the freshly charged batteries were topped off with pressure-compensating oil, which takes up a lot less space than individual pressure chambers.

At 8:15 A.M., it was all systems go. Ralph Hollis, co-pilot Dudley Foster, and I, having removed our shoes, descended the ladder leading down through *Alvin*'s red fiberglass "turret," designed to keep waves from splashing water into the open hatch while the sub bobs on the surface. Then we climbed down into the seven-foot-diameter pressure sphere, careful not to brush against the well-greased hatch. (The grease is needed to ensure a good seal and is next to impossible to get out of your clothes.) Once we were inside, expertise in yoga or contortionism would have helped as we now had to wad ourselves into balls and squeeze into the tiny cabin, hemmed in on three sides by panels of instruments and boxes of virgin video-tape waiting to record some history. For the duration of the voyage, none of us would have room to stretch out or stand up — three sardines in a spherical can.

Ralph then closed the hatch from inside the sub as I turned on our oxygen tank — the sole source of air — slowly bleeding its life-supporting contents into the sphere. Already the sub was becoming stuffy, as Ralph turned on the lithium hydroxide blower that recycles the cabin's air and removes dangerous carbon dioxide.

Outside our tiny craft, the A-frame had begun to swing us out over the fantail, rocking us gently like a pendulum. The point when the sub is suspended half over the deck and half over the water is always one of the most dangerous moments of a dive. Should *Alvin* suddenly fall, there could be severe damage to the sub and injury to the occupants.

As soon as the sub hit the water and the lift line was released, divers swarmed over *Alvin*'s hull, checking that everything was ready for descent. Inside, Ralph was rapidly rechecking all systems now that the sub was "wet." Each phase of the operation was carefully directed by the surface control team in the top lab on board the *Atlantis II*, in radio contact both with the interior of the sub and the inflatable rubber dinghy waiting to pick up the divers.

At 8:35 A.M., the surface controller — always a pilot from the *Alvin* team — gave Ralph clearance to flood our air ballast tanks and begin our descent. The four weights attached to *Alvin* would now send us straight to the bottom. These worked on the same principle used by sponge divers: grab a rock, jump into the ocean, and let the rock get you down as fast as possible without having to expend valuable energy; when you arrive, drop the rock and go to work. With *Alvin*, when we wanted to head home, we dropped two more weights and started up. The idea was to minimize the use of the propellers — and battery power — both on the way down and on the way up.

I felt completely confident with Chief Pilot Ralph Hollis at the controls. I'd known him ever since he joined the Alvin Group in early 1975. And I'd known Dudley Foster even longer; we'd met during Project Famous, 12 years before. Between us, we had approximately 500 dives' worth of experience.

In many ways the backbone of the 1986 expedition was the Alvin Group of deep-submersible pilots. Most of them had joined long after I'd begun diving in the sub in the early seventies, but collectively they had enormous experience in the deep ocean. I also knew that some of them, most notably Ralph Hollis, resented the way my Deep Submergence Laboratory was now capturing the headlines — and the fact that I had more than once predicted publicly that *Argo* and *Jason* would someday make *Alvin* obsolete.

Over the years, Ralph had come to embody the soul of *Alvin* and now took any comments against the sub personally. He and many others in the Alvin Group had never forgiven me for an interview I'd done a few years back for the local Woods Hole newspaper. The article had read: "Ballard says manned submersibles are doomed." Understandably, Ralph and his colleagues hadn't let me forget that one. In fact, their sub was in no immediate danger of being out of work; it simply represented technology that had had its day in the sun.

As the sub slipped silently below the surface, a translucent jellyfish drifted past my viewport, its stinging tentacles dangling down several feet. I glanced at the *Jason Jr.* control panel. Today *JJ* would stay in his specially constructed garage on the front of *Alvin*, but tomorrow Martin Bowen would be on board to pilot our cute little "swimming eyeball" over the wreck. Like the yet-to-be-built *Jason, Jason Jr.* was a remotely operated vehicle (ROV) — an underwater robot. And unlike *Jason, JJ* was light enough to be deployed from a manned submersible. Both would operate on a 250-foot tether and have a telemetry system, imaging cameras, and propulsion plant. But *JJ* didn't have the heavy arms and multiple color eyes we planned for *Jason*. If *JJ* worked as planned, we would be able to investigate many places on the wreck that *Alvin* couldn't safely reach.

Today, we would find out if 12,500 feet of freezing salt water gave *JJ* cold feet. But the main purpose of this first dive was to see how dangerous the *Titanic* would be for *Alvin*'s cadre of seasoned pilots — and to get a good look at the ship up close.

During our time on the bottom, I hoped to survey the bow section from high above the wreckage. We would do this using one of *Argo*'s highly sensitive black-and-white SIT cameras, which we had mounted on *Alvin*'s undercarriage for this mission. On subsequent dives, we would be able to hover safely out of danger and pick out places to work before risking the sub up close. The fear of entanglement was ever present in our minds. Heaven forbid *Alvin* got trapped in wreckage and was unable to free itself.

Because we were diving without a back-up, I'd had to convince the Navy that we had worked out adequate safety precautions. First, I would only land on pre-surveyed sites, pumping ballast to become heavy and then deploying *JJ* from his garage in front of *Alvin*. Second, *JJ* would take all the really dangerous risks. In the event *JJ* became inextricably entangled, a cable cutter mounted on the garage could cut his tether so that we could move away unharmed.

Alvin also had a last-ditch escape measure in an emergency, recommended only if all other measures failed. This meant jettisoning the entire after two-thirds of the sub and letting the pressure sphere rocket to the surface. We might get home, but most of *Alvin* would be lost. And since this escape plan had never been put into effect, we could only guess what would happen to the passengers on their rapid rise to the surface. The sphere might tumble uncontrollably, treating human beings and instruments like the contents of a washing machine. The sphere would certainly make it to the surface, but would we survive the trip?

On a few occasions, *Alvin* had come close to this emergency bail-out point. The most serious of these was in 1974 during the exploration of the Mid-Atlantic Ridge. For over four hours it was wedged inside a rocky crevice in 9,000 feet of water, where overhanging lava outcrops would have prevented the released pressure sphere from rising straight up — which meant almost certain death. Fortunately, the crevice was in relatively fresh "glassy" lava flows that could be chipped and broken. Finally, the pilot was able to bang the sub back and forth until eventually the rock shattered and *Alvin* broke free.

None of us had been on that particular dive and I pushed such thoughts from my mind as we accelerated downward. Within a minute of leaving the surface, the pitching and rolling of the sub had stopped.

We had sunk 100 feet and daylight rapidly faded into deeper and deeper blues as the sub reached its maximum descent speed of 100 feet per minute. At this rate it would take two and a half hours to reach the bottom — a peaceful free-fall in utter darkness.

Inside our inner space capsule, it was still quite warm and stuffy, but the surrounding ice-cold water would soon cool the titanium-alloy hull and leaning against it would become quite unpleasant. Suddenly, a white-tipped shark materialized outside my window, silently scouting *Alvin* for a moment before swimming away. Attracted by the unusual noise and behavior of submersibles, sharks often appear soon after *Alvin* enters the water. It was comforting to know that several inches of metal protected us.

I wondered what Ralph was thinking. He seldom let anyone know; his grizzled appearance and gruff demeanor kept most people at a distance. We'd been friends — in the way that people who work together are often friends — but that was before I'd left the Alvin Group and had started up the competition. He was the one who'd given *JJ* the derogatory nickname — "dope on a rope" — originally applied to ANGUS.

While Dudley ran a few tests on *Jason Jr.*, I loaded our video recorders with fresh cassettes as Vivaldi's "Four Seasons" played softly in the background. (The music would be switched off once we reached bottom and went to work.) Normally, *Alvin* had only one video camera, a low-light-level camera mounted on the forward bow that helped the pilot see where he was going. Its recorder, mounted in the science rack behind us, also recorded the conversations going on inside the sphere.

For the mission we had three additional videotape decks inside the already cramped space — and all of them would require constant reloading. One was connected to the color camera mounted on *Alvin*'s arm, which would capture our best video images. Since the arm could move within a range of several degrees, it would provide close-up images as *Alvin* crossed the *Titanic*'s deck and would also give us a tracking shot of *JJ* when he was prowling outside his garage. The arm was also loaded with a still camera, strobe lights, and television lights, giving the entire rig the appearance of *Sesame Street*'s famous puppet character, Big Bird, which became the camera system's nickname.

A second tape deck was hooked up to the color video camera in *JJ* and the third was connected to the down-looking black-and-white SIT camera that we would use for our high-altitude surveys of the wreck and to spot suitable landing sites.

Ralph, as pilot, sat on a small stool in the center of the sphere, looking out the forward viewport. Dudley and I half sat, half lay on *Alvin*'s small deck, staring out through the port and starboard viewports respectively. In the first few minutes of the descent, we had all been making our nests in the sphere, arranging blankets and clothes as comfortably as possible. Given the close quarters, Ralph would often crunch my ankle with his foot as he concentrated on driving the sub. At other times, the overhead panel would snag my hair and, if I shifted to try and get more comfortable, the cassette machines would poke me in the back. Then, if inadvertently I let my socked foot hit the hull, it would come away cold and wet. During the long hours in these uncomfortable conditions, my legs frequently fell asleep and occasionally I'd get a bad cramp in my hip. At times like that the pressure sphere took on more the character of a torture chamber than a space capsule.

But the long fall to the bottom is usually a kind of lulling experience. The interior gets darker and darker and begins to cool until, after less than 15 minutes, we have reached a depth of 1,200 feet and total darkness. To conserve power, the outside lights are left off and the only illumination comes from three small red-and-white lights inside the sphere. After being attacked by a swordfish — which actually got its sword stuck in *Alvin*'s hull near a glowing window — I'd learned even these interior lights should be turned off at times.

However, there wasn't time for quiet contemplation today. Almost immediately, we had technical problems to worry about. July 13 was proving unlucky. First, we discovered that *Alvin*'s sector-scanning sonar (originally developed for hunting mines) had stopped working. Either the cold seawater or the rapidly increasing water pressure had somehow gotten to it. Without this sonar, we were blind beyond the few yards we could see and now would have to rely on our surface navigator to guide us to the *Titanic*'s side.

A few minutes later, at about 2,000 feet, we passed through what is known as a deep scattering layer, so named because it shows up as a cloud-like blur on a sonar. In fact, it is composed of thousands and thousands of small creatures that live in this depth range during the day and migrate to feed near the surface at night. Many of them are bioluminescent, their small bodies exploding like fireworks as our pressure wake warns them of an intrusive presence. Chains of individual animals commonly form strings of lights about six to eight inches long. Apparently when they are frightened, each bead suddenly brightens; the flashes begin at one end and travel down the string in a fraction of a second. When I first saw this, I thought it looked like a tiny passenger train passing by at night with only the lighted windows visible.

By the time we passed 5,000 feet, almost one hour into our descent, the sub was cold and we were putting on our first layers of extra clothing. The moisture in the air from our breathing had begun to condense on the now-freezing hull, forming drops of water that dripped from the hatch and ran down the inside wall to collect in the bilge. Seventeen years before, on my first dive in *Alvin*, I'd seen these droplets and become convinced the sub was leaking. The pilot had only smiled and explained to the nervous neophyte what was happening. All I had to do was put a drop on my tongue to discover the water was sweet, not salty.

Over the years, I'd learned how to stay healthy while spending so much time underwater. Today, I was wearing a toque from my sons' hockey team to keep my head warm and I had extra clothes if I needed them. I'd also become adept at staying away from the cold hull. Head and lung ailments are common among those who dive frequently in deep submersibles. I always take an antihistamine before a dive to keep my lungs and sinuses clear.

Ten minutes later, as we hit 6,000 feet, Ralph noticed a salt-water leak into the battery pack that powers the sub and its array of instruments. At first, it showed up on our instrument panel as a small leak, but as the level of seawater in the battery tub rose, the leak turned into a hard electrical ground: this meant the protective oil in which the batteries were bathed was being replaced by short-circuiting seawater. Thankfully, we have a back-up battery inside the sphere for emergency use, so the situation only threatened our mission, not our lives. But if we let the batteries deteriorate beyond a certain point, they would consume themselves and our 1986 *Titanic* expedition would be over. Our bottom time would be awfully short today.

The next hour and a half passed uneventfully. Vivaldi gave way to Beethoven on the sub's stereo and there was little talking as we fell silently, swiftly downward. The interior was getting very cold — in the low 50s — and I'd now put on a sweatshirt over my turtleneck sweater.

As we neared the bottom, the *Alvin* navigator aboard the *Atlantis II* began driving us in squares. Apparently his transponders were sending him confusing data — maybe one of them was malfunctioning. Ordinarily, he should have been able to steer us straight to the wreck. But his directions, echoed down to us on the underwater acoustic telephone, indicated that he too was lost. He was sending us first in one direction, then another.

Our down-looking echo sounder, which was still functioning, indicated the bottom was 600 feet below and we were closing fast. We could have dropped weights then, attained neutral buoyancy, and powered ourselves the remaining distance to the bottom. But Ralph, being a pro, waited until the last minute, conserving power, and only dropped our descent weights 60 to 100 feet above the bottom.

We'd arrived. The only trouble was we had no idea where we were.

As we gently descended the remaining distance with our outside lights now piercing the blackness, the featureless bottom slowly emerged from the dark green gloom. The first thing that indicated its presence was our own shadow, cast by *Alvin*'s light and growing sharper as we dropped lower. We stared out of our viewports, straining to see some sign of the wreck. No *Titanic*, no debris, just a gently rolling countryside of mud, much like an alpine meadow after a blanket of snow has all but erased its features: a bump here, what appeared to be a covered valley over there. Outside the window, a gentle "snow" was falling, underwater particles blown by the current. If the sonar had been working, the *Titanic* would show up as a giant blip on the screen and finding her would be a simple matter.

So close and yet so far away. The ship lay somewhere near us, probably no more than 400 feet, the distance from home plate to the center-field wall in Fenway Park. At the surface, such a distance would mean nothing, but here, more than two miles down below in this Stygian murk, a few hundred feet might as well be a thousand miles.

Then the damn alarm buzzer started, indicating that the short in our batteries had reached a critical point. Ralph was already thinking about returning to the surface. Here I was trapped inside a metal sphere, down on my hands and knees on *Alvin*'s tiny deck, peering at nothing but mud out the side viewport as we hovered three feet off the bottom. It had taken 13 long years to get to this point. Now *Alvin*, the most reliable of my tools, was having a bad day.

None of us wanted to give up and go home empty-handed — least of all Ralph, whose pride in *Alvin* was on the line. There was nothing left to do but guess where the *Titanic* was and blindly go there. The snowstorm of particles was blowing from the south-southeast at between a half and three-quarters of a knot; I figured this must have pushed us to the north of our desired location. After a brief discussion, we began driving south. *Alvin*, now gently touching the bottom with its single runner, was like a one-legged skier gliding over virgin snow, leaving a lonely track behind us. This ski keeps the bottom of the sub from plowing into the muck and kicking up a big cloud of sediment.

Now the alarm grew louder and more shrill as the tension in the sub mounted. Ralph was about to pull the plug, when finally our navigator chimed in from the surface: "*Alvin*, this is *A-II*. Tracking is now working. *Titanic* should bear 50 yards to the west of your present location." We had guessed right and had only just missed the ship. We were running parallel along its side.

Ralph turned *Alvin* to the west as we strained our eyes to see. Suddenly, the bottom began to look strange: though devoid of debris, it began to slope sharply upward — too steeply to be a natural underwater feature. It was as though this mound of mud and small boulders had been bulldozed into place. My heartbeat quickened.

"Ralph," I said, "come right. I think I see a wall of black just on the other side of that mud mound." Ralph did as I asked and inched *Alvin* forward until he was stopped by a sight unlike any he'd encountered in hundreds of deep-ocean dives: directly in front of us was an apparently endless slab of black steel rising out of the bottom — the massive hull of the *Titanic*. I thought of Edmund Hillary standing at the summit of Mount Everest, or some future space traveler peering over the edge of the known universe. Slowly, I let out my breath; I didn't realize I'd been holding it.

But no sooner had I persuaded Ralph to let me look through his forward viewport than he dropped *Alvin*'s weights and we began hurtling toward the surface — soon reaching our maximum ascent rate of 100 feet a minute. I had seen the *Titanic*, but not even long enough to know exactly where on the bow we had come in. If we wanted to dive tomorrow, we had to get back on board and fix our growing list of problems. Thank God Ralph had turned that head-splitting alarm buzzer off.

As we rose swiftly back toward warmth and daylight, I reflected among other things on the past 13 years during which I had spent an average of four months out of every twelve at sea. I had passed countless hours on my hands and knees, working in the dark of the deep ocean. I'd participated in exciting discoveries thanks to the work of *Alvin* and the world's other champion manned deep diver, the French *Cyana*. Now, for less than two minutes, we had glimpsed the *Titanic*'s towering hull. That was all we had to show for six hours' work. I couldn't help wondering how long the repairs would take — or whether they could be made at all. And what if the weather deteriorated? Would this be my one and only glimpse of the *Titanic*? Had I come all this way for nothing? I fought back my black mood, but such depressing thoughts continued to mount.

The ascent is usually a time when rock music is playing on the stereo and the people in the sub joke and

I emerge from Alvin after the shortened first dive of the 1986 expedition.

unwind after a job well done. Not today. For the next two hours we sat in virtual silence, meditating on our failure.

I was still in a grim mood when I emerged from the sub into the waiting crowd on the fantail of the *Atlantis II*. My only comment when asked about the situation was, "I saw the ship for about ten seconds. They're going to be up all night. They've got a sick puppy and they've got to fix it." It was at times like this that I wished Jean-Louis were with me — we had shared disappointment as well as triumph and could commiserate quietly together.

This year, I was in command of a ship and crew of 50 men and women ideally suited for the very specific task at hand. The *Atlantis II* is a slightly smaller ship than the

Knorr and lacks the *Knorr*'s sophisticated cycloidal propulsion system. She's a workhorse, not a fancy Kentucky trotter, and in 1986 that's exactly what I needed.

The team on board, which included a few familiar faces from our 1985 expedition, was drawn primarily from the Deep Submergence Laboratory. Added to these members of my immediate "family" were a few experts from private industry who were working with us in the development of the *Argo/Jason* system.

The core of the 1986 team was Chris von Alt, the Deep Submergence Laboratory's latest whiz kid, and the mastermind behind *Jason Jr.* Chris was equally at home at sea or in the lab, a no-nonsense, can-do type of engineer who wouldn't run from a high-pressure challenge. The precise person for the job.

Chris worked with a small team drawn primarily from the *Argo* group, including Martin Bowen, our resident expert on flying remotely operated vehicles, and Emile Bergeron, techie par excellence. When we arrived on site, we had never tested our new robot at ocean depths and we didn't know whether it would stand up to the pressure, exceeding 6,000 pounds per square inch, found there. But in principle we were sure *JJ* could do the job.

The ANGUS team was also on board, though somewhat out of the limelight. Each night, while most of the crew as asleep, Earl Young, Tom Crook, and Tom Dettweiler would methodically tow ANGUS back and forth across the *Titanic*'s debris field and stern section, which had all but eluded us last year. While *Alvin* dove on the wreck's bow, ANGUS paved the way for our final dives to the stern.

Honorary members of the ANGUS team in 1986 were

Bill Lange and Dr. Elazar "Al" Uchupi. Lange, of course, had been in the control van for the 1985 discovery — one of the first people to see the *Titanic*'s boiler. In preparation for this year's cruise, he had worked with Al reviewing every image taken by ANGUS and *Argo* in 1985. By the time summer rolled around, Al and Bill had become *Titanic* experts and I wanted them both on the 1986 cruise to analyze the pictures we brought up from the bottom.

Al Uchupi's 20 years of field work made him, in my estimation, the most accomplished marine geomorphologist in the world — intimately acquainted with every variant of underwater landscape from ripple marks to landslides. On top of that, he has a photographic memory — which came in handy when poring over literally tens of thousands of still pictures and thousands of feet of video. With Jean-Louis absent, Al was my alter ego, the

Al Uchupi and Dudley Foster chat in the top lab, from where Alvin*'s surface controller would direct the sub to its target.*

one man I felt I could completely rely on to be in charge. While I slept, I knew that he would be getting the job done.

The *Alvin* crew worked all through the night to cure their sick submarine, an operation rarely attempted at sea. Replacing one of *Alvin*'s heavy battery banks was dangerous and difficult in the best of conditions. Fortunately the weather remained clear, the seas flat calm, and I was confident I wouldn't return home empty-handed. Besides, Ralph didn't want egg on his face in the contest with *Argo/Jason*.

Overnight, *Jason Jr.*'s crew also made sure their boy had survived his first deep dive in good shape. They made a number of last-minute checks before giving the thumbs-up. This morning, it appeared that all systems were go.

It was still relatively calm in the North Atlantic, but the sky was overcast and gray.

Ralph Hollis was again our pilot on today's dive, but this time Martin Bowen was along to maneuver *JJ*'s first deep-sea deployment. Martin hadn't forgotten his role in the near-loss of *Argo* the previous year. I knew he was determined to turn *JJ* into the star of our 1986 expedition.

Our dive plan was essentially the same as yesterday's: acquire the *Titanic* on sonar upon reaching the bottom, close to visual range, rise up the hull making sure we avoided any overhanging wreckage, and conduct a detailed survey of the ship using our down-looking *Argo* camera. Then, if all went well, we'd pick a site, land, and then try to launch *JJ*.

As part of my preparation for the 1986 expedition, I had carefully reviewed the 1985 ANGUS photographs, constructing a number of mosaics of possible landing sites on the wreck. Of these, the one I was most interested in was a site near the entrance to the forward Grand Staircase. (A similar glass-domed staircase, though slightly less grand, had existed between the third and fourth funnels. But as far as we knew at this point, that part of the ship was now a hopeless wreck.) I had long been attracted to the forward staircase — not only because it seemed to symbolize the ship's luxury, but because it promised to take me deep inside the first-class compartments of the ship. Luckily, it appeared to be the safest of all potential landing locations, a large flat deck surface stretching between the number 1 funnel opening and the staircase opening.

The roof was still intact over the aft part of the officers' quarters and it was one of the highest decks on the ship. The smokestack was gone and with it the guy wires that might have fouled our craft, as well as a ventilation duct that had once run across the deck. The elegant glass dome that had once covered the staircase had not survived the descent to the bottom, leaving an easy entrance for *JJ*. There were sections of railings left at the port and starboard edges of this deck, but these would be easy to avoid. Overall, it was as if someone had gone down there with a bulldozer and cleared a landing pad for our submersible helicopter.

There was another potential landing point on the Boat Deck forward and to the side of the bridge, next to where the wheelhouse once stood. But here, the ANGUS pictures were confusing and didn't appear to agree with our historical drawings and photos. Both port and starboard bulkheads just aft of the bridge, including those in the area of the captain's cabin, had collapsed outward and the roof was caved in as if a giant had brought his fist down on it. True, the forward mast with the crow's nest — its base crimped but still fitted to the Forecastle Deck — had fallen aft and landed on the port wing of the bridge, but that surely had not been a blow sufficient to account for the devastation. Curiously, a strange, anomalous object on top of what seemed to be the wheelhouse resembled a modern radio direction-finder — but that sort of antenna didn't exist in 1912.

Another likely landing point for us was the *Titanic*'s expansive Forecastle Deck near the opening to hatch number 1. According to our 1985 pictures, all three hatches forward of the bridge were open and in theory suitable for *JJ* penetration — if we could land our sub close enough to them. But two of these were down on the Well Deck — the deck that dips down between the forecastle and the bridge — and it looked scary. Not only did the forward mast traverse it, but a formidable array of nasty-looking cables still connected the fallen mast to the ship. Last year, in our hair-raising attempt to get close enough for clear pictures, we had almost flown ANGUS underneath the mast by accident and had actually grazed the crow's nest. If *Alvin* got caught in those cables it could well be "game over."

Although the surface weather was now beginning to worsen with a storm front approaching and the seas building, the launch went without a hitch. But again problems arose shortly after we left the surface. This time it was *JJ*'s turn: his motors had somehow become flooded, rendering them useless. I could see that Martin, geared up for his first dive, shared my frustration. I could abort the trip now, return to the ship, get the motors fixed, and jump back into the water. But that would reduce valuable time at the wreck. Ralph was adamant that we stick strictly to *Alvin* regulations and leave the bottom no later than 3 P.M. each day, no matter what, so the crew could be back on board in time for dinner. I understood the logic behind the rules — the importance of maintaining a regular work routine (*Alvin* makes an average of 150 to 160 dives a year) — but more than once, I would privately curse the inflexibility that prevented us from lingering longer when we were in the middle of something interesting.

I decided to continue the dive and hope that no other problems got in our way; even without *JJ* a lot could be done. Poor Martin would just have to sit it out. Soon we were falling through pitch darkness toward the seabed far below. By the time we reached the bottom, it was beginning to seem like our first dive all over again. *Alvin*'s mine-hunting sonar was again on the blink and we had another ground on the electrical system. This time, however, there were two big differences: despite the ground, we had no leak indications; and the tracking from the *Atlantis II* seemed to be working fine. As message came from the surface: "Target bears 180°."

Our second view of the *Titanic* was breathtaking. As we glided soundlessly across the bottom on our single ski, out of the darkness loomed the razor's edge of the bow — the great ship towered above us and suddenly it seemed to be coming right at us, about to run *Alvin* over. My first impulse was that we had to get out of the way — but the *Titanic* wasn't going anywhere. Gently, Ralph brought the sub closer until we could see the bow more clearly. It was buried more than 60 feet in bottom mud. Both anchors still hung in place, the port one about six feet above the bottom, the starboard one resting just at mud level. I felt myself smiling. The would-be salvagers were out of luck; the *Titanic* was far too deeply buried for anyone to pull her out of the ooze.

As we moved closer, it seemed as though the metal hull was slowly melting away. Rivers of rust covered the side of the ship, some of it running the full length of the exposed vertical hull plating and pouring out over the bottom sediment where it formed great ponds as much as 30 to 40 feet across covered by a reddish-yellow crust. The blood of the great ship lay in pools on the ocean floor.

Then, as we rose in slow motion up the ghostly wall of the port bow, our running lights reflected off the broken glass of portholes in a way that made me think of cats' eyes gleaming in the dark. In places, the rust about them formed eyelashes; sometimes tears, as though the *Titanic* were weeping over her fate. Near the upper railing — still largely intact — reddish-brown stalactites of rust hung down as much as several feet, looking like long needle-like icicles. This phenomenon, the result of iron-eating bacteria, was well known, but never had they been seen on such a massive scale. I subsequently dubbed them "rusticles," a name that seems to have stuck.

These rust features turned out to be very fragile. If touched by *Alvin* or dislodged by the thrust from one of our propellers, they disappeared in a cloud of smoke. Once the foamy crust had been knocked away, the steel beneath appeared almost perfectly preserved, only slightly pitted. I mused for a moment on what it would be like taking a steel brush to the hull and cleaning the ship to its former smoothness. But I had made a promise to myself to leave the ship undisturbed.

Carefully, I counted the portholes aft from the anchor to locate the position where the ship's name should be, but I could see nothing. If I'd been able to remove the rust, the letters ought to have been visible, since they were cut slightly into the hull as well as painted. In fact, looking later at some of our videotape, we could just barely make out what looked like a faint outline of a "C" on the port bow. But this image did not show up in our still pictures.

Alvin rose farther, cleared the railing forward of the number 1 hatch, and Ralph maneuvered out over the *Titanic*'s mighty forward deck. All at once, I was forcibly struck by the sheer size of everything: giant bitts (usually called bollards in 1912), the huge links of the anchor chains, and even bigger shiny bronze-topped capstans. When you were there, on the spot, it really was titanic. Until now, the ship for me had been somehow ghostly, distant and incorporeal. Now it was very close, very material, very real.

As always when we were working, the three people in the sub exchanged few words that didn't have to do with the job at hand. Martin, stymied by *JJ*'s fickleness, looked through the port window quietly and in awe. There was nothing for him to do except gape and think about tomorrow. I was busy snapping pictures through the starboard viewport and instructing Ralph on where to go.

I strained to get a look at the deck's wood planking just four feet below us. Then my heart dropped to my stomach and I muttered, "It's gone!" Except for a few tidbits here and there, the wood had been replaced by thousands upon thousands of small, white hollow calcareous tubes one to two inches in length — the protective homes of now-dead wood-boring molluscs. Gone was our hope of finding much *Titanic* woodwork intact, her beauty unblemished by the years. Myriad little worms had done more damage than the iceberg, wreaked more havoc than the corroding seawater.

Now I could see beyond the illusion of last year's footage. The appearance of decking in our ANGUS photos had been created by the thin lines of resin and caulking that had originally been between the planks. That had remained, producing a laminated pattern, but the wood was virtually all gone. Immediately, I began to wonder whether the metal sub-deck would support us when *Alvin* made its first landing.

Alvin crossed just above one of the great bronze-topped capstans, and landed on the deck just forward and starboard of the *Titanic*'s mast. We were on tenterhooks, afraid the deck might not support *Alvin*'s weight once we'd pumped enough ballast to rest comfortably. As the sub settled, it made a kind of muffled crunching noise. If the steel plating gave way, we could crash downward belowdecks before Ralph had time to drop our weights. At best, the day's dive would be over; at worst, we'd be trapped in collapsing wreckage. But we settled firmly. That meant there was a good chance the *Titanic* would be able to support our weight at future landing sites.

The deck strength tested, we carefully lifted off and headed aft into the "wind," heading along the starboard side between the center line and the railing. The starboard forecastle railing was remarkably intact, almost unmarred by rusticles. The bottom current blowing across the deck was as strong as the day before — between a half and three-quarters of a knot. Particles suspended in the water blew in our faces, so I switched to our down-looking *Argo* camera in time to catch a panorama of the Well Deck as it passed several yards below us. I could see a clutter of cables and the forward cargo cranes, their booms knocked aft off their supports. This was not the place to risk landing *Alvin*.

Ralph was worried: "This current is strong and I can't see in the haze."

"We're fine," I reassured him, my eyes still on the video monitor. "The bridge should be dead ahead. Come right."

As we passed over the big cranes in the after portion of the Well Deck, I could see that they were surprisingly intact, unlike those in the ANGUS pictures of the debris field. Then the dim outline of the superstructure of the ship came into view, rising in three grand steps to the bridge: first B Deck, then A, and then the forward Boat Deck, location of the bridge and the officers' quarters. As the vague outline of the bridge area appeared, I realized why last year's ANGUS footage of this portion of the ship was so confusing. The wooden wheelhouse was completely gone, probably knocked away in the sinking. Apart from strips of teak wood fitted to the Boat Deck outlining where the wheelhouse had stood, there was no trace of the structure. The object I had thought was a strange-looking radio antenna was in fact the ship's bronze telemotor control, where the wheel was once attached. The wooden wheel itself was gone but, remarkably, the huge bronze base was standing intact and kept polished to a shine over the years by the current. Various conduits and the rudder order indicator arrow were still there.

We landed briefly to test the solidity of the second site. Then Ralph reported to the surface that there was a new leak indication in one of our battery tanks. He'd noted the first one moments before. Talking on the acoustic telephone is rather like having a conversation in a well. There's an echoey quality to the sound and the end of your last message to the surface bounces back to you about the same time as the response. As I listened to his conversation with someone two and a half miles up, I wondered how much time we had left today. There was so much more I wanted to see. Surface control gave us clearance for another 15 or 20 minutes.

"Ralph, I want you to lift up from this site and head directly to the Grand Staircase opening."

I directed him up and aft. A blast from *Alvin*'s prop kicked up the sediment on the wheelhouse floor, temporarily engulfing us in a cloud of dust. Soon we entered clearer water as the current blew the cloud downwind toward the bow. Again I switched to the down-looking video camera, which gave me a good black-and-white picture of the ship beneath us as *Alvin* cleared the gaping hole where the number 1 smokestack once stood. All that remained of the massive funnel were a few jagged sections of metal rising eight feet or so above the deck. In one way I wished the stacks were still there; they would have made the hull look so much more dignified. But their absence, along with their numerous stabilizing guy lines, made working above the ship much safer. Martin and I could barely control

The Collision

At 11:40 P.M. on April 14, 1912 — the fifth night of the *Titanic*'s maiden voyage — an iceberg pierced her starboard bow.

Just after midnight Captain Edward J. Smith (left) gave the order to begin firing white distress rockets. The first rockets went up at approximately 12:45 A.M. (right).

At about the same time, the first lifeboat, starboard boat No. 7, was lowered. By 1:40 A.M., all the port-side boats were away, the Titanic's *forecastle was underwater, and collapsible D was being readied for lowering (below).*

The Sinking

At 2:05 A.M., about ninety minutes after she hit the iceberg, *Titanic*'s stern began to lift out of the water. All the boats had gone but more than 1,500 passengers remained on board.

Discovery

In the summer of 1985 French and American scientists joined forces to try to find and photograph the *Titanic*.

(Above) *The sea was calm as the French research vessel* Le Suroit *steamed out of St. Pierre to begin* IFREMER's *sonar search.*

(Below) *As the end of the French phase of the expedition drew near, both Jean-Louis Michel and I became increasingly discouraged.*

The key to the American phase of the 1985 expedition was Argo, *a remotely controlled deep-sea video vehicle equipped with two sonar systems and five television cameras that could transmit images to us from the seafloor.*

(Above) Jean-Louis Michel and I plot the next Argo *run.*

(Right) Argo *is launched from the research vessel* Knorr.

(Top left) Argo *begins its descent.*

(Top right) *Emile Bergeron in the van, flying* Argo.

(Below) *Early on the morning of September 1, 1985, this image appeared on* Argo's *monitor. A 1911 photograph (right) helped us identify it as one of the* Titanic's *boilers.*

MAIN BOILERS

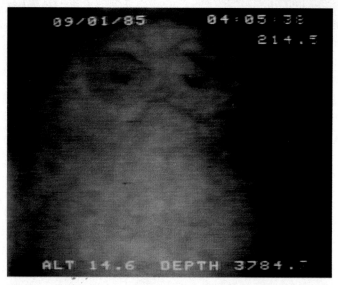

09/01/85   04:05:38
214.5

ALT 14.6   DEPTH 3784.7

Word of our discovery spread quickly throughout the ship, and soon people were pouring into the control van to celebrate and to be among the first in 73 years to see the Titanic. Here we're toasting our success with Portuguese wine in paper cups. Left to right: Stu Harris, Dana Yoerger, Bill Lange, Jean Jarry, and myself.

Visiting the *Titanic*, 1985

(Right) My eyes are riveted to the monitor as we make our first Argo *run over the main wreck.*

(Opposite, top) The huge anchor chains are clearly visible in this picture of the Titanic's forecastle.

(Opposite, bottom) The crow's nest on the fallen foremast.

(Below) Recovering Argo *could be extremely risky in high seas.*

(Above) The Titanic's port anchor.

(Below) JJ explores the starboard forecastle deck, his lights illuminating a rust-topped bollard.

The Boat Deck

JJ looks in the windows of the gymnasium while *Alvin* rests in the distance on the Boat Deck.

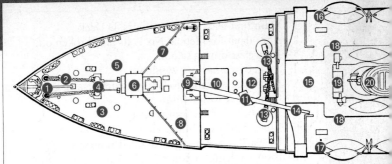

1 Anchor crane.	11 Crow's nest.
2 Anchor chains.	12 Number 3 hatch.
3 Bollards (bitts).	13 Well-Deck cranes.
4 Windlasses.	14 Top of remaining foremast on bridge.
5 Capstan.	15 Steering telemotor where wheelhouse was.
6 Number 1 hatch.	16 Forward davit for lifeboat No. 1.
7 Breakwater.	17 Forward davit for lifeboat No. 2.
8 Crew galley skylight.	18 Peeled-out wall of officers' quarters.
9 Base of foremast fallen on steam winches.	
0 Number 2 hatch.	

The Bow Section
A front view seen from the starboard side

This painting shows how the *Titanic*'s bow plowed int[o]
bottom upon impact, burying itself up to the base of t[he]
starboard anchor. On the forecastle, the anchor chains [remain]
in place between gleaming capstans, and the fallen fore[mast]
still supports the crow's nest, from which a lookout gav[e the]
fatal message, "Iceberg, right ahead!"

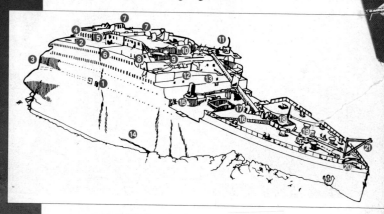

1 Main first-class gangway doors, D Deck.
2 After davit for lifeboat No. 7, its arm broken off.
3 First-class dining saloon.
4 Arched gymnasium windows.
5 First-class entrance to Grand Staircase and gymnasium.
6 Gaping expansion joint.
7 Stokehold (boiler room) vents.
8 Fallen starboard bridge cab.
9 Bulwark rail of bridge wing, fallen forward.
10 Bronze telemotor control.
11 Forward port davit for lifeboat No. 2 which launched
    collapsible D, the last boat to leave the ship.
12 Forward B-Deck first-class staterooms.
13 Still-closed gate between Well Deck (third class)
    and B Deck (first class).
14 Possible ice damage: creased plates with
    horizontally opened seams.
15 Cargo crane.
16 Bollards (bits).
17 Steam winch.
18 Number 1 hatch.
19 Windlasses.
20 Center anchor stowed in its well.
21 Anchor crane.

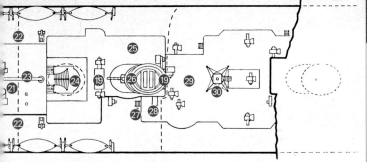

19 Stokehold vents (4).
20 Number 1 funnel opening.
21 Officers' bathroom skylight.
22 Forward expansion joint.
23 Marconi office skylight.
24 First-class forward staircase.
25 Collapsed roof of gymnasium.
26 Number 2 funnel opening.
27 Accommodation vent fan and motor housing.

28 Raised roof over reading and writing room.
29 Area where decks slant downward.
30 Compass platform amidships (missing).

A *Titanic* Bow Section Mosaic

Our deep-towed sled ANGUS made dozens of passes over the *Titanic* wreck and the debris field, taking more than 53,000 photographs from a height of approximately 25 feet. After the expedition, we began the painstaking task of trying to create a photographic "mosaic" of the intact portion of the *Titanic*'s forward section. Woods Hole technician John Porteous spent months assembling a jigsaw puzzle of adjoining images — an extremely complex task given the range of distances, camera angles and lighting conditions. More than 100 images were selected, adjusted and re-assembled in collaboration with the National Geographic Society to create the mosaic shown above.

The Bow

Covered with rust, the *Titanic*'s enormous bow seems to be plowing through the mud of the seafloor.

(Above) JJ's headlights look back at us as Alvin illuminates the knife edge of the bow.

(Opposite, top left) The point of the bow from the port side.

(Opposite, top right) JJ illuminates a windlass on the starboard bow.

(Opposite, bottom) The prow, adorned with rusticles.

Boilers

For years, many historians assumed the *Titanic*'s massive boilers broke loose and crashed through the hull when the ship was upended. In fact, only five single-ended boilers were located in the debris field. The remaining 24 boilers presumably are still within the bow section of the wreck.

(Above) The distinct pattern of the boiler facings made them easily recognizable in the underwater photographs taken by ANGUS.

(Below left) A rectangular piece of metal debris has landed on the face of this boiler.

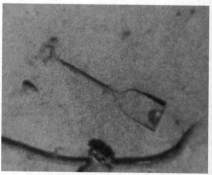

(Above) A tin cup and a doorknob assembly rest by a circular furnace door on one of the boilers.

(Left) This photograph of stokers aboard another ship of the Titanic era gives an idea of what the Titanic's boiler rooms looked like. A stoking shovel, similar to the one found on the ocean floor by ANGUS (opposite, bottom right), leans beside a pile of coal.

The Bridge

The telemotor that once held the ship's wheel stands alone on the devastated bridge.

(Top left) This is the only existing picture of Captain Smith standing on the Titanic's *bridge. Through the window, one of the bridge telegraphs can be seen.*

(Left) The bronze steering telemotor from the wheelhouse. (Top right) How it looked with the wheel in place.

(Above) A painting of the bridge area showing Alvin illuminating the telemotor while JJ takes a closer look at the crow's nest.

(Left) The shadow of the foremast can be seen in this photo of the Titanic's bridge.

The First-Class Lounge

The *Shipbuilder* described the first-class lounge as "...a noble apartment in the Louis Quinze style, the details being taken from the Palace of Versailles."

(Right) This statuette, which once adorned the mantelpiece (below), was photographed by Alvin *lying near boulders dropped by passing icebergs. It is a reduced copy of the classical statue, the "Artemis of Versailles," which is in the Louvre.*

(Right) This photograph was taken at the White Swan Hotel in Alnwick, England, which is furnished with fittings from the Titanic's sister ship, the Olympic. This leaded window from the Olympic's first-class lounge helped identify the one in the Titanic's debris field (above), which still has some of its panes intact.

The First-Class Dining Saloon

The largest room afloat, the *Titanic*'s first-class dining saloon could seat more than 500 people in Jacobean-style splendor.

(Below) One of the side dining areas of the first-class saloon.

(Bottom left) Although subject to 6,000 pounds per square inch of pressure, the cork and lead wrap around the neck of this champagne bottle are still in place. (Bottom right) A silver-plated serving platter from the first-class dining saloon.

(Top) A fragment from the leaded glass windows seen in the photograph on the facing page and in the bay window (right).

(Left) Battered but still shiny, a silver-plated soup tureen lies next to a broken steam pipe.

The Grand Staircase

Designed as the showpiece of the ship's first-class section, the ruined Grand Staircase provided an opening deep into the heart of the ship for *Jason Junior*.

(Above) The A-Deck foyer of the first-class Grand Staircase.

(Right) A feathery sea pen juts from a dangling light fixture similar to those shown at the top of the photograph above.

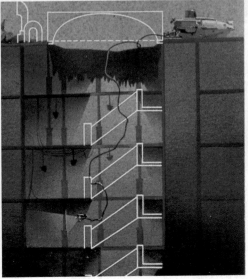

(Above) The area of the Grand Staircase and Alvin's landing site. JJ is exploring the remains of the staircase foyer.

(Left) JJ managed to penetrate as far as B Deck and shine his lights right down into C Deck.

The Staterooms

One of the goals of the White Star Line in building the *Olympic* and the *Titanic* was to make their passenger accommodations superior to anything previously seen afloat. From the period decor of the special B- and C-Deck suites to the brass and mahogany of the berths in the second- and third-class cabins, White Star brought a whole new world of passenger comfort to the transatlantic crossing.

(Below) The white porcelain of this iron bathtub has been almost completely overtaken by rust, in stark contrast to its pristine appearance when new (right).

(Above) The bed in this 1912 photograph of suite B-57 has a brass and enamel footboard identical to the one shown at left.

(Right) Although not quite as luxurious as a first-class suite, this stateroom still had two marble-topped sinks and a space heater next to the bed, similar to the one below.

The Stern Section
A starboard-side view

The stern appears to have struck the bottom with such force that the decks collapsed down on each other and the hull literally blew apart. Particularly striking are the two high-pressure cylinders from the reciprocating engines that are still upright and in position despite the fact the ship broke in two at this spot. Beneath the folded-back Poop Deck, where the *Titanic*'s passengers huddled in the final moments of the tragedy, the interior remains of the third-class smoking room and staircase now lie open to view.

1. Second-class purser's safe, discovered in 1986 and raised in 1987.
2. Hull shell plating.
3. Foundation for No. 4 funnel.
4. High-pressure cylinders of reciprocating engines.
5. Boilers.
6. Underside of decking peeled back aft.
7. Exposed interior decks where shell plating has blown away from hull.
8. Turbine engine room.
9. Aft davit for boat No. 16, lying down on the deck.
10. Second-class entrance deck house.
11. Main mast.
12. Underside of Boat Deck above A-Deck promenade, now peeled up and aft and hanging over the side.
13. A-Deck cargo crane.
14. Windows of second-class enclosed promenade.
15. Poop Deck peeled back and over on itself.
16. Evaporator from turbine engine room.
17. A main condenser from the turbine engine room.
18. Funnel remains.
19. Steel decking.
20. Large section of D-Deck shell plating.

The Bow Section

A rear view seen from the port side

When the *Titanic*'s bow section hit the bottom, the decks nearest the tear collapsed down on top of each other.

1 Missing gangway on B Deck where *JJ* briefly entered on final dive.
2 Where we found a doorway leading to a crew staircase.
3 Forward davit for lifeboat No. 2.
4 Telemotor from wheelhouse.
5 Officers' quarters.
6 Remains of after part of No. 1 funnel.
7 Electric winch for raising lifeboats.
8 After davit for lifeboat No. 8.
9 Vent for first-class elevator shaft.
10 First-class entrance.
11 Collapsed first-class Grand Staircase area.
12 Open D-Deck gangway door.
13 Remains of No. 2 funnel.
14 Collapsed roof over gymnasium.
15 Fallen first-class lounge roof.
16 No. 3 funnel casing.
17 Bilge keel.
18 Plating torn open at first-class dining saloon.

The Gymnasium

Situated on the Boat Deck near the starboard first-class entrance, the gymnasium provided a warm refuge for passengers on the night of the disaster while the lifeboats were being loaded.

(Top) This photograph of the Olympic's gymnasium shows a mechanical horse on the left by the arched window. A front view of the horse appears on the facing page (top). (Bottom) The arched windows of the gym are now draped in rusticles.

(Above) A fragment of the protective mesh that surrounded exercise machinery such as the electric horse (top) can be seen through this gym window. (Below) In his white flannels, the Titanic's gym instructor T. W. McCawley demonstrates the rowing machine.

The Kitchens

As the *Titanic* sank, thousands of pots, pans, dishes and utensils from the combined first- and second-class kitchens on D Deck hurtled to the ocean floor.

(Below) This copper sink no doubt came from one of the sculleries or may have been used in the kitchen for washing pots and pans.

(Right) Purser Herbert McElroy and Captain Smith in front of the officers' quarters.

(Below) This window matches the ones behind McElroy and Smith above.

(Left) This 1912 photograph of the Titanic *shows the open forward A-Deck promenade which can also be seen (bottom) on the* Titanic *wreck.*

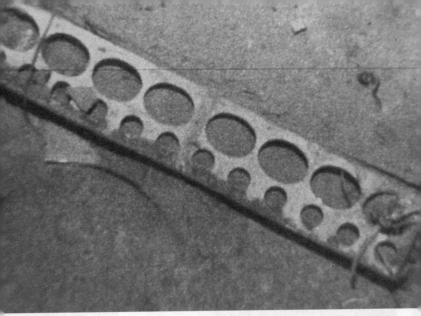

(Above) A section of one of the range tops, showing oval openings where burner covers once sat. An intact range top can be seen in the photograph of the pantry (opposite, top).

Corrosion seems to have had little effect on metal kitchen items like this copper stockpot (middle).

(Bottom) This plate from the third-class dining room bears the White Star emblem on its rim.

Lifeboats

The empty lifeboat davits still standing on the Boat Deck provide a poignant recollection of the night they were used for the first and last time.

THE
"WELIN QUADRANT" DAVIT
OVER
4000
FITTED or FITTING on vessels of all Nationalities.

TYPE DAY
As fitted on S.S.'s "OLYMPIC" & "TITANIC" (White Star Line), and many others.

Manufactured in **30** *Distinct Sizes.*

(Above) A crab scuttles along the arm of a lifeboat davit that last saw use at 1:10 A.M. on April 15, 1912, as it lowered lifeboat No. 8.

(Opposite, top) The same davit can be seen holding lifeboat No. 8 behind the passenger at the rail.

(Opposite, bottom) The Titanic's Welin davits were designed to carry 32 lifeboats, but they held only 16 — the number legally required by the British Board of Trade.

The Debris Field

Like a silent underwater museum more than two miles down, debris lies scattered over the ocean floor near the *Titanic* wreck. Most of the debris is concentrated near the severed stern section which is 1,970 feet away from the more intact bow section.

(Left) This plain headboard from third class or the crew's quarters provides a strong contrast to the more elegant enameled footboard shown on the opposite page.

(Below) A grenadier fish and Alvin's arm inspect a third-class coffee cup bearing the White Star emblem.

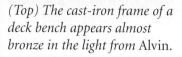

(Top) The cast-iron frame of a deck bench appears almost bronze in the light from Alvin.

(Above left) A toilet bowl lies next to a liquor bottle.

(Above right) A painted metal footboard from a first-class stateroom.

(Bottom) These wooden stairs may have taken third-class passengers from the Well Deck to the Poop Deck. Probably made of teak, the stairs are remarkably well preserved.

R.M.S. *Titanic*: Then and Now

Although the funnels are gone and the hull is broken, the wreck and debris field of the *Titanic* reveal fascinating glimpses of the great ship that was.

(Left) The port-side Boat Deck of the Titanic. *In the left foreground can be seen one of the "Sirocco" ventilation fans and its motor.*

(Above) The fan and motor housings still rest in their original position after 74 years.

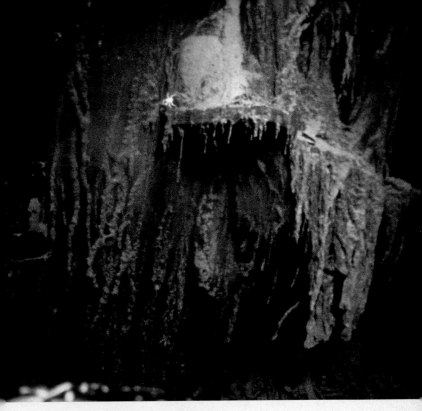

(Above) Rivers of rust flow off the port-side anchor.

(Left) The anchor as it looked when the ship was launched.

The Stern Section

A port-side view

This painting of the *Titanic*'s stern section shows the Poop Deck peeled back and partly overhanging the stern under which *Alvin* is exploring. Moving forward, the after Well Deck has been torn away and shell plating and framing have peeled outward from the hull. The fallen main mast and the starboard A-Deck cargo crane are still fitted to the ship as is the

second-class entrance deck house on the Boat Deck.

The large piece of debris in the left foreground is a section of deck from the galley. In a trail of debris leading back to the ship are broken hull and deck sections, three cargo cranes, two lifeboat davits and many other items.

The Losses

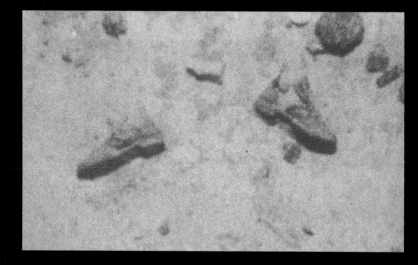

"Did you see any bodies?" is one of the questions asked most often of those who took part in the 1986 *Titanic* expedition. Although any human remains have long since disappeared, many poignant relics such as this pair of shoes lying side by side where a body once lay (above) are strong reminders that the *Titanic* wreck is indeed a gravesite, one which I have long believed should be left undisturbed. Subsequent salvage attempts have altered the wreck site irrevocably and damaged the ship's hull. Our 1986 visit proved that images like this one are far more compelling than the odd artifact removed from its emotional and historical context.

our excitement as the ship unfolded beneath us.

We quickly crossed the deck aft of the smokestack hole and arrived over the Grand Staircase opening.

"It's gigantic," commented Ralph. "We don't need *JJ*. I can take *Alvin* down that opening."

He was half joking, half serious, but I didn't rise to the bait. "That's all right, Ralph. I think we'll stick to the original plan and land *Alvin* on the deck and let *JJ* go down that hole, not us." But that mission was for a later dive and a healthy robot. Today I wanted to continue the tour.

Heading west, *Alvin* cleared the port side of the ship and the Boat Deck fell behind us into darkness. At my request, Ralph now pivoted our sub back around, dropped down, and came in along the A-Deck windows, the enclosed first-class promenade. As we did this, the hull of the ship began to act as a "windbreak," protecting us from the current. Clearly, the port side of the ship was the best place to work when the current was strong.

Huge rusticles hung from the overhang made by A Deck. These partially obscured the smaller windows looking into B-Deck staterooms just below. As I peered entranced through my viewport, I could easily imagine people walking down the promenade, looking out of the windows I was now looking into.

Here I was on the bottom of the ocean peering at recognizable, man-made artifacts designed and built for another world. I was looking through windows out of which people had once looked, decks along which they had walked, rooms where they had slept, joked, made love. It was like landing on the surface of Mars only to find the remains of an ancient civilization similar to our own — a live episode from *The Twilight Zone*.

Ralph now began to bring *Alvin* toward the Boat Deck. Suddenly the sub shuddered, made a clanging noise, and a waterfall of rust covered our viewports.

"Ralph, we've hit something!" I exclaimed. "What is it?"

"I don't know," replied the pilot. "We should be clear of any overhang. I'm backing off."

Unseen overhangs are the nightmare of the deep-submersible pilot. Gingerly backing out from the hull, Ralph brought us slowly upward. Directly in front of our forward viewport, a big davit block slid by — only inches away. That was what we'd hit. It was attached to one of the *Titanic*'s long, curved lifeboat davits which had fallen onto the deck and hung several feet out over the side. This was the after davit for lifeboat No. 8 — a sight to chill the heart of the hardiest explorer. No. 8 was the boat Mrs. Ida Straus had refused to enter, the boat steered through much of the night by the doughty Countess of Rothes.

We continued rising and headed aft once more, in search of the severed end of the bow section. Just beyond the number 2 funnel opening, the deck plunged at a precipitous angle and Ralph tried to chase it down, crossing diagonally toward the starboard side of the ship. But our sub was now being buffeted by the full force of the current and Ralph was having trouble holding *Alvin*'s head to wind. As we turned south into the current, what I saw out the starboard viewport I didn't like. The graceful lines of the ship had disappeared in a maelstrom of twisted and torn steel plating, upturned portholes, and jumbled wreckage protruding in our direction, too close for comfort, ready to poke out *Alvin*'s right eye.

"Swing back to the left! I have wreckage just out of my viewport and it's getting close. Swing left!" It was moments like these that all deep-submariners lived in fear of.

"It won't come around into the current!" Ralph returned.

"Then come up. Let's get out of here! It's too dangerous. Continue driving forward until we clear the tear. Let's go along the starboard side of the ship to the bow."

It was probably worse for Martin, stuck at the left-side viewport and unable to see the danger. He said nothing, but the tension must have been getting to him.

Once again *Alvin* was acting up and Ralph informed me that I'd better start thinking about going home. We had been on the bottom less than two and a half hours. Surface control informed us that the weather topside was getting worse. Every minute we now delayed would make *Alvin*'s surface recovery more dangerous. But I couldn't bear to leave the ship until the last possible minute — not now that I'd finally found her.

Ralph reluctantly agreed to make a few high-altitude runs back and forth between the midships tear and the bow so I could determine other places to land tomorrow when I planned to make our first penetrations with *JJ*. Few words were spoken as we passed back and forth along the length of the lifeless hull.

Suddenly that infernal alarm went off again, indicating that the battery grounds were steadily getting worse. Surface control chimed in to inform us that the weather upstairs was deteriorating. Our time had run out. Ralph drove *Alvin* away from the wreck, dropped our weights, and we began our ascent.

I popped a cassette in the stereo — the soundtrack from *Flashdance* was my favored music for the way up. Upbeat music fits in well with the feeling of accomplishment after a good dive and spurs the joking and small talk that seem to flow at such times.

Two and a half hours later, as we approached the shallow, daylit layers, *Alvin* began to heave as the seas at the surface made themselves felt. When we broke the surface, the sub suddenly pitched forward, throwing an array of bottles, tissue boxes, and videocassettes crashing down on my head.

Suddenly Ralph yelled, "*JJ* is out of his garage!"

We were helpless inside the wildly pitching sub as *JJ* fell downward. *Alvin*'s heaving action was causing his tether to snap like a whip, and the cable was chafing against the cable cutter and in danger of severing. If that happened, *JJ* would be lost forever, before even having one chance to perform. Ralph grabbed *Alvin*'s radio mike to contact the surface controller as divers swarmed out of their dinghy onto the sub, oblivious to the crisis.

"*A-II*, this is *Alvin*. Get the divers in the water immediately and put a safety line on *JJ*!"

But his directive was lost in the confusion. Bridge, surface control, launch coordinator, and the rubber boat carrying the support divers all had radios and everybody seemed to be talking at once as preparations were made to recover the sub. Vainly I tried to signal them through the viewport. No luck. The divers were too busy getting ready to attach safety lines to the front of the sub. At last, we got in touch with the support boat and Ralph practically shouted, "Get a safety line on *JJ* now!" The divers rushed to rescue *JJ* and soon he was safely on the support boat. Since the water was too rough for the divers to manhandle *JJ* back into his garage, the only alternative was to cut his tether. With frightful ease, the cable cutter did its work, the crisis was over, and we were soon all back safely on board the *Atlantis II*.

We had spent a total of two hours and fifty minutes examining the *Titanic*'s entire forward section from the bow to the forward base of where the number 3 funnel once stood, marking the aftermost part of the broken-off bow section. Soon our video studio was jammed with people eager for their first glimpse of the *Titanic* close up. We didn't disappoint them.

Meanwhile, Chris von Alt and his team had *JJ* on the table preparing for an all-night operation. Not only did they have to replace the cut tether cable, they wanted to get to the root of *JJ*'s poor performance on his debut voyage and to eliminate a "noise" we'd noted was interfering with the video signal. As well, they wanted to prevent him from again coming loose from his garage when we hit the surface.

As I collapsed in my bunk, I vowed that if *JJ* was working properly we'd go down the Grand Staircase tomorrow. Each dive could be our last and, given *Alvin*'s battery problems, there wasn't time to warm up to the challenge. Tomorrow we would go for broke.

While I slept, the *Jason Jr.* team did its work. Chris even rigged up an ingenious way of keeping *JJ* in place during rough launches and recoveries: an inflated air bladder

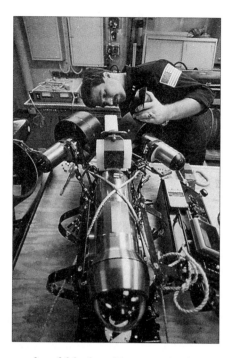

Lt. Mike Mahre works on JJ's after thrusters.

made of black rubber — similar to an inner tube — placed in the front of the garage. At the surface, it would keep our boy snugly stowed. On the bottom, the water pressure would compress the air inside the bladder, collapsing it flat and freeing *JJ* to move in and out of his garage on command.

The main storm missed us and by morning the weather had improved, but again my hopes for the perfect day quickly vanished. As we readied for launching, Chris checked out *JJ*'s system from inside the sphere only to discover that one of his four motors had jammed. It had been running fine when tested out of its housing; now it was hitting the protective shroud.

Although Dudley Foster would be piloting today, his boss, Ralph Hollis, was quick to remind me that any delay meant time lost on the bottom — we would still have to be back on the surface in time for dinner...

For the next three hours I stood around in mounting disbelief as one glitch appeared after another. Once *JJ*'s port motor was fixed, the starboard one failed to function. While Martin replaced a capacitor in *Alvin*'s arm camera, Chris changed a blown-out bulb in *JJ*'s strobe.

Finally, at 11:18 A.M., *Alvin* was falling toward the bottom with *JJ* nestled snugly in his garage. Martin Bowen would finally get to operate our eye-on-a-string — if it was still working when we got to the bottom.

It was nearly two o'clock when we neared the seafloor and I put my favorite arrival tape on the sub stereo — the Boston Pops playing the themes from *E.T.*, *Chariots of Fire*, and *Raiders of the Lost Ark*. This was the perfect music to psych everyone up for the dive (we used to joke that *E.T.* was *JJ*'s song for our expedition.) With the orchestra going full blast, Dudley dropped the descent weights and leveled off just below 328 feet altitude off the *Titanic*'s port side. It was a beautiful underwater day for diving, with only a gentle current blowing. We moved quickly through a field of light debris full of white third-class china coffee cups bearing the insignia of the White Star Line. Within moments, the *Titanic*'s massive hull emerged from the darkness. We were coming in on the port side, this time near the aftermost part of the bow section.

With so little time, Dudley piloted us quickly up the ship's side and across the port Boat Deck toward the staircase opening. Barely clearing the rail on the deck above, we jumped up to the area where I wanted to make our landing.

I pointed out the big opening above the Grand Staircase.

"Got it," was Dudley's reply.

"Now, spin the sub slightly to the right and land next to that small vertical pipe." The pipe, centered amidships, had been a vent for the large elevator shaft below it and us.

I directed the pilot to move forward to the very edge of the opening and set down *Alvin*, facing aft, with *JJ*'s garage next to the elevator vent. We landed gently on the deck and Dudley turned on the ballast pumps, their squealing noise echoing through our tiny sphere. Slowly, our rocking motion disappeared. We didn't want to be too heavy, just enough to stay firmly in place.

Alvin now rested quietly on the topmost deck of the R.M.S. *Titanic* directly above the shaft where three elevators had carried first-class passengers from belowdecks should they not wish to climb the elegant Grand Staircase. We, however, would take the stairs.

Martin was extremely nervous, not so much because he felt a lack of experience but because this was the first real test for *JJ*. Almost all his attention would be focused on a video monitor inside our sub while he projected his mind away from his body and inside a single remotely controlled swimming eyeball.

The *JJ* control box sat on Martin's lap. With his right hand he operated the joystick. When Martin pushed the lever in any of 360 directions, *JJ* would go the way he pushed. If he twisted it clockwise, *JJ* would spin clockwise

Martin Bowen concentrates intensely as he prepares to maneuver JJ *down the* Titanic's Grand Staircase.

on his axis, and so on. His left hand clutched a pistol-grip control. When he pushed away on the button near his thumb, *JJ* would go down; pull it toward him and *JJ* would go up. When he pulled his trigger finger once, the cable would start to unwind from its reel; pull it again and the cable started pulling *JJ* back into his garage. If he rolled a knob with his finger, *JJ*'s eye rolled up and down within a range of 170°. If he pushed another knob with the same finger, *JJ*'s strobe light flashed on and a color picture was taken by a still camera mounted next to *JJ*'s video eye. Martin had spent many hours practicing these maneuvers with *JJ* in a pool back at Woods Hole. Now that training would be put to the test.

Cautiously, *JJ* left his garage. Then Martin turned him around to look back at *Alvin* resting on the deck. It was the first time we'd actually seen ourselves on the video monitor, through *JJ*'s eye. There we were inside a tiny submersible surrounded by darkness and incredible pressure, our running lights looking like the eyes of a deep-sea monster.

JJ turned away and slowly floated out over the staircase. For an instant he swerved drunkenly until Martin got him under control. As I watched *JJ* on Big Bird's video screen, I thought for a second that he was going to fall over the edge. Instead, four small motors turned *JJ* into an underwater hovercraft as he inched out over the yawning blackness.

I glanced at the red safety cover protecting *JJ*'s emergency decoupling switch. We'd already had to lift that cover once and cut *JJ*'s tether. That switch might save our lives, but if we had to use it down here, it would mean *JJ* was gone for good and half a million dollars down the drain. I fervently hoped we wouldn't need it again.

Our best route down appeared to be along the near or forward wall of the staircase opening, where an elaborate ornamental clock, decorated with the figures of Honor and Glory crowning Time, had once hung. It had graced the landing between the Boat Deck and A Deck. This route promised the least potential for obstruction and Martin hugged it closely as he paid out more cable and *JJ* dropped down. At first, *JJ* could see nothing but the rusty orange crust of the vertical bulkhead with rivets still visible. Hardly a trace remained of all that oak woodwork and paneling. Dudley inched *Alvin* forward so that Big Bird's camera could track our little explorer as he dropped deeper and deeper. But soon *JJ* was lost from view and Martin was completely on his own. I turned now to concentrate on the images appearing on *JJ's* video screen in the back of the sub. Dudley stared too. This was the tensest moment of our dives so far.

A room appeared off the port side foyer on A Deck, defined by the dim shapes of pillars. Martin swung *JJ* around for a closer look and suddenly he saw something off in the distance. "Look at that," he said softly. "Look at that chandelier."

Now I could see something too. "No, it *can't* be a chandelier," I said, more to myself than to Martin. "It couldn't possibly have survived." It was difficult to believe my eyes. The ship had fallen two and a half miles, hitting the bottom with the force of a train running into a mountainside, and here was an almost perfectly preserved light fixture! Soon we could see more of them in the distance. "My God, it *is* a chandelier," I crowed. Indeed, that was what it looked like.

I told Martin to try to enter the room for a closer view. This would be the truest test of *JJ's* maneuverability: how close could we get without disturbing our object of study? Our robot left the stairwell, entered the room, and headed toward the fixture, in the process brushing up against rusticles hanging from the ceiling. The rust dissolved upon impact and suddenly *JJ* was engulfed in an orange murk, visibility zero. But by pitching *JJ's* eye up we could again see our "chandelier." Martin moved closer until he was less than a foot away. A feathery sea pen sprouted from the light fixture, turning it into a crystal crown with a feather on top. We could plainly see the delicate designs in the brasswork surrounding and above the fixture, still bright and shiny. And there was the actual socket where a bulb had been fitted! "Take a still picture, this is fantastic," I exulted.

"Bob, we are running short of bottom time. We have to return to the surface."

Dudley's words cut through my excitement like a knife. We were deep inside the *Titanic*, down the Grand Staircase, the fulfillment of a dream, and Dudley wanted to go home for dinner! I knew Dudley was just following orders, but I wanted to shout in protest. We had been at the bottom less than one hour — lots of battery time left. I could see Martin shared my frustration as he gently maneuvered *JJ* out of the room and back up the vertical wall.

Emerging from the black hole, our proud little robot soldier, an R2D2 of the deep, shone his lights toward our sub as we watched him approach on Big Bird's video. For a moment, I felt as though we were being visited by aliens. Instead of us looking out into an uninhabited world, something was looking back at us. Then *JJ* maneuvered in front of *Alvin*, his lights sweeping across our three viewports and bathing the interior in an unearthly glow. It reminded me of the scene in *Close Encounters of the Third Kind*, when the alien spaceship hovers over a truck, shining lights into its windows. Flying saucers aside, *JJ* had just walked on the surface of the moon and returned safely.

LAST RESTING PLACE

TWO AND A HALF HOURS AFTER LIFTING OFF FROM THE Grand Staircase, three aquanauts emerged from their underwater space capsule onto the fantail of the *Atlantis II*, where a crowd of colleagues had gathered. Word of our successful dive had already spread and people were eager to hear firsthand about what we had seen below. If the expedition had ended now, I'd have had few regrets. We'd proved what we came here to prove. JJ had strolled in the first-class compartments of the *Titanic*!

Martin and I were ebullient, still hyped up from our trip down the staircase, as we attempted to recreate for those on the surface the experience of entering the *Titanic* for the first time. At one point, Martin quipped with forgivable exaggeration, "We went dancing in the ballroom!" I echoed his words. It didn't matter that there was no ballroom on the *Titanic*, or that the "chandelier" was a fairly ordinary light fixture, only one of nearly a hundred like it on the ship; the phrase simply captured our mood.

Alvin *holds a broom to indicate a "clean sweep" after our trip down the Grand Staircase.*

I gave Martin a bear hug as the onlookers applauded.

The crowd on deck followed us into the video studio for our première presentation of "*Jason Junior* Descends the Staircase." Martin and I watched it with them, none of us tiring of the repeated showings. There before us on the video monitors, as *JJ* wheeled around the staircase well, we could now plainly make out the shape of the balconies and various deck levels. While the light fixture we had most closely studied was on the port side, others appeared on the starboard — then more and more of them, visible back into the darkness. Like the first one we'd seen, each had dropped from its original position in the ceiling and was hanging by its electrical wire. Some were intact with the cut-glass exteriors still fitted in their holdings. Others retained only the brass mounts.

More of the oak woodwork remained than I had first

thought, giving rise to speculation that woodborers might not have completely decimated the interior wood deep in the ship. Some of the support columns still retained the decorative wood sheathing at their bases, their design just discernible. And horizontal wood trim was still visible on the edge of each deck level facing the stairwell. Unfortunately, we could see no trace of those beautiful wrought-iron balustrades I had admired in the old photographs. Maybe they were lying nearby covered with fallen rusticles; more likely they had fallen down the stairwell beyond the point we had dared venture with *JJ*. Or perhaps they had simply rusted completely away.

That evening, after supper and sunset, with *Alvin* and *JJ* being prepared for the next day's dive, I sent my daily report, describing our underwater exploits, ashore via satellite phone link. Then I dealt with the media, one network and wire service after another. Like last year, they were clamoring for news and I was amazed yet again by the intensity of the public's continuing fascination with the ship. Question after question was thrown at me. "Have you seen any bodies?" "How big is the gash?" "How dangerous is it down there?" "What is the most exciting thing you've seen so far?" "Have you found any valuables? Did you bring anything up?"

The question about salvage was asked again and again, but prior to the cruise I had ruled out bring back anything from the bottom. There had been long discussions with everyone from Woods Hole's director of research, Dr. Derek Spencer, to the Smithsonian Institution. Naturally, the temptation was great. Maritime collectors around the world would have paid thousands of dollars for a piece of the ship.

And artifacts could be easily recovered with *Alvin*'s powerful robot arm, designed to collect biological and geological samples in the deep sea. How I would have loved a bottle of *Titanic* champagne for my own wine cellar. But from all our discussions it became clear the *Titanic* has no true archaeological value. Although it is tempting to make the comparison, the *Titanic* is not a pyramid of the deep. We knew exactly how the ship was built and what was on board. Recovering a chamber pot or a wine bottle or a copper cooking pan would really just be pure treasure-hunting. My major funder, the Navy, wasn't interested in using taxpayers' money for this purpose. Nor was I.

Post-dive checks on *Jason Jr.* had given him a clean bill of health, *Alvin*'s battery troubles appeared to have been solved, and this morning's launch began to look routine. Even the weather, which had been mostly good to us so far, continued to cooperate — grudgingly. Again the sea was calm, but a dense fog had rolled in. Nonetheless, dive number four, July 16, started with a spurt and a sputter. *Alvin* had hardly lifted from its deck cradle when Will Sellars, our pilot for today, noticed a problem with one of *Alvin*'s cameras and decided to land back on deck to get it fixed. Fortunately, only ten minutes later we were over the side and free of the ship.

The fog, however, added an element of danger. *Alvin*'s turret-like fiberglass "sail" is transparent to probing radar, and a ship bearing down on us in this pea soup would never see us. So, while Will swiftly completed his final surface checks, the *Atlantis II* stood guard, its radar scanning for

The fourth dive of our 1986 expedition began in a dense fog.

intruders. Only one large blip appeared on the screen, the Navy's rescue ship USS *Ortolan* out of Charleston, South Carolina. *Ortolan* was keeping us friendly company.

Safety checks completed, Will flooded the tanks and *Alvin* sank into safer and quieter waters. It was odd to think that it was less dangerous sinking 12,500 feet down than hanging around on the surface — but given the thick fog, it was. For Martin and me the trip to the *Titanic* was becoming old hat, but this was Will Sellars's first time. Will hadn't been around as long as Ralph Hollis or Dudley Foster, but quite long enough to become an experienced pilot. I also knew that like his colleagues he'd follow the book: he had no choice. When it was time to leave, he'd leave, whether we were in the middle of some momentous discovery or not.

When the *Titanic* once again came into view, we headed for the wheelhouse area. Conning *Alvin* into position, I asked Will to land near the brass remains of the steering mechanism, which glinted in our bright lights. Since the current was stronger than yesterday, Will had to control his excitement at seeing the *Titanic* for the first time in order to make a precise landing without damaging the wheel pedestal — or our sub.

At my request, he spun the sub around to face the wheel and the port side of the ship, setting down just outside the rectangular wooden frame on the deck where the wheelhouse had been. The upper part of the *Titanic*'s foremast was just beyond our forward lights and ahead to our right; where the ship's outer bridge had once stood with its many gleaming instruments, the deck just stopped, ending in a jagged, bent-down edge. It had been wrenched away, perhaps when the forward funnel fell during the sinking.

"All right, Bob. It's all yours," said Will with an audible sigh of relief.

Actually it was all Martin's, who now coached *JJ* out of his garage and toward what was left of the ship's wheel.

A well-preserved running light on the fallen foremast. Its glass lamp was still intact.

Then he headed to the mast. Through *JJ*'s eyes we could see a brass running light still attached to the mast, and the fine metal wires inside the intact glass lamp.

Now I directed Martin to drive *JJ* along the sloping mast toward the crow's nest, warning him to watch out for the cable. If he stayed slightly above the mast he should be okay. *JJ* promptly disappeared from our viewports as his yellow cable paid out into the darkness and I watched the video monitor spellbound as our little friend did his tightrope walk.

Martin's skill with *JJ* was almost as fascinating as what we were seeing. He played the control console like a concert musician, his fingers moving with quick precision across its array of knobs, levers, and switches. Suddenly, the crow's nest loomed into *JJ*'s view. He was now at the very spot where Frederick Fleet and Reginald Lee had been standing when they saw the iceberg appear without warning in the *Titanic*'s path. And *Alvin* was resting at almost the exact place where Sixth Officer James Moody had received the lookout's alarm call, and relayed it to the watch commander, First Officer Murdoch. Thirty-seven seconds later came the impact. Looking out of *Alvin*'s window, I could imagine the helmsman turning the wheel hard-a-starboard in a vain attempt to avoid the collision.

The wonderful clarity of *JJ*'s video vision now revealed that the hole in the mast just above the twisted crow's nest, which we had previously assumed was the lookout's telephone hook-up, was actually much larger than we'd thought. It was in fact the hatch through which the lookouts climbed to enter and exit the crow's nest.

Now *JJ* dropped down beneath the crow's nest into

the no-man's-land of the Well Deck. In front lay the two large cranes used to load luggage into holds number 2 and 3. The scene was beautiful — the lines of windows looking out onto the Well Deck, the cables draped gracefully across, the detail of the cranes themselves — but dangerous. JJ was hemmed in by superstructure, cables, booms, and wreckage. And just as we'd feared, we encountered our first serious problem.

Martin drove JJ up to the forward bulkhead of C Deck, just abaft the port crane in the Well Deck, to take a look at a gate in the bulwark railing that kept third-class passengers from entering first class. The gate was still closed. Then he flew JJ along the row of B-Deck windows facing the bow looking for a broken one to peer into. The window to first-class cabin B-3 was gone and JJ glimpsed inside… But no furniture or fixtures were visible, just the metal channels defining the ceiling and walls. As JJ passed from window to window along this forward end of B Deck, he could see the large steel doors that gave onto the deck. They were closed tight, their hinges and portholes intact.

But JJ had gone too far. Suddenly Martin noticed that his cable had become hung up on one of the jagged pieces of metal protruding from the bridge. Martin tried taking in the tether, but it began chafing against a piece of torn steel plate. "That's no good," he whispered, and tried driving JJ up and away in an effort to take the loops out, drawing it straight. JJ was turned toward us so he could watch the effect of this maneuver. As the distance widened between us and our robot, the tether finally came free.

"Bring him home," I said. This place was simply too risky. "Let's try another site."

With *JJ* safely in his garage, *Alvin* rose up from the wheelhouse, pivoted left, and crossed over what once was Captain Smith's cabin on the starboard side, its exterior bulkhead collapsed outward and lying on the deck. The interior side of a window passed within inches of my viewport and I could see a shiny brass worm gear used to open and close the upper portion of the window. Was this, I wondered, a window that Captain Smith had cranked open to let a little fresh air into his bedroom before turning in for the night?

"Watch it," I warned. "We are too close to a piece of railing. It's coming right for my viewport."

Will kicked *Alvin's* stern around, rotating us free of the obstacle, and began to drop onto the starboard Boat Deck. *Alvin* was now facing aft toward the midships tear. The current, for some reason, had gone slack. I swung *Alvin's* mechanical arm to the right and trained Big Bird's cameras on the windows lining the Boat Deck. As we glided along, I felt as though I were visiting a ghost town in the Wild West where suddenly one day everyone had closed up shop and left. Some windows were open, others closed.

A lifeless boat davit stood high on the starboard side, not cranked out after its last launch, but standing almost erect. This davit had seen more use than any other that night, having lowered both lifeboat No. 1 and collapsible C. Then it was cranked back in for yet another launch — collapsible A. But the *Titanic* had given a lurch and suddenly A was floating on its own. Steward Edward Brown jumped in, severed the lines just before a wave washed the boat clear of the ship, partially swamping it. A number of swimmers later gained its safety. Now we could see the davit still standing tall, waiting in vain for another boat launch. Ahead, an electrical winch sat slowly rusting on the deck and, along the deck's outer edge, I could see the row of chocks on which the *Titanic*'s lifeboats had rested.

It was on this very deck that the full spectrum of human behavior was played out in the three short hours between 11:40 P.M., when the ship hit the iceberg, and 2:20 A.M., when she disappeared beneath the waves. Alfred Rush, who had turned 18 during the voyage, refused to climb aboard a lifeboat with the women and children because he was now a man — and went down with the ship. Bruce Ismay, the wealthy president and managing director of International Mercantile Marine, which owned the White Star Line, had hopped into the partly filled collapsible C as it was about to be lowered away, and lived to regret his instinct for survival. After his public vilification as J. "Brute" Ismay, he became a recluse and eventually died a broken man. And from here you could have heard the *Titanic*'s brave band playing cheerful ragtime music to boost the crowd's spirits as the slope of the deck grew ever more alarming.

We had landed *Alvin* just aft of where Ismay had entered the boat, near where lifeboat No. 5 had once sat. Now we sent *JJ* over the side, following the same precarious route the lifeboats themselves had taken down to the water. One of them almost dumped its passengers before being righted. A pretty young Frenchwoman almost didn't make it into boat No. 9 and another woman completely missed boat No. 10, falling between the dangling lifeboat and the side of the ship. But some quick thinker grabbed her ankle and, as she hung indelicately over the side, people on the deck below hauled her into the promenade.

Passenger Lawrence Beesley described what it was like to leave the towering ship in a tiny lifeboat: "It was exciting to feel the boat sink by jerks, foot by foot, as the ropes were paid out from above and shrieked as they passed through the pulley blocks, the new ropes and gear creaking under the strain of a boat laden with people, and the crew calling to the sailors above as the boat tilted slightly, now at one end, now at the other, 'Lower aft!' 'Lower stern!' and 'Lower together!' as she came level again… It certainly was thrilling to see the black hull of the ship on one side and the sea, seventy feet below, on the other, or to pass down by cabins and saloons brilliantly lighted…"

Looking through *JJ*'s eye into the A-Deck promenade, I could imagine the first-class passengers waiting patiently below, herded there by Lightoller, who had the good idea of speeding things up by loading some of the boats from the promenade. But the windows had been closed and many passengers had shuffled back up onto the Boat Deck. Eventually, however, the windows were opened and lifeboat No. 4 was loaded and lowered from A Deck.

JJ kept descending, moving below the first-class state-room windows of B Deck. As he passed, he peered in and caught a brief glimpse of the interior of cabin B-49. The aft wall and overhead were clearly visible, the steel channels bare where the decorative ceiling used to be. The walls appeared to be painted white and seemed fairly clean, but there was no sign of any wood paneling or furniture. As *JJ* continued down, the windows gave way to a steel wall punctuated by an endless row of viewports — C Deck. A few were open, some undoubtedly unlatched by first-class passengers after they had felt the ship's engine stopped, and who had peered out of them to see what, if anything, had happened. Some people in lifeboats recalled watching the seawater swirl in through these same open ports. By the time this part of the ship was underwater, these rooms had long been evacuated.

Martin brought *JJ* back to home base and then we sent him for a stroll aft along the Boat Deck. As he wended his way along, he looked in the windows of several first-class cabins and down now-exposed passageways until he came to the twin entrances to the Grand Staircase and the gymnasium. As *JJ* moved aft toward these entrances, he looked into the windows of the foyer of the Grand Staircase. Although the roof had crashed in beyond a few feet, making his view only a short one, pillars could plainly be seen. Mounted high on the protective weather housing around the doorways was the fitting that had held an electric sign bearing the words "First Class Entrance." *JJ* peeked into the doorway of the entrance to the Grand Staircase, spotting the door between its vestibule and the gym, before kicking up a dust storm and retreating.

As *JJ* slowly passed by the gymnasium windows, remnants of the equipment could be seen amid the rubble, including a piece of metal grillwork that had protected the works of such contraptions as the electric camel, a turn-of-the-century exercise machine. Also visible were various wheel shapes and a handle. The ceiling was festooned with rusticles and collapsed downward on the inboard side. It was in this deserted gym that Colonel John Jacob Astor had calmed his pregnant young bride by explaining to her how a lifevest was packed with cork as he cut one open with a small pocketknife.

As I looked out of *Alvin*'s forward viewport, I could see *JJ* far off down the deck, turning this way and that to get a better view inside the doorways and various windows. It was almost as if our little robot had a mind of his own, seeming so deliberate and inquisitive. Martin was now controlling *JJ* with such skill that this floating eyeball had almost become an extension of his own body.

As Martin brought *JJ* home, I was thinking about going back to the Grand Staircase. Martin had done such a great job of getting us to within inches of that "chandelier" on our last dive, but we'd later discovered to our dismay that the still camera had jammed. We had a good videotape, but no stills at all.

The next day we again landed next to the remains of the elevator-shaft vent — this time on its port side — and again facing aft. *JJ* headed back down the stairwell. As *JJ* retraced his steps, I asked Martin to check several of the rooms on the starboard side of the ship. But we could see all sorts of wires drooping along under the ceiling and

The base of this pillar still bears some traces of its original oak woodwork.

decided not to risk an entry. Finally, we relocated the light fixture we'd first seen, with its feather-like sea pen jauntily protruding, and Martin nosed *JJ* in close as I snapped off one still picture after another. Then Martin ventured even farther into its depths. Very little was recognizable — except the columns, light fixtures, and wires — in the jumble of fallen rusticles scattered several inches deep on the floor. There was certainly no sign of the luxurious furniture that once graced the room.

We were now dangerously deep in the interior of the ship, and there was no sense taking any more chances with *JJ* than we already had. This fourth dive was turning into a banner day for *JJ*. We were doing exactly what we'd set out to accomplish — landing on one site after another and letting Martin and *JJ* do their thing. Our next stop was the bow.

Alvin landed gently on the bottom sediment a few feet from the knife-edge of the bow that towered overhead. Again I was awestruck by the size and majesty of the ship, its mighty prow plowing through the mud. From our vantage point there was no evidence this behemoth had been bothered by a mere iceberg. In a few moments, *JJ* was out of his cage and off to explore, a tiny figure against the great black hull. *JJ* flew up to the port anchor, resting at an angle in its hawsepipe, rust flowing off in a frozen cascade, then rose farther to look once more in vain for the *Titanic's* name. Next he went higher and passed over the Forecastle Deck railing, across the auxiliary anchor crane to one of the large bronze capstans nearby. Maneuvering to within an inch, Martin pitched *JJ*'s optical eye down and easily read the manufacturer's plate: "Napier Bros. Ltd., Engineers, Glasgow."

Reluctantly, Martin brought *JJ* home. It was time to head for the surface. We had landed at four separate sites, successfully deploying our robot on each occasion. The three of us were exhausted but elated as we headed for the surface to the sound of rock music. The floor of our cabin was a sea of videocassettes — our priceless *Titanic* salvage — as we joked and kibitzed, reliving the highlights of a fantastic day.

There are easy dives and hard dives and our fifth visit to the *Titanic*, on July 17, turned out to be a frustrating three hours and fifty-three minutes. Martin got the day off so that Chris von Alt, *JJ*'s architect, could try out his baby. Paul Tibbits, a recent addition to the *Alvin* team, was our pilot.

The current on the bottom was the strongest so far and the water was clouded with sediment. When we attempted to land on the bow, the sub smacked against the opening to number 1 hatch and a nearby capstan before we settled down. The thought of wreckage punching a hole in a viewport was a constant fear in our minds as the view-ports are the only weak spots on the sub. Then we watched as *JJ* was blown like a kite in the submarine wind, his tether in danger of getting hopelessly wrapped around railings or wreckage. Having decided to keep *JJ* in his garage, we fared little better ourselves as we tried to investigate the region of the tear, the place where the bow had broken off, just forward of the number 3 smokestack. Yawing perilously close to the ugly wreckage, we were thrown dangerously out of control by the current. But we saw enough to know that the decks of the ship had collapsed in on one another like a giant accordion. It was time to get out of here before the current swept us onto this treacherous shoal.

Paul was exhausted when we finally started for the surface, and all three of us were relieved to be floating peacefully upward after being tossed around by the storm below. Back on board the *Atlantis II* we were tired and disappointed — especially Chris, who'd been denied his one and only chance to drive *JJ* in the deep.

That evening, I sat down with Al Uchupi to review the still-camera footage he and the ANGUS team had been gathering each night after *Alvin* and *JJ* returned from the bow section. Our next dive would be our first to the debris field and I wanted to make maximum use of the limited time that remained — only seven days. I had therefore asked Al to work up a map identifying the more interesting targets. I would carry this chart with me on the sub. That way we could save some time as the surface navigator led us from target to target.

ANGUS had so far mapped only a scattering of debris along the 1,970 feet separating the bow and the large stern piece we'd located last year. Most of the heavy debris seemed to be concentrated around this stern section and to the east of it, including all of the ship's smaller single-ended boilers. Al and I believed these had fallen out of the mid-portion of the ship when it broke in half at or near the surface. We surmised that these heavy round objects had fallen straight to the bottom. In the vicinity of the stern section, there were additional pieces of large wreckage scattered in a larger field of lighter debris. As well as the boilers, ANGUS had spotted three ship's telegraphs.

This lighter material included some of the coal carried by the *Titanic* and many small fragments of wreckage including cups and plates, silver platters, and countless floor tiles apparently carried east of the stern section by the strong surface current running that night. I wondered what we would find went we went in for a close-up look.

My work with Al that evening was interrupted by a call from the radio room. Peter Jennings wanted to interview me for ABC News. Like so many before him, he asked the inevitable question about the chances of finding human remains. "Well, Peter," I replied, "if we are ever going to find any bodies, it will come on tomorrow's dive to the debris field." In fact bodies were highly unlikely, but I thought there was a faint possibility of human skeletons. Certainly any sign of human remains was a chilling thought.

The morning of July 18 was another lovely sunny summer day. But as I reclined quietly by the starboard viewport inside our little sub — my home away from home — pondering Al's map, I couldn't help feeling edgy about the day's mission. I was anxious about what we would find down there. At least the risks in the debris field would be minimal for Jim Hardiman and his trainee co-pilot, John Salzig.

This was to be an *Alvin* training dive and JJ had been left behind. To ensure a steady flow of well-trained new drivers, there is a rule that on every seventh dive we have to give up one seat to a pilot-in-training.

Today, our sixth descent to the bottom proved uneventful — no battery grounds, no malfunctioning sonar, no ominous alarm buzzers — and we found our target easily. Landing to the west, we approached the debris field along the ocean floor. As the first fragments of wreckage began to appear, it was like entering a bombed-out museum. Thousands upon thousands of artifacts littered the rolling fields of sediment, many of them perfectly preserved. The entrails of the *Titanic* spilled across the ocean floor in seemingly endless quantity. In stark contrast to the grandeur of the broken bow, this was a grisly mixture of beauty and destruction.

Then, without any warning, I found myself looking into the eyes of a small, white smiling face. For a split second I thought a corpse had actually materialized — and it scared the hell out of me. Then I realized I was seeing a ceramic doll's head, its hair and clothes gone. My initial shock changed to sadness as the poignancy of the image sank in. Who had owned this toy? Had the girl been one of the survivors? Or had she clutched it tightly as she sank in the icy waters?

We moved on and I glanced at my two companions. They, too, were engrossed in the amazing scenery passing

For a split second I thought this ghostly doll's head was part of a human skeleton. Experts have identified it as a bisque head of French or German origin.

by our viewports. The contents of the *Titanic*'s kitchens were laid out on the seafloor, copper pots and pans (and lids) polished to a sheen by the current, serving dishes, plates, cups, and even a copper sink. One pan even had a big piece of pink floor covering sitting in it. There was a wine and spirit cellar that would have fetched a fortune laid out before us — including champagne bottles, many with the corks intact. Soon it became difficult to keep track; all the sundry accoutrements of shipboard life were on display, their very ordinariness making them all the more haunting.

Occasionally the juxtapositions were dramatic. In one instance, an ugly twisted piece of iron wreckage sat just inches away from a lovely glass window from one of the bays in the first-class lounge, still in one piece. In another instance, we were exploring the face of a boiler, and there, on top of it, rested an upright rusty metal cup of the type used by the crew, as if placed there by a stoker moments before water had burst into the boiler room. Beside it was a doorknob, the wooden door itself long gone.

At first, we moved slowly around the debris field in systematic fashion using Al Uchupi's map as a guide. We looked and looked but couldn't find the ship's telegraph, so clear in the ANGUS stills. But as time wore on, we began to follow our instincts and our senses, turning to pursue objects caught in the outer edge of *Alvin*'s lights. Whenever something interesting appeared in my viewport, we'd slow down so I could snap a picture. The sheer scale of this "museum" was overwhelming.

Around noon, we spotted a safe. Quickly, I told Jim to bring the sub to a halt and immediately we were engulfed in a giant cloud of sediment. Driving *Alvin* slowly across this muddy bottom was like driving a Land Rover at 70 miles an hour across salt flats with a rooster tail of dust streaming out behind. Visibility was good as long as we kept moving, but the minute we stopped, our dust tail caught up.

Since the current wasn't that strong today, I knew it was going to take a while for the mud cloud to clear. And I wanted to take a close look at that safe, which appeared to be in good condition. My first impulse was simply to photograph it. The safe was now about 65 to 100 feet behind us and to the right, so I told Jim to swing around 180° and move closer to its position, figuring we might as well stir up more mud now and then wait for it all to settle while we ate lunch. Soon our tiny cabin was filled with the smell of peanut butter as we excitedly discussed our safe and what it might contain.

Sixteen years before, when I'd first dived in *Alvin*, the traditional lunch was a bologna sandwich. In fact, those early lunches had become legend. In October 1968, *Alvin* had slipped its moorings with three people aboard, filled with water through the open hatch, and sunk in 5,200 feet of water. The crew just managed to escape in time. Ten months later when the sub was recovered, the bologna sandwiches were still edible. This triggered a whole new field of research in microbiology since this new evidence suggested that the rate of decay of organic material at these depths was much slower than previously assumed. It was because of this accident with *Alvin* that many people held out hope that the *Titanic* would be much better preserved than she turned out to be.

By the end of a long day in a tiny submersible, the

atmosphere can become, well, close. You pray that your diving companions have taken a nice long shower that morning and that they didn't eat garlic or beans for dinner the night before. And with no room for a toilet, we have to resort to facilities similar to those used by weightless astronauts. (Our plastic urine bottle is nicknamed HERE, an acronym for human endurance range extender.) At least, unlike astronauts, we don't have to spend days at a time in our capsule.

As we finished our repast, the safe began to emerge at the edge of the arc illuminated by our headlights. Very gently, so as not to disturb more mud than necessary, our pilot swung us around until the object of our interest was directly outside my starboard window. It sat with its door face-up. The handle looked as if it was made of gold, though it had to be brass.

I directed Jim to bring *Alvin*'s sample-gathering arm around for a picture. As he did so, I realized the claw was going to practically touch the safe's handle — why not try to open it? So I watched as the arm's metal fingers locked on the handle and its wrist began to rotate clockwise. To my surprise it turned easily, then stopped. But the door wouldn't budge, its flanges apparently rusted shut. It would be so easy to bring the safe back with us to the surface. We'd lifted heavier things with *Alvin*.

I looked at Jim and he looked at me.

"What now?" he asked.

There was a long pause as I considered the possibilities, and imagined what the safe might contain. What would I have done if we'd opened it to discover something valuable — the bejeweled *Rubaiyat of Omar Khayyam*, for

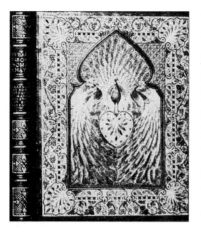

We wondered at first whether the safe we found might contain this copy of the Rubaiyat of Omar Khayyam, *which was being shipped to New York on the* Titanic *and whose binding was studded with over 1,000 precious stones.*

instance? I probably would have called to the surface and told them to radio Woods Hole: "Have found priceless *Titanic* artifact. Please advise." Fortunately, my vow not to return with *Titanic* salvage wasn't put to the test. Probably the safe was empty, anyway. I remembered Bill Tantum telling me once that, supposedly, the ship's second-class safes had been opened by the crew and emptied during the final moments before the *Titanic* sank. Since it was apparent on closer examination that this was clearly one of the safes from the second-class purser's office, it was unlikely that it had ever held real treasure. Perhaps it contained some money and not-too-expensive jewelry. It would have been wonderful to find out.

"Let go of it and let me take some more pictures," I finally replied. If I could pass this souvenir up, I could pass up anything. (When I later examined the photos I took, I could see that the bottom of the safe had rusted out. Any contents ought to have been visible on the sediment underneath, but we saw no sign of them.)

Two days passed before I again descended to the *Titanic*. It was now time for one of the young Navy submarine officers to have a turn down below while I took an inventory of what we'd found so far. Actually I was ready for a break. We'd reached the halfway point in the expedition and we'd already gone a long way toward getting the *Titanic* on film — both video and high-quality still images.

But Navy Lt. Jeff Powers had to wait an extra day for his trip because *Alvin*'s battery charger had accidentally been left turned off overnight. So instead of heading for the bottom, *Alvin* spent July 19 aboard the *Atlantis II* having its batteries juiced up. The next morning, July 20, dive number seven departed as planned with Lt. Powers on board and Jim Aguilar at the controls. Martin went along to help Jeff handle *JJ*. Despite a strong current on the bottom, the sub managed to land on the *Titanic* and take some pictures, but *JJ* again had problems: this time his video wasn't working. After performing beautifully in our early dives, *Jason Jr.* was becoming a problem child.

After two days' rest, I was raring to go. Ralph Hollis was back at the controls and the third member of the crew was Ken Stewart, a graduate student working in the Deep Submergence Laboratory. Ken had been in charge of *JJ*'s development before Chris von Alt joined our team and he was looking forward to driving *JJ* in for a close-up look at the propellers — if they were there.

Today, I was determined to finally lay Jack Grimm's "propeller" claim permanently to rest. We planned to land *Alvin* on the bottom directly behind the stern section and then send *JJ* in under the overhanging hull. Unless the propellers had fallen off during the descent, they ought to still be there. All eyewitnesses agreed that only the forward section of the *Titanic* had actually bashed the iceberg, although a number of the crew members who did not see the berg and had barely felt the collision assumed that the reason the ship stopped was that she had dropped a propeller blade — a rare, but not unheard-of, problem. If only it had been that simple. At any rate there was every reason to expect that the great blades were still fitted to their bosses and that the 101-ton rudder was still in place. The *Titanic* had three huge propellers — the two three-bladed ones on each side measuring 23 feet, 6 inches, while the smaller one in the center was 16 feet, 6 inches. Together they were capable of moving the ship at a speed of over 23 knots. In fact, her maximum speed was never known — Ismay later stated that her top-speed test had been scheduled for Monday, April 15...

This was Ralph's third trip down to the wreck. Instead of skiing along the bottom, we made a breathtaking high-altitude approach over the debris field. Soon the Poop Deck gradually came into view through the eye of the *Argo* SIT camera. This aftermost piece of the *Titanic*'s stern was recognizable at least, rimmed by big fairlead rollers — spool-like guides for the mooring lines. But instead of landing on this deck, which was dangerously cluttered with debris, Ralph steered us aft and down beside the wall of the stern, hovering briefly while Big Bird searched in vain for some sign of the *Titanic*'s name or her home port, Liverpool. The rusticles just were too thick.

Then we dropped farther and Ralph made a soft

landing on the bottom, pumping ballast so that we could deploy *JJ* from a solid base. This was what Ken Stewart had been waiting for but he wasn't showing his excitement. I knew he felt it, though — this wasn't his first dive in *Alvin*, but it was his first look at the *Titanic*. *JJ* was hardly out of his garage when it became apparent that something was wrong. He was going in circles. One of his motors, which had worked fine on the surface, was gone.

"Damn," I said. "We've come all this way. We are sitting where we want to be and *JJ* won't work." This was the only trip I'd scheduled to the heavily damaged stern section and it looked like a washout. I sat glumly staring out my viewport at the muddy bottom and feeling sorry for myself. Suddenly, the mud started to move! Ralph was slowly inching *Alvin* forward on its single ski, in under the stern. Was he crazy? What if a piece of wreckage came crashing down? Ralph was breaking the first rule of *Alvin* piloting: never go in under a man-made overhang. He was going to prove that *Alvin* could do anything *JJ* could do better. He still thought he could win the battle against unmanned robots.

Looking out my porthole, I could see ahead of us the line that marked the beginning of no-man's-land: the area covered with the rust that had fallen from the stern above. Up to that demarcating line the ocean floor was clear; beyond it was a pile of hundreds of foot-long rusticles. Crossing that line was like accepting a dangerous dare; once on the other side, there was no sure route of escape in an emergency. I prayed Ralph knew what he was doing, but I said nothing. I wanted to see those propellers. None of us spoke. The only sound in the sub was our breathing.

Quietly, I reached over to a point just by Ralph's right elbow — the control for *Alvin*'s arm — and began to maneuver Big Bird's camera to look upward. If a problem was going to occur it would come from the corroded hull hanging above us. I turned my back on the viewport and concentrated on the color video monitor in the rear of the sphere. At first, all I could see was a stream of particles, but slowly a massive black surface began to inch down toward the lens. Soon the entire monitor was taken up by a single giant section of steel plating, the rivets clearly visible. If we went much farther, we'd wedge ourselves under the stern. I didn't usually feel claustrophobic in the sub, but this was different — the hull seemed to be coming in at us from all sides.

"I see the rudder, Bob, but I don't see any propellers," Ralph reported in a matter-of-fact voice. If he was nervous, he wasn't showing it. He had stopped *Alvin* dead.

I moved up to his viewport and gazed out into the dark. There directly in front of me and in every direction was the stern rising from the seafloor, its curved hull plating disappearing up and out of sight. From here, it looked in almost perfect condition, as if it were in dry dock to have its bottom cleaned — but the bottom was clean! There was hardly any rust and virtually no marine growth — apparently the steepness of the hull provided little purchase for rusticles.

Like the bow, the *Titanic*'s stern section was buried deep into the mud — 45 feet or so — with the mudline resting well above the position of the propellers. Only about 16 feet of her rudder could be seen rising out of the ooze, as if the ship were floating on the surface of the sea.

I was sure the propellers were down there, but I couldn't prove it. I could almost hear Jack Grimm's chuckle. I knew he wouldn't believe it.

There was nothing more we could do and Ralph had proven his point. "Let's get out of here," I said.

The pilot turned *Alvin* around, and ever so gently retraced the path left by our lone ski mark. *Alvin* recrossed the demarcating line of rust and passed out from under the stern. At last we could relax, our sense of relief almost palpable, though no one said anything. All of us, including Ralph, were glad our adventure was over.

In the time remaining on this eighth dive to the *Titanic*, I intended to complete one mission that had long been on my mind. I wanted to place a memorial plaque on the stern in memory of my friend Bill Tantum and to all those lost on the *Titanic*. More than anybody else, Bill had kept my *Titanic* dream afloat. And a memorial to him would also be

The plaque placed on the stern in memory of Bill Tantum and those who perished on the Titanic.

a tribute to the members of the Titanic Historical Society, who have done so much to keep the memory of the ship alive. Bill's wife, Anne, had liked the idea, and on the day we sailed had presented me with a handsome bronze plaque.

I had originally thought of putting the plaque on the more nobly preserved bow. But those who died on the *Titanic* had gathered on the stern as the ship tilted bow first. The stern had been their final haven.

We rose up the wall of steel and Ralph carefully maneuvered *Alvin* onto the edge of the Poop Deck next to two of the steel fairlead rollers. There was so little space that Ralph could only rest the forward part of the sub on firm decking while our tail hung out in space, like a rock teetering on the brink of a cliff. With great care, *Alvin*'s arm plucked the plaque from its quiver strapped to *JJ*'s garage. Then Ralph rotated the arm and gently released it. The three of us watched on the video as the plaque sank quietly onto the thin veneer of sediment covering the hull.

Now Ralph lifted off and we began rising upward, Big Bird's camera keeping the plaque in view as long as possible. As we rose, it grew smaller and smaller until finally it was swallowed up in the gloom. Fading from our sight was a picture of the last spot where people had stood on dry *Titanic* deck, now peaceful and deserted. There was little talking in the sub. We were all emotionally drained as we headed back toward sunlight.

Time was now getting short and our next two dives proved especially frustrating. After working so well during the first half of the expedition, *Jason Jr.* had been plagued with recurring problems. Despite yeomanly efforts by Chris von Alt and his team, *JJ* failed to work properly on either July 22 or July 23. That meant that for four days in a row we'd been without our swimming eyeball, and denied access to the other places inside the wreck I'd wanted to explore.

On July 22, we photographed the entire exterior of the bow and took a close look at the area where the iceberg supposedly tore a gash. From the bow to a point roughly even with cargo hatch number 2, the hull below the water-line was buried in the mud. Aft of this point, we could begin to see the area where the gash should have been, but no tear was visible. Instead, as we moved aft, descending along the mudline, we passed two large and dramatic vertical buckles in the hull plating. The one farther aft was particularly interesting: there, the steel hull had folded out at an angle of almost 90° and then back in on itself with no evidence of a torn seam or a popped rivet. These vertical buckles were clearly the result of the bow's crash into the bottom, which had left the forward part of the ship bent down several degrees. Farther aft, however, about even with the bridge and just above the turn of the bilge, we could see some horizontal buckling and creasing of hull plates, the plates themselves slightly separated at the seams, and we could see the holes where rivets had popped out. We were now well within the area damaged by the iceberg. Were we looking at a fragment of the *Titanic*'s mortal wound? If so, where was the great gash we'd been led to expect? Perhaps there was an actual hole in the hull farther forward, but from what we could see, it appeared perfectly possible that the famous gash had never existed.

On July 23, the two other Navy submariners on board, Lt. Mike Mahre and Lt. Brian Kissel, got their turn to dive. On the port side of the bow section at D-Deck level, they discovered a large, first-class gangway door that was wide open — probably jarred out on impact. They shone *Alvin*'s lights through the hatchway and into the entrance foyer beyond. All that could be seen was a bulkhead and the ceiling disappearing into the darkness. What lay beyond the limit of the headlights? This would have made a wonderful point of entry for *JJ*. He could easily have ventured into the first-class reception room, viewed the three elevators, traveled forward into passenger companionways or aft into the first-class dining saloon. But once again our little robot petulantly refused to cooperate.

On the eve of our final dive, I was determined that *JJ* would have one more successful deployment. So I asked Chris and his troops to work through the night in an effort to find and fix the problems. Then, just before midnight, Chris came to my cabin and handed me a piece of smashed wire. Emile had found it tucked up inside the tether take-up reel. Apparently, during the original assembly, this small wire had been damaged just enough to break its protective plastic jacket without severing the actual wire. On the surface nothing had shown up; but at the tremendous pressures on the ocean floor the wire had sometimes grounded. So the problem would be there one day and not the next, and so on: a technician's nightmare. We'd caught and killed the gremlin, but that piece of smashed wire had cost us three dives worth $60,000 in total.

Now, finally convinced that all was well, I slept soundly and bounced out of bed on the morning of July

24, ready for our final dive and what I knew would be my last look at the *Titanic*. Will Sellars, who'd piloted us on our banner fourth dive, was to take us down, and Martin Bowen was on board to take a final turn with *JJ*. Miraculously, the weather still held, our spirits were good, but within seconds of a perfect launch euphoria turned into despair. Martin Bowen gave me the bad news. "Bob, I have a hard ground on *JJ*."

"You've got to be kidding. Tell me you're kidding," was my only response.

There was no choice but to resurface and see if we could fix the problem. Today, we had even less flexibility than usual. Before the morning's launch, Captain Baker had stressed the importance of being back in time for our scheduled departure for home. The powers that be wanted us to arrive at Woods Hole for a carefully orchestrated welcoming ceremony and the captain didn't want to be late.

For an hour, Martin, Will, and I baked inside the pressure sphere as it sat on the gently rolling deck of the *Atlantis II*, while Chris and his cohorts attacked *JJ* once more. As the heat rose inside our tiny compartment, I couldn't tell which was its main source: the hot sun on our metal hull or my rising annoyance. Mercifully, the delay turned out to be a false alarm — minor electrical grounds in each of *JJ*'s four motors that added up to a seemingly serious ground when taken together. *JJ* should work fine when we got to the bottom.

Finally, shortly after 10 A.M., we were back in the water and headed toward the bottom as fast as our descent weights would take us. At noon, as we neared our destination, we ate the last peanut butter sandwiches of the 1986

Titanic expedition. Just after 12:30, we approached our now-familiar forecastle landing site. We placed a second plaque (given to us by the Explorers' Club of New York, of which I am a member) on one of the bow's beautiful bronze-topped capstans. The inscription asked all those who follow to leave the ship in peace.

As we lifted off and headed for the port A-Deck promenade, Martin reported that *JJ* seemed fine. On previous trips along the port side, I'd noted an opening on B Deck I thought was big enough for *JJ* to enter — just abeam of the bridge. It was a gangway opening in the bulwark railing, its door now missing, two decks below one of the remaining lifeboat davits.

After we'd spotted the opening, I directed Will to land *Alvin* on the Boat Deck just above it — a landing spot on the port side I'd first noticed on our second dive — beside the collapsed officers' cabins. Once over the rail, we moved forward along the Boat Deck, passing the windows on the port side of the Grand Staircase until we were beside the expansion joint, just after of the number 1 funnel opening and the officers' quarters. The superstructure of the ship had actually cracked open along the expansion joint and I could see all the way through and out the starboard side; there were tantalizing glimpses of the interior. Inside one cabin, I could see a small coal-burning stove, which appeared to be coated in a green ceramic glaze. Perhaps it had warmed the officers' pantry.

We moved slowly forward toward the forwardmost davit on the port side, the davit for lifeboat No. 2, where we intended to land, right beside First Officer Murdoch's cabin. It was the only davit still standing on the port side.

Will could see the davit now — and quite a bit of wreckage ahead to the right, where the wall of the officers' quarters had collapsed outward. Landing near there would be tricky. Just aft of the davit, a few metal stanchions, which had once lent support to a short bulwark rail along the side of the ship, jutted out a couple of feet. But Will landed safely and brought *Alvin* in as close as he could.

This would be *JJ*'s last hurrah. In all likelihood none of us would ever sit on the deck of the *Titanic* again. "Let's go for it, Martin. It's now or never," I said.

With accustomed skill, but some nervousness, Martin maneuvered *JJ* down the two decks and then back and forth, scanning the opening I'd chosen. Would it prove big enough? Martin thought so and cautiously inched forward, clearing the railing on either side of the gangway opening into B Deck and carefully going in. Unfortunately, there was nothing much to see. Sediment and falling rusticles filled the water and Martin soon gave up.

Stymied in our first attempt to enter the promenade space, Martin flew *JJ* back up onto the Boat Deck to inspect boat davit number 2, taking some wonderful close-up stills that show marvelous detail. Its worm gear was as bright and new as the day it was made. Both lifeboat No. 2 and collapsible D were launched from this spot. Collapsible D, the very last one to be launched from the ship, was the one Lightoller had protected with a ring of crew members who had locked arms around it to prevent a stampede. Among those who had left in this boat were the two little Navratil boys, kidnapped by their father from his estranged wife. When the *Carpathia* arrived in New York, it had taken days before their identity was known. (The father, who went down with the ship, had been listed on the passenger roster as a Mr. Hoffman.) Many other children were not so lucky.

Martin now took JJ over the rail again to search for a way into A Deck, steering him into an "open promenade" enclosure at the forward end of the first-class promenade just above the disappointing B-Deck gangway. Here there were doorways leading in two directions. On the outboard side of the large door in the bulwark separating us from the enclosed promenade, there was a sizeable window. Rusticles dangled down menacingly over both, so Martin moved toward a second open door, apparently leading to the interior of the ship. As he did so, I spotted a brass plate to the right of it and he zoomed in for a closer look. It read, "This door for crew use only." As it turned out, the door opened into an inner stairway that led to the Boat Deck just above, next to the bridge, or down to B Deck — not to interior cabins.

As JJ rose up for an even closer look, he banged into a large rusticle suspended from the overhanging deck and suddenly his eye went blind — JJ was spinning around and we became disoriented. Then JJ's tether got hung up on something. I thought of Stan Laurel's famous line: "Well, Ollie, you really have us in a fine fix now." And now Will Sellars decided to remind me that it was almost time to head back to the surface.

Finally JJ was able to see his own tether in the rusty water. It was hung up on a jagged piece of steel. Martin brought JJ up, freed the cable, and we breathed a sigh of relief as I gave my final command.

"Bring him home, Martin. We have proven our point. All final objectives have been reached. Now get him back in his garage and let's go home." As *JJ* maneuvered out of the open promenade and rose back up to the Boat Deck, he spied a little hose plug (hydrant) at the edge of the deck near the stanchions. The red paint was still visible.

With *JJ* safely home, Will lifted off from the deck and moved slightly away from the ship so that our ascent weights would drop harmlessly into the mud. The sub paused for a moment, as if reluctant to leave the *Titanic* for the last time. Then we began to drift upward, accelerating toward the surface. I watched the video screen as the Boat Deck of the ship faded into the gloom; the last things I saw were the squashed roof of the officers' quarters and that lonely lifeboat davit…

Suddenly it was over. The *Titanic* disappeared from view as Will turned off the incandescent headlights, and we floated silently upward in the blackness. For once, I didn't put the *Flashdance* tape on the stereo — instead I played something soft and classical — there was none of the usual talking and joking, none of the customary unwinding after hours of intense concentration. Each of us sat quietly with our own thoughts.

I knew I had visited the ship for the last time. In the unlikely event I ever did return, it would not be in *Alvin*. *Argo* and *Jason*, my remotely controlled underwater imaging system, would replace our sub. Certainly it would be an advance for science, but I knew something would be lost — gone would be the immediacy, the intimacy that I had known over the last 12 days.

A melancholy feeling of emptiness came over me. How could I be experiencing this sense of loss, I wondered? After all the *Titanic* was, in the final analysis, only a big wreck in deep water. Our mission had been a technological success. I should be feeling jubilation. Instead, I felt like a high-school senior saying goodbye to his steady girlfriend before heading off to college. I wanted to look to the future, but I couldn't help looking back.

Two and a half hours later, when we reached the surface, there was no time for celebration and reflection. Everyone had a job to do as we recovered the transponders, stowed the sub, made sure *JJ* was comfortable, and prepared to head for home. Later that night there would be a party in the lab, but through it all I would still be thinking about the *Titanic*: of the people who had built her, sailed on her, and died when she went down.

The Royal Mail Steamship *Titanic* had yielded up many of the secrets she had guarded for 74 years. Our two expeditions had been a remarkable accomplishment. The *Titanic* had been found, and now she had been paid a respectful visit. But had we put the ship finally to rest, or merely opened a whole new era of speculation about her fate and attempts to rob her grave?

TITANIC RECONSIDERED

PART OF MY ORIGINAL FASCINATION WITH THE *TITANIC* WAS the simple fact she was there. The vanished ship was the Mount Everest of my world (the deep ocean), a peak that no one had scaled. As I became familiar with the story of her building and her fateful first voyage, I was caught in the grip of the story of human tragedy and by the larger morality tale of technological arrogance leading, as if inevitably, to disaster. And the events of that night are so tantalizingly studded with what-ifs and might-have-beens. What if the ship had been traveling more slowly? What if the lookouts had been issued with binoculars? What if the moon had been out or the night had been less calm, the collision head-on instead of a glancing blow? What if the radio operator on the *Californian* had not gone to bed minutes before the *Titanic* sent out her first distress signal?

In reflecting on our efforts, I find it interesting that in one key respect the *Titanic*'s tragedy and our success in

Aboard the Atlantis II, *I try to recreate what happened during the* Titanic's *sinking.*

finding her are linked: technology. The technological achievements of the time made it possible to build this "practically unsinkable" ship. In turn, it was sophisticated technology in our day that allowed us to find and then photograph her in such stunning detail. In a sense our discovery of the *Titanic* brought one chapter of history to a close, while at the same time opening another. After the *Titanic* sank, the world was never quite the same again. As a result of finding her, I believe the exploration of the deep ocean has moved into a new era. Finding and photographing the ship enabled us to test our new deep-sea imaging technology, which will allow us to explore many new submarine frontiers. It also gave us new information that allows us to reconsider some of the circumstances of the *Titanic*'s final hours and to reconstruct what happened after she disappeared from sight — not to be seen again for almost three-quarters of a century.

THE "GASH"

We'll probably never know for sure the exact nature of the damage inflicted by the iceberg on the starboard side of the *Titanic*'s bow. Too much of it is buried too deep. But what we did see confirmed that the damage was nothing like the gash many had believed resulted from the impact with the ice. Of course, as some serious *Titanic* buffs knew — and as Walter Lord points out in his book *The Night Lives On* — a continuous gash or tear in the ship's hull was virtually a physical impossibility.

There were enough eyewitness accounts of where the water had entered the ship to conclude that damage to the hull extended from the first through the fifth of the ship's 16 watertight compartments, and slightly into the sixth — a distance of as much as 249 feet. At the British Inquiry in 1912, Edward Wilding, one of Harland & Wolff's naval architects, made some calculations on the damage. On the basis of the evidence given at the Inquiry about the times at which the water had reached various decks within the hull spaces affected, he figured that the ship took in about 16,000 cubic feet of water during the first 40 minutes. He then used a formula to calculate the total area of the openings and came up with about 12 square feet. Assuming a continuous gash about 200 feet in length (enough to account for all the evidence of damage), he divided this figure into the 12 square feet, yielding an average width of about three-quarters of an inch. This result naturally struck Wilding as highly unlikely. He therefore concluded that the damage to the hull was probably intermittent, not continuous.

Our examination of the wreck tends to confirm Wilding's conclusion — at least in part. But the ship as it now lies is buried deeply in the mud from the bow to just aft of the forward Well Deck, so we couldn't see most of the damaged area. All we can say with certainty is that the damage we were able to observe and photograph seemed quite minor: a number of separated and horizontally creased hull plates, the openings ranging from less than an inch to six inches in width. On the basis of the portion of the damaged hull we were able to see — from a point just aft of the Well Deck to its farthest aft point a couple of feet into boiler room No. 5 (roughly between hull frames 58 and 80 forward) — Wilding's hypothesis that the damage was intermittent seems to be supported.

His theory that the damage probably consisted of a number of punctures in the hull is not. What we were able to see was plates knocked apart at their riveted seams. If this was all that happened — a number of ruptures, not punctures, at the joints between the hull plates — it could still account for the water seen by the various witnesses. Of course, we couldn't see the bottom of the hull or the forward part of the bow where much damage occurred, so we'll never know for sure. But it seems likely that the outright punctures, if any, were few, and that the impact of the iceberg simply caused the riveted plates to separate, water rushing in through the resulting cracks.

A metallurgical engineer has written to me to suggest that the *Titanic*'s steel hull may have been particularly susceptible to high stress at cold temperatures. Professor H. P. Leighly of the University of Missouri suggested that some turn-of-the-century steel became brittle below a certain temperature and would have begun to crack under pressure from the weight of the berg. This cracking would have progressed "catastrophically" — an apt word — causing rivets to pop from their sockets. It might even have contributed to the fact the ship broke in two. It's an intriguing theory and, indeed, some of our photos show portions of the hull that have cracked like an eggshell and blown apart — rather than tearing along the plate joints as one would expect.

Whatever the exact nature of her ice wound, it was enough to sink the ship — barely enough, given a design that allowed for the simultaneous flooding of the first four, but not all of the first five, watertight compartments. It is important to stress that the tragedy should not be allowed to overshadow the fact that the *Titanic* was a relatively safe ship, not only according to the standards of her time but of ours. According to English naval architect K. C. Barnaby in his book *Some Ship Disasters and Their Causes*, "It is very

A 1912 artist's conception of the ice field the Titanic *encountered on her last night.*

doubtful if modern subdivision rules make present-day liners any safer than the *Titanic*." Indeed, from Barnaby's accounts of the sinking of the *Andrea Doria* in 1956 and the *Shillong* in 1957, it appears that damage fatal to these two ships would have proved no more than a nuisance to the *Titanic*. The fault lay not in her construction but in her failure to avoid hitting an iceberg at almost full speed. In defense of the ship's builders, it must also be said that no ship before had ever experienced a glancing blow such as the iceberg gave, running over a quarter of the ship's length. (Unless, of course, in the age before wireless when ships sank without a radioed distress call, none survived to tell the tale.) Nor has such an accident occurred since. The odds against this particular kind of collision happening were extremely high.

THE TRUE POSITION OF THE *TITANIC* AND THE QUESTION OF THE *CALIFORNIAN*

There is no longer any reason to keep the exact position of the *Titanic* wreck a secret. Originally I hoped to protect the wreck from treasure seekers, but too many people now know where it is, or could figure it out. And we are bound as responsible scientists to give out enough information so that another serious expedition could find the wreck with relative ease. But until that happens, the main interest the true position of the wreck holds is the possible insight it can provide into the controversy that still surrounds Captain Lord and his ship the *Californian*, believed by some to have been close enough to the scene that night to have rescued most if not all of those on board the *Titanic*.

Those who support Captain Lord and feel that the

Captain Stanley Lord, master of the Californian.

British and American inquiries made him into a convenient scapegoat are known in *Titanic* circles as "Lordites." They believe that the ship seen by some people aboard the *Titanic* while she sank was not the *Californian*, and that the ship the officers and men on the *Californian* saw was not the *Titanic*.

For readers unfamiliar with this aspect of the *Titanic* story, it can be briefly recapitulated. Around 10:20 (*Californian* time) on the night of April 14, 1912, the 6,000-ton steamer *Californian* stopped after being blocked by a large field of ice. She remained with her engines stopped, drifting with this ice for the rest of the night. Based on dead reckoning after a celestial sighting taken at sunset, Captain Lord calculated his position as 42°05'N, 50°07'W — or 19 miles north-northeast of the *Titanic*'s CQD position. It was not long after stopping that the radio operator on the *Californian* contacted the *Titanic* and attempted to give her an ice warning, but was rudely brushed off by Phillips, who was busy "working Cape Race."

Around 11 P.M., the *Californian*'s third officer, Charles Groves, saw the lights of a steamer coming up from the southeast. At 11:30, the ship's radio officer went to bed, exhausted after a long day. At about 11:40, the stranger stopped. After midnight, white rockets were seen, just above or beyond the stopped ship. Both *Californian*'s Second Officer Stone and Apprentice Officer Gibson suspected that the strange ship was in trouble. Stone, now on watch, remarked to Gibson: "She seems to look queer now." Gibson took a look through the bridge binoculars and concurred: "She looks rather to have a big side out of the water." At 1:40 A.M., an eighth and final rocket was observed. Sometime after 2 A.M., the stranger disappeared completely, appearing to have steamed away to the southwest.

Despite various discrepancies between the testimony of those on board the *Titanic* and the *Californian* — for instance, as to the times when the rockets were fired — both the British and American inquiries held that the ship sighted from the *Californian* was indeed the *Titanic* and condemned Captain Lord's inaction as verging on criminal negligence. Lord had gone below after the ship steamed into view, but before the first rockets were sighted. When informed of the rockets, he had done nothing except to ask what color they were and tell his men to attempt to signal the vessel by Morse lamp. They received no answer. The radio operator was not wakened.

Captain Lord maintained to his dying day that a third ship, not the *Titanic*, was the one sighted from the *Californian*. He claimed that she didn't look like a passenger ship (one of the officers on board the *Californian* disagreed on this point) — and that she disappeared still afloat. Of course, even if he was right — and no mystery ship has ever been positively identified (although the Lordites claim to have turned up all sorts of ships in the vicinity that night) — the presence of a third ship does not change the fact that rockets were seen around the time the *Titanic* was firing them — rockets corresponding in character to distress rockets — and that no move was made to rouse the *Californian*'s sleeping wireless operator in order to clarify the situation. (To justify the skipper's inaction, the Lordites point out that all sorts of rockets and flares were used in 1912, that procedures covering distress signals at sea were in a state of flux, and that some company signals were white.)

Until now, the two great unknowns in the tale were the actual position of the *Titanic* and the actual position of the *Californian*. At least now the *Titanic*'s final position can be stated with reasonable certainty — assuming the wreck lies pretty well directly below it. Since the stern and boilers likely fell almost straight down, these probably are closest to the ship's surface position at the time of sinking. The stern section sits on the ocean bottom at 49°56'54"W, 41°43'35"N and the center of the boiler field is at 49°56'49"W, 41°43'32"N. (The center of the bow section is located at 49°56'49"W, 41°43'57"N.) This means the *Titanic* sank roughly 13.5 miles east-southeast of her CQD position. She is just south of her calculated course, but well to the east. So the navigators on board overestimated the *Titanic*'s speed by roughly 2 knots: instead of traveling at 22.5 knots as Fourth Officer Boxhall had supposed, she was moving at about 20.5 knots. This position therefore puts the *Californian*'s logged position 21 miles to the north-northwest.

After she struck the iceberg, the *Titanic* undoubtedly drifted somewhat south and west in the current, but so likely did the *Californian*, already stopped in field ice. And since the *Californian* stopped sooner, she would already have drifted south from her course, given the current, nearer to the course the *Titanic* was on when she actually struck the berg. The drift that night was noted by, among others, Third Officer Groves.

The true position of the *Titanic* does cast the *Californian*'s stated position in a new light — but does not decisively weight the scales for or against Captain Lord. All witnesses on board the *Californian* agreed that the ship they saw "disappeared" to the southwest. But we now know that the *Californian*'s stated position was west, not east, of where the *Titanic* went down. As long as the old CQD position was accepted, this put the *Titanic* west of the *Californian* so that her sinking could have been mistaken as sailing off to the west. This appears to give the Lordites a boost.

But the *Titanic* was so far east of where she thought she was — at least in part because of the current that night — that we must consider the strong possibility that the *Californian* was also roughly on course, though south of it — but well east of her calculated position. In sum, given the new evidence, the weight of probability is that the *Californian* was not more, and probably less, than 21 miles from the *Titanic*'s position. Equally probable is that she was considerably farther away than the five or six miles estimated by Boxhall and Lightoller on board the *Titanic* when they saw the lights of a ship to the north — causing them to send up distress rockets.

All of this only supports the likelihood that the white rockets seen by the officers on board the *Californian* were indeed the same ones sent up by the *Titanic*. Whether the two ships were 21, 19, or even fewer miles apart, rockets could certainly be seen on a calm night over that distance. Later that morning, the *Californian* spotted rockets that almost surely came from the *Carpathia* as she raced to the rescue — considerably farther away than the *Titanic* could ever have been.

Of course, the *Californian's* true position will never be known and Captain Lord's case will never be settled. Even if he had wakened the radio operator at the first sighting of rockets, learned the *Titanic* was in distress, fired up his boilers, headed for the ship he could see, and discovered that it was indeed the sinking liner, he might have arrived in time only to fish a few half-dead bodies from the water. But the telling fact remains that he and his officers failed to act when action was called for.

THE BREAK-UP

On the basis of many previous wrecks that have been found in shallow water — including large ships, older and more poorly built — most people held considerable hope that the *Titanic* was lying on the bottom in one piece. Certainly, until we discovered the *Titanic*, most people believed that she had left the surface intact. Although several witnesses testified to the contrary, this was the finding of the two inquiries in 1912, that's how she was

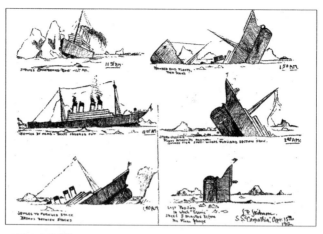

Aboard the Carpathia *on the way to New York, 16-year-old Jack Thayer (left) described the* Titanic *breaking up while sinking to L. D. Skidmore of Brooklyn, who made these sketches. Although inaccurate in many ways, the drawings refute the findings of the two inquiries that the ship sank in one piece. From what we observed, it seems almost certain the ship broke apart at or near the surface.*

pictured in the movies made about the tragedy and, until very recently, that's how all authors including Walter Lord have described the sinking. But Walter Lord changed his mind after examining in more detail the testimony given at the British and American inquiries, testimony ignored in the official reports. The inquiries gave particular credence to the testimony of Second Officer Lightoller, Colonel Archibald Gracie, and Third Officer Herbert

Pitman, all of whom described the vessel as sinking whole. Lightoller, Gracie, and Lawrence Beesley (who also backed this version) also published authoritative accounts of the disaster. None of them, however, was in a good position to see the ship's final moments (Gracie was actually underwater and didn't see it at all). On the other hand, many eyewitnesses agreed that the ship in fact had broken in two, the bow plunging down while the stern briefly righted itself before turning almost vertical and sinking a few moments later.

Given the facts — a 1,970-foot distance between the two main pieces of the hull on the bottom, the cluster of additional wreckage in the vicinity of the stern, the absence of a skid mark between the two pieces, and the fact that they are pointing in different directions and upright on the bottom — it does seem almost certain that the ship broke apart at or near the surface. As the bow sank and the stern rose ever higher out of the water, the pressure on the keel became increasingly unbearable until it finally snapped at a weak point in the structure between the third and fourth funnels in the area of the reciprocating engine room hatch. It was weak there because of the large open spaces in the decks above — the aft Grand Staircase and the air shaft from the reciprocating engine room. The ship did not break at either expansion joint — these were part of the superstructure and did not continue down into the hull of the ship. But the hull does show vertical buckling below the forward expansion joint, which therefore may have been a factor when the bow hit the bottom. The after expansion joint had nothing to do with the tearing of the hull below — that was caused when the keel bent and snapped — but as this happened the after expansion joint was probably the place where the superstructure first gave way.

The bow and stern sections that now lie on the bottom of the ocean account for most of the keel. The seven hull segments, 130 feet to 260 feet northeast, east, and southeast of the stern — which included at least one stack and possibly a second one — represent a V-shaped chunk of the hull and superstructure at a point just aft of amidships. The Boat Deck area aft of the number 2 funnel — where the large brass ship's compass platform stood — is still there but collapsed down at an angle. The compass itself has not been found.

THE FINAL PLUNGE

About 2:15 A.M., the stunned passengers of the *Titanic*'s lifeboats watched in horror as the ship's bow sank ever more deeply and the stern lifted farther and farther up out of the water until it reached an angle of at least 45° (according to eyewitness accounts). Then the bow broke off or split down (perhaps remaining for a few moments attached at the keel) "with a sound like thunder," in the words of one survivor, and soon began its plunge. It was closely followed by various pieces of the ship that crashed into the ocean as the hull and superstructure pulled apart. The heavier these were, the more quickly they fell. The keel definitely snapped right under the forward part of the reciprocating engine room (between stacks 3 and 4); and the two forward low-pressure cylinders, ahead of the break, must have fallen straight to the bottom like bombs, along with all the single-ended boilers from boiler room

No. 1. The two high-pressure cylinders and the rest of the engines, aft of the break, remained bolted to their bedplates and survived the plunge and the impact with the bottom. The heaviest piece of all was the intact bow section, which had slowly filled with water over the previous two and a half hours and now planed down and away from the surface still upright and at a slope, gathering speed. (Given enough depth to stabilize, all shipwrecks should rest on the bottom on their keels, since these are the heaviest parts of the ship.)

Some people have theorized that when the bow reached a certain angle the boilers broke loose from their fittings, crashed through the bulkheads, and fell forward, possibly piercing the bow and dropping ahead of it down to the bottom. If this were even possible (naval architects generally have scoffed at the notion of boilers bursting through the *Titanic*'s hull), it now seems unlikely this occurred. Assuming the bow broke off at or close to the surface, it never reached the extreme angle of the stern and apparently never exceeded the maximum tilt it had when it left the surface. We know this because the condition of the bow indicates it didn't crash nose-first almost vertically in the mud. Therefore the boilers couldn't have ended up in the forwardmost part of the bow. If they had crashed through the hull, we would certainly have found some of them on the ocean floor. (We found only five single-ended boilers, which all came from the boiler room nearest to where the ship broke in two.)

Shortly before 2:20 A.M., while the bow began its descent, the stern temporarily righted itself, then turned sternmost straight up in the air before it too disappeared.

What some people assumed was the whole ship standing almost on end was actually the stern alone. When the stern turned up, whatever was loose fell into the water — and can now be found in the debris field. Mysteriously, not much of what we found there can be definitely linked to the stern. What can be found includes "Orex" spring and chain mattresses from third-class berths and metal-slat or ribbon mattresses from crew and steerage areas. The engine-room equipment we saw also came from the stern section, and we found cranes, bench supports and cowl vents from the stern decks.

All sorts of lighter debris from the damaged midsection floated down at various speeds, some of it taking several hours to reach the bottom. Some of it we found, some we didn't, but a sampling of the items included the following: tons of coal from the two breached boiler rooms and the bunkers on G Deck, along with stoking shovels, pails, and other tools; pots, pans, and utensils from the kitchens; stacks of plates and casserole dishes; thousands of bottles of wine, champagne, and other beverages (including 15,000 bottles of ale and stout); patterned linoleum floor tiles from many different rooms; many sections of wrought-iron and gilt-bronzed balustrades from the after Grand Staircase; crumpled sections of the leaded glass windows from the first-class dining room and stained glass from the first-class smoking room; a wall sconce from the first-class lounge, light fixtures, bathtubs, washbasins, toilets, bedsprings, head and foot-boards, deck benches, dustpans, chamber pots, stateroom fans, milk containers, baseboard-vent grills, silver serving trays, hairbrushes, hand mirrors, and all sorts of passengers' effects — from items of clothing to toys and suitcases.

These items all fell or drifted in the wake of the plummeting stern — which most likely fell straight down. Unlike the bow, the stern hadn't filled with water before it began its plunge. After the break, water began to pour in, probably crushing the weaker bulkheads and wreaking considerable havoc in the interior. Air escaping from the stern may have contributed to the fact that the Poop Deck peeled up and over onto itself. But this may have been the result of the force of the water rushing aft and scooping under the deck as the stern plunged into the ocean. As the stern accelerated straight down, it probably turned slowly (something subs like *Alvin* do during their free-fall descent), accounting for its orientation away from the bow on the bottom.

Any estimate of the maximum speed of the *Titanic*'s descent is largely speculative. There are simply too many variables involved. Based on the evidence of a later ship that was scuttled and clocked during its fall, the two large hull sections may have reached a speed of as much as 25 or 30 miles an hour. Depending on how quickly that speed was reached, they could have fallen in as little as six minutes. We simply don't know enough about the weight of the two big hull pieces or the plunge — but it probably took at least several minutes for these huge hull pieces to reach their terminal or maximum falling velocity.

The bow probably hit before the stern, prow first and at a slight angle, its tremendous forward and downward momentum driving it deep into the mud to a depth of over 65 feet at the anchors, the plowing action bending and buckling the forward part of the bow section downward. Seconds later, after the bow had dug in, the part aft of the forward expansion joint slammed down into the bottom, possibly accounting for some additional "tweaking" in the hull at a point beneath the expansion joint. The impact worsened the damage caused by the surface break-up of the hull, the decks inside the aftermost part of the bow section collapsing on top of each other like a stack of pancakes.

Writer Charles Pellegrino, who has been working on his own book about the *Titanic*, has a plausible theory that may help account for the devastation of the area around the bridge, which, when I first saw it, looked to me as if it had been squashed by a giant's fist. A large, heavy object accelerating through water at the speed of the bow would create a sort of slipstream effect similar to an airplane passing through air. When the bow abruptly stopped dead, the water following it would have come crashing down, most powerfully at the center of the bow section — exactly where the bridge was. This "downblast" of water may partly explain the current state of the wreck.

Alternatively, the damage in the area of the officers' quarters may have happened near the surface. Some eyewitnesses noted a sudden lurch just as the bridge was dipping under the water. If the bow sank rapidly for a few seconds when this lurch occurred, the wave of water rushing aft might have flattened the bridge area fairly symmetrically — the walls peeling outward, the roofs of the still-water-free cabins smashing down.

A few minutes after the bow came to rest on the bottom, the stern hit even harder, about 1,970 feet to the south, sinking about 45 feet into the mud. Since it had already been weakened by the havoc caused by the water rushing in at or near the surface, the effect of the impact of the stern with the bottom was more devastating as the upper decks all pancaked down. (Any downblast would have abetted this process.) The entire deck area of the stern is now utter devastation. Most of that damage happened both at the start of the plunge and at the moment of impact.

For the next several hours, pieces of debris fell; the lighter ones carried by the below-surface current southeast, but most settling near the stern. First, the low-pressure cylinders, the boilers, and the other heavier pieces of wreckage crashed into the bottom mud — then, a shower of medium-heavy debris; and finally, the lightest items such as shoes, teacups, perhaps a pack of waterlogged playing cards fluttering down. By the time the survivors were all on board the *Carpathia* six hours later, most of the falling objects had settled on the muddy bottom. Some objects, including bodies (which sink once the lungs fill with water), may have floated awhile before falling to the seafloor far from the original wreck site. But some human beings — those without lifevests who drowned quickly or were trapped inside the sinking hull and escaped too late — would have sunk down to join the debris. (In cold, deep water, gas cannot form and lift the body back to the surface.)

The trail of debris and wreckage that we actually found on the bottom represents in fact two overlapping debris fields — one trailing southeast from the bow to the area of the stern; one trailing southeast from the area of the stern. Each of these fields is between 2,000 and 2,600 feet long — less than the mile I was expecting. When you add them together they are about a mile long, however. Because the two fields overlap in the area of the stern, you get a combination of heavy and light debris there.

THE PASSING YEARS

The deep ocean is a quiet and relatively stable place. After the *Titanic*'s tumultuous final hours she found herself at a depth of 12,460 feet in an environment where most changes happen over decades rather than days. First to disappear would have been any soft organic material such as food or bodies — the flesh and bones rapidly devoured by bottom-feeding fish and crustaceans (any bones they missed would soon have been dissolved by the salt water). Clothing would have taken much longer, probably years. In some cases leather shoes have survived, sitting side by side where once a body rested. Perhaps the chemicals used in the shoe-tanning processes are unappetizing to bacteria.

At some point, weeks or months later, wood-boring molluscs, the larvae of which were probably borne by the submarine currents, found their way to the wreck. They settled, metamorphosed and then dined on the soft pine wood of the *Titanic*'s decks and gradually migrated inside the openings in the hull. Within a few years, the decks were mostly eaten away and, inside the ship, the lavish wood furniture, fine carvings, elaborate tapestries, and Axminster carpets were all but gone, along with the wood paneling and the oak banisters of the grand staircases.

These molluscs play an important role in deep-submarine ecology, breaking down wood and thus increasing the cycling of nutrients. But by the time we visited the ship, these creatures were likely dead and gone; all that was left were the calcareous tubes characteristic of a particular species of wood-borer — the one that likely played the major role in devouring the ship. While these molluscs thrived, so did the species of fish and crustaceans that prey on them, making the ship an underwater oasis.

We can only speculate why some of the wood on the *Titanic* and in the debris field remained intact. Teak, being a very dense wood, is generally resistant to the borers, and teak has survived rather well on the *Titanic*. All teak railings, topcourses, and roof trim appeared to be in almost mint condition. But these creatures don't generally respect wood that has been treated with anti-weathering material; so why was that set of stairs we saw so well preserved? Perhaps it, too, was teak. Not long ago, an ancient ship buried under Mediterranean bottom mud was found with much wood intact. Once uncovered, the wood remained impervious to wood-borers while fresh wood left nearby was devoured. Apparently something happens when the wood is buried, but we don't know what. And since the wood on the *Titanic* was never covered, this can't explain the selective preservation there.

Other types of organisms, such as bacteria and other tiny animals, would have attacked the remaining organic material on the ship. Unlike the wood, most of these items — such as clothing — would have deteriorated very slowly: mattresses (probably made of horsehair), bed linen, the cloth body of a doll. Thus, as the years passed, most of the organic contents of the ship and the debris field gradually disappeared and the *Titanic* became an even quieter place. But she continued to be a haven for a few deep-ocean creatures, mainly galathean crabs, starfish, and various bottom-dwelling rat-tail fish, who found shelter in the roomy wreck.

The main exception to all this was and will continue to be the iron-eating bacteria responsible for the rusticles.

These are tiny organisms that use ferrous iron as an inorganic source of energy; they oxidize the iron and leave rust particles behind as a waste product. Because conditions in the deep ocean are not acidic enough to suit these bacteria, they manufacture a more favorable environment in which to live. They do this by secreting a highly viscous slime that protects them from surrounding seawater. As the slime is produced, it flows outward and away from the metal surface, carrying with it dead cells and ferric oxides (rust) and hydroxides. These are what form the rusticles. They grow and grow until, if left undisturbed, they eventually fall off from their own weight.

Since these rusticles are very fragile — they broke off when touched by *JJ* and *Alvin*, or even when disturbed by the wake of our little sub — they are testimony to the stability and tranquility of the deep-ocean environment. It is unclear just how much damage the iron-eating bacteria have done over the years. When we brushed them away, the steel underneath seemed in quite good shape — but this is partly because, unlike chemical oxidation, bacterial oxidation actually "cleans" the metal, leaving a smooth surface. Woods Hole's expert on iron bacteria, Dr. Holger Jannasch, thinks the ship has probably already corroded to the point that any attempt to raise her would result in the hull breaking into many pieces.

On November 18, 1929, 17 years after the sinking, the general area where the *Titanic* rests was rocked by the Grand Banks Earthquake. This far from the epicenter, whatever mudslide the tremor set off was blocked by Titanic Canyon, saving the wreck from possible burial. We have no way of knowing what damage, if any, the quake did to the ship, but it does not seem to have done much. We do know that we could see many things that looked "as if" they hadn't moved since the day of the sinking. The cup that still rests on the boiler is a good example.

Since the earthquake, apart from the rust bacteria (and perhaps bacteria that have gradually worked their way deep inside the ship), the *Titanic* has remained undisturbed and virtually a dead place. Only a few creatures of the dark lurk in her corners and crevices.

REMAINING QUESTIONS

We now know a great deal about the *Titanic*. We can plausibly reconstruct what happened as she sank and settled. But mysteries remain. A number of artifacts that we should have found easily either escaped our notice or were hidden from view. Where, for instance, is the big brass compass platform that must have fallen off the top deck between number 2 and number 3 funnels? It ought to have survived in good shape, yet we found no trace of it. And while we found numerous sections of wrought-iron and gilt balustrade from the aft Grand Staircase, along with floor tiles from that area, where is the famous large bronze statue of a boy holding a light standard that stood at the B-Deck landing? It was one of two nearly identical statues, the other on the A-Deck landing of the forward staircase. Also missing was any sign of the ship's bells, bridge instruments, first-class chinaware, or small silver items such as knives and forks. Surprisingly, we saw very little that came from the first-class smoking room, which was right under the fourth funnel. And there is precious little from the stern, which ought to have emptied all sorts of articles when it turned end up before it plunged.

Who knows what we might find if we could walk the corridors of the wreck at will? Perhaps the wrought-iron grillwork of the first-class elevator doors is still in place. And maybe in the first-class dining saloon on D Deck we might still see the remnants of the breakfast settings scattered on the floor. The innards of the piano that graced the first-class reception room are probably still there, though badly out of tune. And down inside the forward cargo hatches are the remains of the Renault and all sorts of other freight — maybe even the fabled *Rubaiyat* with its cover studded with emeralds and rubies. Maybe fish now swim in the *Titanic*'s small swimming pool; perhaps the tiles still gleam inside the Turkish baths. Likely no one will ever know.

THE FUTURE — SANCTUARY OR SALVAGE?

As long as the wreck is left unmolested by treasure-hunters, the *Titanic* won't appear to change much in my lifetime. The prevailing currents, which gave us so much trouble on some dives, will continue to build up a sediment around the "windward" sides of the large pieces of wreckage, but complete burial under sediments falling from above would take less than a thousand years for the smaller pieces, nearly one million years for the two large hull sections. Before then, iron-eating bacteria would have finished their demolition work. Sedimentary deposition this far out in the ocean is very slow and even the smallest objects we saw, such as the doll's head, showed very little evidence of burial despite the passage of 74 years. Since the ship sits in an area of underwater sand dunes, the surrounding terrain will shift as the dunes migrate, revealing currently buried pieces of debris and covering up things we saw.

In the longer term, the rusticle-forming bacteria will continue to do their work. Gradually, the ship will be eaten away until its remaining structural integrity is threatened. My colleague Holger Jannasch predicts that in another 75 years, perhaps a little longer, the R.M.S. *Titanic* will likely be a jumble of rubble, its noble bow section only a memory. Certain things will still be there to see — mostly in the debris field: ceramic, bronze, and brass remains; lumps of coal. But it will not be a pretty sight.

For now, the greatest threat to the *Titanic* clearly comes from man, particularly in the form of crude dredging operations. There are all sorts of fishing boats and drill ships that could be hired to go out to the site and attempt to bring up pieces of wreckage. But most artifacts of any value lie scattered in the debris field and would have to be salvaged by a sub with a mechanical arm. But apart from *Alvin*, there are only two submarines that could dive this deep — the U.S. Navy's *Sea Cliff*, and France's *Nautile*.

The legislation passed by the United States Congress and signed into law by the President, calling for the wreck to be made an international memorial and left unmolested, should discourage most treasure-seekers. At least it guarantees them bad publicity. My simple wish is that any who do mount new expeditions to visit the wreck will respect the site as I have.

Now that the wreck's true position is known, its ownership could well become an issue. It lies within the offshore waters claimed by Canada, a claim not recognized by the United States. Fortunately, the Canadian government has strongly indicated it would oppose salvage. But in whatever jurisdiction the wreck falls, the *Titanic* belongs to all of us.

LOOKING BACK

The loss of the *Titanic* was as traumatic to the people of that time as the assassination of John F. Kennedy was to ours. Perhaps the most recent and closest parallel of our day is unquestionably the loss of the space shuttle *Challenger*. In both cases, there was unjustified overconfidence in technology. In both, the power of the natural environment was underestimated. And, in both cases, this led to negligence by those in high command. Apparently, we still have something to learn from the *Titanic*.

Finding and filming the *Titanic* doesn't compare in historical importance with the tragedy of 1912, but it represents a turning point of another sort. For one thing, it demonstrated the effectiveness of a visual search in deep water. As a result of our success, it seems likely that future searches for sunken wrecks will at the very least combine acoustic and visual imaging. Sonar search works best on a flat, featureless bottom. But the ocean floor is complex, full of mountains and valleys that present many false acoustic targets. In order to ensure complete coverage with sonar, you must overlap ground covered and, even then, you can't be 100 percent sure about what you've seen or missed. Only a camera's eye can tell you that a particular sonar target is really the thing you're looking for.

More important than any contribution to underwater search techniques, however, the video exploration of the

Titanic was a pioneering super-high-tech job done in the deep sea. For the first time, a remotely operated vehicle was crucial to the success of a deep undersea mission. Seventy-five years from now, I'd like to be around to find out just how important this scientific achievement appears. Will we look back and see the *Titanic* expedition as the beginning of genuine exploration of the deep? So far, man has barely visited the two-thirds of the earth covered with seawater, and these regions remain mysterious at best.

The oceans represent the last truly unexplored areas of our planet. With the exception of a few obscure tracts of tropical rainforest and a few remote mountain peaks, human beings have pretty thoroughly visited the earth's exposed and dry surface. Climbing Mount Everest — though still dangerous enough — has practically become routine. If you've got the money, you can take a day trip to the North Pole. But our knowledge of the deep ocean remains primitive. For true adventure we must look either to outer space or inner space — that unknown world beneath the waters.

We've expended so much scientific energy and money on the exploration of outer space in comparison with the discovery and exploration of our own planet. In part, we've taken the seas for granted. In part, oceanography has never captured the public's imagination in the way the conquest of space has — and it will likely never be as glamorous. But there are very good reasons for increasing our knowledge of the oceans.

The most obvious of these is that water is both the most abundant and the most precious substance on earth, the blood of our planet. Understanding the whole ocean system is increasingly essential because of the rapid dissemination of pollutants. We are poisoning that lifeblood. The oceans determine our weather, affect the amount of oxygen we breathe, and conceal beneath them the dynamic forces that shape and modify our planet.

There are other reasons. As long as there are global rivalries between superpowers, the seas will be of great strategic importance and deep-sea exploration will have military significance. Also, the sea may one day become a major source of resources, although this possibility seems to be receding as we become less dependent on primary metals.

Our *Titanic* expeditions also demonstrated to the doubters that science and showmanship can make a successful mix. Traditionally, scientists have been interested in science, not publicity. Sometimes it has seemed that they've gone out of their way to keep their discoveries from the public. But I believe if you can get the public interested, and get their support, then it's much easier to raise money for your research.

Perhaps in a few generations the *Titanic* will be forgotten by all but a few — but somehow I doubt it. Long after her hull has decayed to rubble, I have a feeling people will still be drawn to the events of the night of April 14, 1912.

EPILOGUE
TO THE 1995 EDITION

WHEN I SAILED AWAY FROM THE *TITANIC* WRECK SITE IN August 1986, I did so with the reasonable hope that the ship's last resting place would be left undisturbed. In the first edition of this book, I wrote: "My simple wish is that any who do mount new expeditions to visit the wreck will respect the site as I have." However, the lure of *Titanic* "treasure" proved even stronger than I guessed. And now a new chapter of *Titanic* history must be written. As it has always been with this most mesmerizing of lost ships, the latest episode is full of contradictions and human foibles — not to mention the competing demands of science and sensationalism.

TITANIC VISITATIONS

In August 1987, an impressive new expedition arrived at the *Titanic* site. A number of American investors had formed a consortium with France's IFREMER, my partner in the 1985 discovery. This organization's declared purpose was to salvage artifacts from the wreck. IFREMER provided its deep submersible *Nautile*, as well as its video and salvaging technology and considerable oceanographic expertise. The Americans provided the money — roughly $6 million according to George Tulloch, one of the principals. In 1986, we had one ship, the *Atlantis II*, and could afford a mere 12 days on the site. During our 11 dives with *Alvin*, we had a total of 33 hours to investigate the wreck and the debris field. The 1987 *Titanic* expedition spent more than six times as many hours on the bottom, but most of this was used up in the laborious process of deep-ocean salvage, in all raising 1,800 objects from the seafloor.

Sadly, the 1987 salvagers did serious physical damage to the wreck in their eagerness to bring back booty — despite promises from those involved that the ship itself

This cartoon by James Morin appeared in the Miami Herald *when the 1987 expedition began raising artifacts from the wreck site.*

would not be harmed in any way. As millions watched the
subsequent television special aired from Paris, *Return to the
Titanic… Live*, the damage was obvious. The mast light
that lay on the table of artifacts next to host Telly Savalas
had been wrested from the foremast (it was firmly attached
when I last saw it), and the upper section of the intact foremast that angled above the Boat Deck had been crushed
flat — presumably in this same effort. Rigging hanging
over the port-side edge of the forecastle was cut, perhaps
so *Nautile* could get close enough to clean the *Titanic*'s
name on the bow. A block that we saw dangling forlornly
from the davit lying on the bridge in 1986 is now missing,
as is part of the port Boat Deck outward bulwark. Most
tragic of all, the crow's nest is now gone, utterly destroyed
— almost certainly in the act of getting at the ship's telephone that was inside.

All this was visible to us in just the few minutes of
video made available after the 1987 salvage expedition.
Since then the world has seen many more underwater
images of the *Titanic*, which have not only confirmed the
damage done but showed us the wreck more clearly than
before. In June 1991, a Canadian-Russian-American team
arrived at the *Titanic* site on board Russia's *Akademik
Keldysh*, mother ship to the world's two newest and most
advanced research submersibles, *Mir I* and *Mir II*, which
are a lot roomier and more comfortable than *Alvin*. Under
the direction of filmmaker Stephen Low, these two
submersibles worked together to take the breathtaking
images of the wreck that can be seen in the 1992 IMAX film,
Titanica. As those of you who've watched the film know,
the highlight is the spectacular underwater footage shot

using recently developed undersea high-intensity HMI lights — but that footage is all too brief. The movie is less about the *Titanic* and her story than about the eccentric characters who came together to film her. Among this large cast were Ralph White and Emory Kristof, two refugees from our 1985 discovery expedition. In 1991 Ralph was the resident *Titanic* expert. Emory had a major supporting role while busily shooting stills and 3-D video footage that someday may show up on movie or television screens.

The 1991 IMAX team neither damaged the ship nor removed anything from the debris field. This was exactly the kind of "use" of the *Titanic* wreck I had envisioned when, following the discovery, I and others worked to promote an international agreement to protect the *Titanic* site. Unfortunately the most we have been able to achieve is the R.M.S. *Titanic* Maritime Memorial Act, passed by Congress in 1986, which called for cooperation between the United States, Canada, France, Britain and "other interested nations" to come up with an agreement that would make the wreck site into an "international maritime memorial" with clear guidelines for all future visitors. Until such guidelines were in place nothing would be done to "physically alter, disturb or salvage the R.M.S. *Titanic*." Unfortunately this law had no power to stop George Tulloch and friends, recently reconstituted under the name RMS Titanic, Inc., from continuing to remove arti-facts from the site. In fact, in the summer of 1994, an American court designated this company the "salvor in possession," effectively granting it exclusive ownership of all objects salvaged from the wreck site.

In the summers of 1993 and 1994, two more salvage

expeditions visited the *Titanic* and raised another 1,800 artifacts. In the wake of the public outcry after 1987, these
recent expeditions have left the wreck alone, opting instead
to mine the debris field for all it's worth. By now there can't
be much left worth taking. In all, 3,600 items from this great
lost liner and its cargo have been brought to the surface and
undergone elaborate preservation. But to what end?

If you're a *Titanic* buff, you probably watched the
news reports of the first salvage, the ensuing television
special and the subsequent reports of each new expedition
with very mixed emotions. On the one hand, each new
object that was raised from the deep carried strong asso-
ciations with the 1912 tragedy: a ship's telephone (was this
the one used by the lookouts to call the bridge when the
iceberg was sighted?); an officer's megaphone (did Captain
Smith use this bullhorn to issue the order to "abandon
ship" or to admonish his crew, "Be British"?); the ship's
bell from the crow's nest (which sounded three clangs
when the iceberg was sighted). On the other hand, each
relic dislocated from its deep-sea resting place lost some
of its meaning and mystery and diminished the dignity of
the wreck we had found.

I have argued long and hard that the *Titanic* is a
gravesite that should have been left undisturbed, except by
visitors like the 1991 IMAX crew who come with even better
cameras to explore and wonder. Whether or not one agrees
that salvage was wrong, it has to be admitted that a teacup
brought to the surface and restored to "mint condition,"
with its red White Star Line insignia gleaming as good as
new, is still little more than a teacup. However, a teacup
resting on a boiler at the bottom of the ocean, as if set there

moments ago, is a moving reminder of the *Titanic*'s fate. Personally I'd rather see that teacup left where it is.

The *Titanic* site is a place of historical importance rather than archaeological significance. True, people would pay handsomely to own a *Titanic* fork or plate or silver tray — but their interest is sentimental, not scientific. The objects raised during the three salvage expeditions revealed precious little that was new or thought-provoking. And the act of raising them has altered the wreck site irrevocably.

NEW DISCOVERIES

But the story of the three salvage expeditions is not all bad. Despite the damage done and the disrespect shown, the salvage operations did make some new discoveries and these must be given their due. But in my opinion, the real treasure they brought back was captured on film and videotape. In 1987 *Nautile* filmed a gaping hole in the starboard bow that we had missed. Like a similar hole on the port side, this almost certainly occurred when the bow section collided with the bottom and buckled at a weak point just forward of the C-Deck superstructure.

The major video find in 1987, however, was of the port propeller sitting close to its original position at the stern. Readers may well ask how we could have missed such a massive object when we came within a few yards of it on our own white-knuckle foray under the starboard side of the stern. But investigating the wreck in a deep submersible was very much like exploring a haunted house at night with nothing more than a flashlight. We could only see what the arc of *Alvin*'s "flashlight" revealed. (It was only months after we'd returned to Woods Hole and, with the help of Ken Marschall, analyzed the 75,000 ANGUS images that the overall condition of the wreck began to take shape. In fact, we learned more about the ship after we'd returned to port than during our 11 dives.) When we found no evidence of the starboard propeller, we mistakenly assumed that the port one was buried also.

Although *Nautile*'s video footage shows the propeller seemingly in its proper position, it has clearly been wrenched up, probably on impact. The mudline at that part of the stern is above the ship's waterline, and all the propellers were, of course, well below water. Nonetheless, seeing one of Jack Grimm's missing propellers still almost in place at the stern provided one of the few moments of satisfaction I've gained from the various salvage expeditions.

Incidentally, Jack Grimm has recently taken one more brief turn on the *Titanic* stage. In the summer of 1992, a ship he hired sailed to the *Titanic* site while the Texas millionaire was in a Norfolk, Virginia, courthouse challenging the claim of RMS Titanic, Inc. to sole salvage rights. Grimm pleaded with Tulloch and company for at least one fragment of the wreck he had spent so much energy and money failing to find, but to no avail. Grimm's ship, which was equipped only with deep-sea dragging equipment, turned back without recovering a single object.

In 1993, IFREMER's tethered robot *Robin* (the French answer to *Jason*) retraced *Jason Junior*'s footsteps down the Grand Staircase and got a closer look at the dangling light fixtures *JJ* had glimpsed at a distance. In pursuit of bigger game, they also sent *Robin* down the number 1 hatch in an attempt to find the purser's office and to look for some of the ship's most famous cargo: William Carter's Renault or perhaps the famous jeweled edition of the *Rubaiyat of Omar Khayyam*. But *Robin* saw little inside the hull except extraordinarily long and slender rusticles that had formed in the quiet, currentless interior.

The four expeditions since 1986 have also made modest contributions to underwater science. They have investigated how a deep-sea wreck becomes an underwater oasis and the ways different materials deteriorate in the deep sea. Among the more surprising recoveries were various pieces of paper—newspapers, banknotes, letters, calling cards and an almost entirely readable copy of the *Home and School Standard Dictionary* with bookmarks still in place. Paper, being a fragile organic material, doesn't normally survive very long on shipwrecks. Even more fascinating, metal objects found quite close to each other had corroded to drastically different degrees. Why? In some cases the answer lay in the existence of microclimates created by the wreck and the debris field. For instance, even inside a single suitcase, objects may have fared differently due to small differences in temperature, salinity and oxygen.

ARTIFACTS ON DISPLAY

Ever since the the the first salvage expedition in 1987, we've been hearing promises that the objects recovered would be kept together and put on display, but over the ensuing six years only a modest number had shown up in exhibitions in Europe. This changed in October 1994, when the National Maritime Museum in London opened the first major exhibition of *Titanic* artifacts — 150 in all — as part of a show called "The Wreck of the *Titanic*." These objects are the centerpiece of an ambitious display that takes visitors through the whole *Titanic* story, from its sinking to its discovery and exploration, to the preservation of recovered artifacts and the debate over the wreck's future.

Those who saw this exhibit report that it will disappoint anyone hoping for new and startling revelations from the deep. Almost all the objects on display had already been shown in Paris in 1990 and few add anything to our knowledge of the story. One of the most interesting items I've heard about is a letter — badly damaged but still readable — from an ostrich-feather merchant predicting that feather boas will soon go out of fashion.

As you can imagine, I have very mixed feelings about this exhibition. It's wonderful that the *Titanic* story is receiving such royal treatment and that so many visitors will experience it anew or for the first time. But the people who stand to profit from this exhibit and the traveling roadshow to follow are the original salvagers. While they claim that the revenue they earn will merely recover their costs — and these have been considerable — I'm sure they expect to turn a tidy profit in the long run. But to me, the real lesson of this latest development is that the public remains as fascinated as ever by the *Titanic*'s sinking. In the final analysis the ship and her story will always triumph. As Walter Lord so aptly put it in the title of his second book about the tragedy, *The Night Lives On*.

THE FUTURE

No doubt there will be more expeditions to visit the last resting place of R.M.S. *Titanic*: she will haunt our imaginations for a long time yet. But now that the wreck and the debris field have been picked clean perhaps we can dare to hope that the salvage chapter has been brought to a close. If so, the wreck can revert to its rightful role as a memorial to those who died and as a deep-sea museum that will once in a while be open for public viewing.

I hope someday to lead a new expedition to the *Titanic*'s grim North Atlantic gravesite, to walk the *Titanic*'s deck and tour what's left of the debris field. Only if I do I will visit the wreck without ever leaving my surface ship and broadcast the pictures live around the world.

This is a technique we have perfected in the years since the *Titanic*'s discovery. As of spring 1995, I will have hosted six live broadcasts from distant locations, beamed via satellite to students in Canada, Bermuda, Britain, and the United States as part of an educational enterprise called the Jason Project. My dream was to use *Argo/Jason*'s remote television presence, or "telepresence," to interest young people in science. That dream seems to be coming true. Hundreds of thousands of students have now participated in our various Jason Project expeditions and gained hands-on experience of scientific discovery. They have taken the controls of *Jason* as he moves in for a closer look at a giant tube worm or talked to a diver at the exact moment he explores a coral reef.

But as I look forward to the spring 1995 *Jason* expedition, my mind is turning to fresh challenges. Chief among these is the planning for a new Institute for Exploration to be established in Mystic, Connecticut. The institute will be both a backer of new underwater expeditions and a major museum of marine exploration, built as part of a scheduled expansion of the Mystic Aquarium. As I now see it, the highlight of the museum will be a simulated dive down to the *Titanic* recreated with the latest in special-effects technology. With luck and funding, I hope to be at a ribbon-cutting during the summer of 1998.

And there are still a few lost ships I'd like to find. I want to go back to the Mediterranean and conduct more sophisticated remotely controlled archaeology. I want to hunt for some of the many sunken wrecks in the Black Sea, which is where the mythical Jason and his Argonauts actually sailed in search of the Golden Fleece and which with the end of the Cold War is now open to exploration.

One modern shipwreck that fascinates me is that of the USS *Indianapolis*, the heavy cruiser that carried the key components of the first atomic bomb dropped on Japan near the close of World War II. After delivering her deadly cargo to the island of Tinian in the Marianas, the *Indianapolis* was torpedoed and sunk by a Japanese submarine. Of the nearly 1,200 men on board, roughly 800 made it into the water, where they waited three and a half days for rescue. Only 320 made it home; many of their comrades had been eaten by sharks.

Another dream is to set up the world's first *in situ* marine museum. For this to work, the wreck must be in clear water, close enough to shore to be in some country's territorial waters — so that clear title can be established — but deep enough to have rested out of reach of scuba-diving scavengers. Right now, I am setting my sights on the *Titanic*'s sister ship *Britannic*, which was sunk by a torpedo in the Aegean Sea off the Greek island of Kea in November 1916.

In the summer of 1995, I plan to explore the *Britannic* with the help of the U.S. Navy's nuclear-powered submarine

NR-1. (Unlike my Jason Project expedition, we won't be broadcasting on-site, but will be taking film for future use.) My idea, which I've already tested with *NR-1* on the *Andrea Doria* (she sank south of Nantucket in 1956), is to land the sub on *Britannic's* hull and use the side of the ship as a stable roadway for a mobile lighting platform. (Like the *Andrea Doria*, the *Britannic* is lying on her side.) The key to spectacular underwater pictures — as the IMAX expedition to the *Titanic* showed — is the use of two powerful light sources. *NR-1* will be that second set of lights as *Argo/Jason* photographs the wreck and explores inside the huge explosion hole near the bow.

In the future, if the Greek government goes along, the *Britannic* could become the world's first maritime museum that's actually under water. A fiber-optic cable would link deep-sea cameras to an onshore broadcast site, connected by satellite to museums — or even classrooms — around the world. I can foresee the day when anyone will be able to "tune in" to the *Britannic* and a host of other *in situ* submarine museums.

I can't guess how I'll feel if and when I return to the *Titanic*. But I know that nothing will ever match my first real look at her — on our second dive in *Alvin* in 1986. Suddenly, out of the submarine night, a huge black shape loomed up — the knife edge of the great ship's bow plowing the bottom mud into a great wave and coming right at me...

The *Titanic* lives on in our imaginations, not because of a slew of artifacts brought back to daylight but because her story is universal. I still cherish the hope that the wreck our Franco-American team found and photographed will someday be turned into an internationally protected memorial. But protected or not, the *Titanic* will always stand as a haunting monument to the heavy price of human arrogance.

I will always picture her as I see her now in my mind's eye, upright on the bottom, dignified despite the decay and desecration and, finally, at rest.

Photograph & Illustration Credits

Every effort has been made to correctly attribute all material reproduced in this book. If any errors have unwittingly occurred we will be happy to correct them in future editions.

All *Argo*, ANGUS and *Alvin* photos are by Robert Ballard and Martin Bowen/WHOI. All paintings are by Ken Marschall.

CE — *Cork Examiner*
EK/NG — Emory Kristof © National Geographic Society
HW — Harland & Wolff
ILN — *The Illustrated London News*
JCC — Joseph Carvalho Collection
KMC — Ken Marschall Collection
PT/NG — Perry Thorsvik © National Geographic Society
RS/NG — Richard Schlecht/National Geographic Society

PAGE 2: Eric Sauder Collection CHAPTER 1: 10: EK/NG CHAPTER 2: 16: Father Francis M. Browne, S.J., Charles Haas/John Eaton Collection 19: HW 21: JCC 22: CE 26: Bettmann 29: ILN 31: (Left) Marconi Co. Ltd., (right) ILN 35: ILN 38: ILN 41: Walter Lord Collection CHAPTER 3: 46: Dann Blackwood, WHOI 51: WHOI 53: WHOI 55: Anne Tantum 61: WHOI 62: WHOI 65: Robert Ballard CHAPTER 4: (All) Anita Brosius, courtesy of Lamont-Doherty Geological Observatory CHAPTER 5: 84: EK/NG 89: EK/NG CHAPTER 6: 96: EK/NG 100: WHOI 107: EK/NG 108: WHOI 112: EK/NG 124: EK/NG 127: EK/NG 131: EK/NG CHAPTER 7: 140: EK/NG 145: EK/NG 153: *Toronto Sun* 155: EK/NG 160: Joseph H. Bailey © National Geographic Society 162: WHOI CHAPTER 8: 167: PT/NG 181: PT/NG 183: PT/NG 198: PT/NG CHAPTER 9: 206: PT/NG 209: PT/NG 217: Still courtesy of National Geographic Society 226: F. Sangorski & G. Sutcliffe Ltd. CHAPTER 10: 242: PT/NG 245: ILN 252: (Top) ILN, (bottom) From *The Doomed Unsinkable Ship* CHAPTER 11: 270: James Morin, *Miami Herald* 288: Kate Odell, courtesy of Jeremy Nightingale COLOR INSERT: i: Painting by Ken Marschall, Rustie Brown Collection ii: ILN iv–v: Painting by Ken Marschall, David Hobson Collection vi: EK/NG vii: EK/NG viii: (Top right) EK/NG, (middle) HW ix: EK/NG x: EK/NG xii: (Top) PT/NG xix–xxi: (Mosaic) WHOI, (diagram) RS/NG & Ken Marschall xxiv: (Top) HW xxv: (Bottom) Ken Marschall Collection xxvi: (Capt. Smith) British Newspaper Library, (telemotor) Bill Sauder Collection xxvii: (Bottom) ILN xxviii: (Middle) Howard Holtzman Collection, (bottom) HW xxix: Roy Varley xxx: (Top) Ken Marschall Collection xxxi: (Middle) *The Shipbuilder* xxxii: (Top) JCC, (bottom) Still courtesy of National Geographic Society xxxiii: (Bottom) RS/NG xxxiv: (Top) HW xxxv: (Top) HW, (bottom right) Byron Collection, Museum of the City of New York xlii: (Top) HW xliii: (Top) Ken Marschall Collection (Bottom) Father Francis M. Browne, S.J., Charles Haas/John Eaton Collection xliv: (Top) Ken Marschall Collection xlvi: (Top) CE, (bottom) *The Shipbuilder* l: Kate Odell, courtesy of Jeremy Nightingale li: (Top) CE lii: (Top) *Syren and Shipping Magazine*, Titanic Historical Society liii: (Bottom) HW

INDEX

DESIGN AND ART DIRECTION: Andrew Smith Graphics Inc.

PAGE DESIGN AND COMPOSITION: Joseph Gisini

EDITORIAL DIRECTOR: Hugh M. Brewster

PROJECT EDITOR: Ian R. Coutts

EDITORIAL ASSISTANT: Lloyd Davis

PRODUCTION DIRECTOR: Susan Barrable

PRODUCTION CO-ORDINATOR: Sandra L. Hall

COLOR SEPARATION: Colour Technologies

PRINTING AND BINDING: Metropole Litho Inc.

The last photograph ever taken of the Titanic *as she steams off from Queenstown on her fateful maiden voyage.*

THE DISCOVERY OF THE TITANIC was produced by Madison Press Books under the direction of Albert E. Cummings.

609L